THE CLOSEST
EXIT
MAY BE
BEHIND YOU

Memoir of a Fearful
Flight Attendant

Kathi Davidson Davis

Paperback: ISBN 979-8-9924275-0-9

First paperback edition 2025

Edited by Sharon Schmid
Cover design by Ann Weinstock
Layout by Euan Monaghan

Printed in the United States of America

www.kathidavis.com

Dedicated to all sojourners of the sky — past, present, and future

Flying is learning how to throw yourself at the ground and miss.
DOUGLAS ADAMS

Contents

Introduction

I never dreamed of being a flight attendant. I wasn't one of those little girls who looked at magazine travel ads and longed to join the ranks of the smiling, uniformed cabin attendants. On the contrary, I was terrified of flying. No one understood why, least of all me, because I'd never even been on an airplane. I don't remember seeing photos of fiery crashes in newspapers (although there would have been plenty of them) or hearing on the evening news about an engine falling off an airplane. The spate of hijackings to Cuba didn't occur until the 1960s, when I entered my teens, and that wasn't what scared me anyway. It was the idea of hurtling through space with no assurance I would return safely to Earth. Despite this overwhelming fear, I spent nearly thirty-five years working in the sky.

My career began in 1970 at the tail end of the so-called Golden Age of Flying. Many passengers (those who could afford the hefty fares) still regarded an airline trip as an exciting, luxurious experience and dressed accordingly—women in hats and gloves, men in suits and ties—and brought only a briefcase, purse, or small tote bag into the cabin. With the loosening of government regulations in 1978, there was a considerable decrease in the cost of tickets. More people could afford air travel, and they brought all sorts of things on board. The unwritten dress code of previous years vanished, gradually replaced by an "anything goes" attitude.

Society was on the cusp of significant changes in the way it viewed women, and women themselves struggled with self-definition. I had one foot planted firmly in the norms and expectations of the past, a traditional career (if one at all), a life-long marriage, and children. But with the other, I dipped my toe into the more progressive ideas of liberated women. Hemlines might be shorter, and most women wanted to look nice, but they shunned being objectified and judged on their appearance. They demanded equality in the workplace, the choice to marry (or not), or to have more than one partner at a time, and they repudiated one-sided relationships in which men held all the power. At age twenty-one, I was simultaneously attracted to, and repelled by, these new possibilities, and I straddled the divide.

When Delta Air Lines hired me, the airline industry was clearly in the traditional camp. Stewardesses were required to look appealing, be unmarried, and comply with strict standards of appearance, which included height minimums and weight maximums. Liberated women did not write airline ads during the late 1960s and early 1970s. Instead, the slogans intimated that a passenger could expect much more than a cocktail and a meal from *his* stewardess.

Today, flying is nearly unrecognizable when compared to the final thirty years of the twentieth century. Because airline travel has changed so much since I last demonstrated to passengers how to fasten their seatbelts, I wanted to give readers a look at what flying was like in the "old" days. I wrote a collection of stand-alone true airline stories. Every flight attendant has them—meal services that went awry, medical emergencies, difficult passengers—and, I thought I would publish them some day. However, I realized the stories were more meaningful in the context of other things that were going on in my life at the same time, relationships, dreams, love, heartbreak, messiness, and joy. You'll do a bit of sightseeing and learn about Flight Attendant Face, Bad Ice, and my near-disastrous experiences in the air and on the water.

I remind those I flew with, who may disagree with some of the book's details, that memory is not a videotape. Time and experiences filter recollections, but the content of this book is *my* truth. Likewise, conversations are not transcripts but represent the essence of the exchanges. To those who still object to what I have written (and even those who don't), I encourage you to open a blank page on your computer and type "Chapter 1." Everyone has a story to tell.

Prologue

"Whoop, whoop! Pull up! Whoop, whoop! Pull up!

The mechanical voice blared from the cockpit only a few feet away from my jumpseat at the right front door. The other flight attendants and I had taken our seats in preparation for landing in Dallas/Fort Worth when what felt like a giant hand began to pull the L-1011 aircraft toward the ground. Unlike the engines' familiar sounds on a typical approach, they screamed for more altitude.

The Flight Attendant in Charge sat on the opposite side of the plane. I couldn't see her because the center first class galley blocked my view, but I heard her shaky voice. "Kath?"

I forced down a wave of panic and feigned a neutral expression to benefit the passenger who sat directly opposite me. She eyed me nervously, searching for clues as to whether she should be terrified. From the corner of my eye, I saw treetops. They shouldn't be there. I felt surprisingly calm as I accepted that we were only a few seconds away from crashing.

Ironic how things turned out, I thought. *If I had listened to my eight-year-old self, I wouldn't be here right now.*

Chapter One

"Is it safe now?"

I had flung myself from the back seat of the Chevy Bel Air to lie prone across the transmission hump on the floor. It felt like the car was going downhill, but I had to be sure. I propped myself on my elbows to look up at my big sister Sandy, her legs stretched into the space I vacated, but she continued to read her movie fan magazine as though I weren't there. From a folded-back glossy page, Marilyn Monroe smiled down at me and, for a second, I forgot my distress.

Louder. "Is it safe?"

I spotted the bright yellow Juicy Fruit gum wrapper I had tossed on the floor before the crisis began. Rip, rip, rip into tiny pieces. Another momentary distraction.

"Mom, she's on the floor again," Sandy said, not taking her eyes from the page. My behavior was not noteworthy, just a routine occurrence to report.

My mother craned her neck to peer over the front passenger seat. "Kathleen, get up," she demanded. "Sandra, move your legs so she can sit down." She turned to my dad and shook her head. "I don't know why she does that, Bill."

He glanced at her and shrugged. "Me neither."

They never asked *me* why I did it, and even if they had, I couldn't have explained the overwhelming panic I felt at those times. My excitement at visiting Grandpa Davidson evaporated when we approached the one spot I dreaded on the two-hour drive from Waterloo, Iowa, to his home in Crawfordsville in the southeastern part of the state. Familiar landmarks alerted me that we were almost there, and I would have to move quickly. There it was, the dreaded sign. "Hiawatha 5 miles." My panic reached its peak. Mouth dry as dust, heart pounding, breathing difficult, stomach flip-flopping.

Soon, we would climb the steep railroad overpass and possibly career over the side. *No way around it. Can't look. No, I'll stay right here on the floor until I'm absolutely sure I'm safe.*

"But Mom, are we over the bridge yet?"

Fear of heights robbed me of the pleasure of many childhood experiences. Once, on a family trip to Chicago, I spent the morning mesmerized by bizarre-looking stingrays and playful otters at the Shedd Aquarium. After lunch, Dad navigated north to the John Hancock Building, where I expected more interesting sights.

Dad led us toward a bank of elevators in the lobby, and I felt my stomach somersault. I could barely drag my feet across the glossy marble floor. As we sped to the ninety-fourth floor, my ears popped, and the doors opened onto a glass-enclosed lobby. I was breathless (and not in a good way) when I saw the tops of skyscrapers and clouds at eye level. Elevator doors closing! No escape!

"Come on, Honey." Mom took my hand as we headed to the door that led to the open air. "Kathleen, your fingers are freezing! What's wrong?" She cradled both of my hands between hers and rubbed them vigorously, then released one and, with the other, led (pulled!) me outside.

Dad and Sandy were already several feet away. "Look, there's the Chicago River," Dad exclaimed as Sandy turned to look where he pointed.

"Kathi, come look!" Sandy yelled. *I'll take her word for it.* Cotton balls in my mouth. Lots of them. Can't swallow. Muffled traffic sounds confirmed what I had already suspected—we were miles above the unseen cars. *So far to fall!*

I pushed away Mom's hand and plastered myself against the lobby wall. With an exasperated sigh, she walked to the glass by herself and "oohed and aahed" at the view of the city from the dizzying height.

When my active imagination took over, I conjured up numerous other fearful objects and situations that became real enough to overwhelm me. While planning a summer vacation, Dad opened a road map on the dining room table for Sandy and me to see. "Here's where we'll get on the Pennsylvania Turnpike," he said. "See that green line?" *Turnpike. What's that?* I said the word out loud and there it was, a narrow road that twisted and turned over a canyon. One wrong movement of the steering wheel and we would tumble into its depths.

Mom and Dad discussed an upcoming family trip to the West Coast that would take us through mountainous parts of the country. My stomach always felt uneasy when we drove over the rolling hills of southeastern Iowa to Grandpa's. But, they were like kiddie rollercoasters compared to the mammoth mountains we would encounter out west. My friends and I painted tempera pictures of them at school—tall triangles with steep sides topped with pointed snowcaps. Driving over them would surely end in catastrophe—the car climbing one side, teetering wildly back and forth on the peak, and plummeting down the other at breakneck speed.

My most perplexing source of anxiety was my fear of flying. The only time I ever saw airplanes was from a distance when

Mom, Sandy, and I picked up Dad at our small airport after his business trips. From the safety of Dad's hug, I eyed the green and white Ozark Airlines plane that squatted on the tarmac like a giant grasshopper about to jump. I couldn't shake the image of being inside when it shot into the air, the ground disappearing below and clouds swallowing it whole. How could Dad be so relaxed, having just escaped a potential calamity? My parents might force me to take car trips that involved both real and imaginary hazards, but I was confident they would never shove me into an airplane against my will. Would they?

In the early summer of 1956, I occasionally spotted Mom and Dad speaking in hushed voices. I caught the words "trip," "Florida," and "tickets" before they suddenly ended their conversation upon seeing me. It must be about our upcoming vacation, but why were they whispering? They always told Sandy and me everything we would do and see. I didn't know that Mom and Dad were adding another segment to our vacation: a dream trip to an exotic destination they had read about in *Holiday Magazine*. It was the epicenter of the Xavier Cugat rumbas and the Perez Prado mambos they had learned in their Latin dance classes at the Elks Club. They made sure I didn't hear the part about flying to Cuba.

We set off in the third week of July, just after my eighth birthday and just before Sandy's fourteenth. Dad, who always gave in when Sandy and I pleaded, pulled off at caves, historical markers, putt-putt golf courses, rock gardens, trampoline centers, souvenir shops, wildlife attractions, and nearly every Stuckey's along the way, where we stocked up on pecan log rolls sweet enough to make our teeth ache.

When we stopped for the night, Sandy and I ensured the motel met our requirements. "Not that one! It doesn't have a swimming pool." Dad dutifully moved on until he found one that did. When he unlocked the door to our room, Sandy and I raced to put on our bathing suits and jump into the water to cool off after a hot day in a car that had only 4-60 air conditioning (all four windows rolled down, going sixty miles per hour). At our Miami Beach hotel, we sputtered when we got unexpected mouthfuls of salt water instead of the familiar taste of chlorine.

When we reached the Florida Keys, the clear blue-green water, sometimes visible on both sides of the car at once, enchanted me. With its sturdy-looking safety rails, the road presented no threat of our vehicle sliding off its sides, so I felt relaxed and secure.

I enjoyed the drive so much that when Dad pulled into a motel earlier in the day than usual and announced, "Here we are in Key West, the end of the line," I was surprised and slightly disappointed. Then, through the lobby's glass doors, I spotted the sparkling water in a vast swimming pool and realized Dad had saved the best for last.

At dinner that night, as I licked the last traces of a hot fudge sundae from my spoon, Mom said she and Dad had something to tell me. They exchanged nervous looks, and I braced myself for—what? Sandy averted her eyes; she already knew what they would say.

Mom cleared her throat. "Tomorrow, we'll all get on an airplane to fly to Havana, Cuba. Won't that be fun? We'll see so many interesting things and…." She trailed off when she saw my stricken face and massive tears threatening to roll down my cheeks. *No!*

"Yes," Dad chimed in, not looking at me directly. "We'll have a wonderful time." His remark wasn't so much a prediction as a demand. He had carefully planned this once-in-a-lifetime trip, and it wasn't cheap. The four airline tickets alone cost $132 ($1,500 today) on top of all the motel rooms, meals, entrance fees, and gas. He loved me, but his tone told me my "ridiculous" fear of flying would not spoil this trip for everyone.

I crossed my arms defiantly. "I'm not going."

"But Honey, you have to come with us," Mom said, half pleading, half annoyed. "We can't leave you here by yourself."

"I won't be by myself." My family looked at one another, puzzled. "I'll stay with Mr. and Mrs. Johnson." They were the couple who managed the Hibiscus Motel, where we had checked in that afternoon. "Mrs. Johnson likes me. She asked me how old I was and what grade I'd be in."

"She was just being friendly," said Mom.

"No! She likes me! She'll love having me stay with her and Mr. Johnson." Mom and Dad's subtle smiles caused my assertiveness to plummet when I realized I would not win this battle. "But she gave me a slice of key lime pie," I whined as proof of Mrs. Johnson's fondness for me, ignoring that she had given each of us a slice.

The tears gave way to a fit of temper, and I balled my hands into fists. "I don't want to go on the airplane! I want to swim in the pool at the motel!"

Other diners turned to stare at us, no doubt wondering what the commotion was about. Dad lost his patience. "That's out of the question. Come on, we're going back to our room."

I shuffled to the car behind the others, and, except for my sniffles, we rode back to the motel in silence. Mom tucked me into bed and kissed me on the forehead, but I rolled over to face the wall so I couldn't see her or Sandy (who was in on this, too), and especially not Dad. I no longer trusted any of them. They were all against me. Anger and fear vied for first place as I fell into a fitful sleep. In the morning, Dad found a small, air-conditioned café where we ate breakfast. I still wasn't speaking to any of them, but I picked at a plate of blueberry pancakes.

When we arrived at the small yellow cinderblock terminal building, Dad parked in the shade of a striped awning, and we went inside to check in for the flight. After confirming our reservations, the uniformed ticket agent said, "Mr. Davidson, the vending machine for life insurance policies is next to the restrooms. Do you need some quarters?" Dad glanced at me to ensure I listened and responded, "No, we won't need insurance because we know flying is perfectly safe, don't we?" *If it's so safe, why are all those other people plunking coins into the machine?*

Like the Ozark planes, the Q Airways plane lurked on the tarmac with its rear end lower than its nose. I felt the same symptoms of fear—trembling, queasy stomach, sweaty hands—that I suffered as we approached the Hiawatha bridge. Nearby, a girl about my age with red ribbons tied to her braids chatted excitedly with her parents. She gave me a cheerful wave, and I shyly waved back. *I wonder why she's not afraid.*

When the agent announced it was time to board, Dad took my hand and led me into the blinding sunshine. We climbed flimsy-looking stairs that extended from the plane's body to the ground. A pilot in a crisp white shirt and navy-blue visored hat stood at the top. "Welcome aboard," he said in an odd accent. The cabin was small, confined, and closed in. Dad had to bow his head slightly to avoid grazing the ceiling. I followed him so closely up the narrow aisle that I stepped on his heels and nearly caused both of us to topple.

A second pilot sat in the cockpit, but where was the stewardess? There was always a stewardess in the magazine travel ads. Seeing her confident smile might make me feel a little safer. In response to my observation, Dad said, "There aren't enough seats to require a stewardess." He was just plain wrong. The real reason was that stewardesses knew better than to step into a tiny metal tube like this.

We reached our row near the front. "You can sit next to me." Dad patted the window seat. "The water will be so blue and beautiful from the air." He leaned across to part the patterned cloth curtains covering the oval window.

7

The window seat will be the first thing sucked out when disaster strikes! No, I will not sit there! I plopped down in the aisle seat and firmly grasped both armrests, forcing Dad to crawl over me. He fastened my seatbelt and cinched it tight. I had never worn this kind of restraint, and the pressure sent the blueberries, now with an unpleasant taste, into my throat. *Maybe if I get sick, I won't have to go.* But I didn't want to embarrass myself by throwing up.

The sudden clunk of the propellers as they wound up prompted me to grasp Dad's forearm and lean into his side as closely as the seatbelt allowed. The plane lumbered away from the terminal, and I ventured a brief peek out the window, where I saw palm trees near the terminal building swaying in the breeze. "Goodbye, it's been nice knowing you," they whispered. I was startled by a whining buzz that slowly increased in volume and pitch until it sounded like a giant enraged bumblebee. The plane picked up speed, bounced over bumps on the runway, and rose at an angle that forced me against my seatback and sent my stomach to my ankles. *I think I'm in the sky now.* Cold, clammy sweat and a wildly thumping heart made me close my eyes and bury my head in Dad's side to avoid seeing the approaching disaster.

From across the aisle, I heard Sandy exclaim, "Look, Mom! Those boats look like toys!" In the row behind us, the girl who had waved at me squealed with delight. "This is fun!" *No one else understands the danger we're in.*

Dad provided unwanted commentary on his view from the window—small islets, fishing boats, sandy shoals, tiny whitecaps on the waves—while I focused on my knobby knees and scuffed sandals. Dad also noticed a not-so-pretty sight—bruises blooming on his arm where my rigid fingers were digging into his skin.

Thirty minutes lasted an eternity. With each slight movement of the plane, I clamped down harder on Dad's arm, and I was acutely aware of tiny changes in the loud droning of the engines. The pilot announced we would land in five minutes. It was almost over, but new worries emerged. The takeoff was terrible enough; what if the plane can't stop? I pictured us plowing through a field, wings on fire, or diving off the end of the runway into that sparkling water Dad thought was so beautiful. My muscles tensed up, and my breath came faster and faster, making my head feel like a balloon about to float away.

Surprisingly, the touchdown amounted to a couple of light bounces. Once it came to a stop, the aircraft turned in the opposite direction and taxied slowly toward the terminal building. It was only then that I peeled my hand from Dad's arm, and he grimaced and rubbed the painful area. My knees wobbled when I stood up and turned toward the open door, where we climbed down the narrow stairs into the midmorning heat and humidity.

We followed the other passengers through a gate in a chain-link fence where vivid exotic flowers lined the walkway. They looked like graceful birds ready to take flight from atop tall, slender perches. Colorful posters on the walls in the baggage claim area previewed exciting tourist attractions. After ten minutes, a large cart piled high with luggage clattered through two swinging doors. The man who pushed the cart had rivulets of sweat pouring down his wrinkled face as he strained against the weight. Once we retrieved our suitcases, we went to the taxi stand, where my recent trauma vanished into the sultry air. "Dibs on the window," I shouted, sliding across the back seat to the driver's side.

As we approached the city, the cacophony of honking horns and drivers shouting at one another in Spanish filled the air. In the heart of this frenetic activity stood our destination, the Royal Palm Hotel. The taxi pulled up to the curb next to the stately entrance of the tall building, which stood diagonally at the intersection of two bustling streets, and a red uniformed bellhop emerged to take our luggage inside. I expected our room to be as ornate as the lobby, but when the bellhop unlocked the door, I saw the room was spacious but disappointingly plain. Mom ran her fingers across the worn brown bedspreads and closely inspected the sheets underneath. "Oh well," she sighed, "we'll be sightseeing most of the time.

My favorite spot on our three-day stay was Morro Castle, the old fortress that had once guarded Havana harbor. My thin-soled sandals were no match for the ancient cobblestones, and I struggled a bit for balance as we climbed to the main entrance.

"There's no telling how many people have walked this path over the centuries," Dad commented. "Everyone from Spanish soldiers to prisoners to British invaders. Now we're following in their footsteps and leaving our imprint, too." I liked that idea.

We took a tour bus ride outside the city to a shady grove where white-haired men hand-rolled cigars and hunched over long tables piled high with tobacco leaves. At the end of the tour, the bus driver steered all the passengers to the gift shop, hoping for a commission from the proprietor for any items we bought. But Dad was a Lucky Strike man, and the driver glowered as my family returned to the bus empty-handed.

As we strolled along the streets of the old section of Havana, we caught sweet, fruity, and spicy aromas wafting from the cafes. Mom chose a small restaurant with a colorful canopy, and we sat at an outdoor table, where, after perusing the menu, Dad pointed out his selections to the waiter. I recognized the rice and beans on my plate but not the charred yellow things. "Those are fried plantains," Mom said. "Try them; they're sweet and delicious." On our final afternoon, we strolled in the dappled sunlight of the Prado, where several shoeshine men unsuccessfully vied for Dad's patronage.

The incredible adventure made me forget we would have to fly back to Key West. But on the taxi ride to the airport, my fears returned, and my body was so tense that I ached when I reluctantly climbed the plane's stairs. Dad said, "Marge, you can sit with Kathi this time." She gave him an irritated look.

When I tried to grab her arm, Mom yanked it away and said firmly, "No, Kathleen. You can hold my hand but not my arm." She would not allow the same unsightly bruises that only now were fading on Dad's arm. "This flight will not be any different from the first one, and you'll be just fine." But I hadn't been "just fine" on the first one. She didn't understand how I felt, dizzy, sweaty, and full of dread. None of my family knew. I didn't choose to feel like I couldn't breathe or that my heart would pound out of my chest. I wanted to feel carefree like that other girl on the plane, but I couldn't.

When the propellors wound up, I leaned into Mom, which elicited no reassurance from her. I looked across the aisle at Dad, who had offered at least some degree of solace on the previous flight, but he was pointing out the window and talking to Sandy. No one cared about me.

After another excruciating thirty minutes of hearing fearsome noises, clutching my upset stomach, and looking at the floor, I listened to the welcome announcement that my ordeal was almost over. This time, the touchdown was practically imperceptible, so I was surprised when the plane turned around to taxi to the terminal. The nearby palm trees seemed surprised to see me as they waved, "Welcome back!" I was safe.

Having survived the trip, just barely, I was sure about one thing. While seeing new places and meeting new people had been fun, I didn't think these experiences were worth my torture. If I did travel in the future, it would be on the ground because I would never set foot on an airplane again!

Chapter Two

Maybe we missed it. The car crept toward Terminal 3 at Chicago's O'Hare Airport. We spotted TWA and Air Canada, and then a tiny sign between American and North Central told us we'd found the right place. Mom pulled over to the curb. Would she say it or not? We had tiptoed around the taboo subject on our four-hour drive from Waterloo but had veered off into safer territory each time. She blurted it out. "Are you sure you want to go through with this? It's not too late to change your mind. I won't be mad."

"It'll be fine," I said, attempting to assure myself as much as her. "I don't think they'll hire me anyway."

"But what if they offer you the job?" she pressed. "Will you tell them the truth?"

I didn't have an answer. It had been only nine days since I graduated from college, but the pressure I felt to find a job had led me to this absurd situation. What made me stand a chance of success in a career that did not just *touch* upon my phobias but would deliver body blows daily?

I leaned across to kiss Mom goodbye, retrieved my small suitcase from the back seat, and watched her drive away. A chilly May breeze made me shiver as the car's taillights disappeared around a curve. I should have accepted Mom's offer to return to the safety and predictability of home, but I didn't. I pulled my shoulders back resolutely, and as I walked inside the terminal, a newsreel documenting the past year of my life played tauntingly in my head: "Waterloo Woman Makes Boneheaded Decisions." And I was about to make another one.

I was a college senior in 1970 and had spent the last four years working on an almost worthless degree. Without grad school (which I couldn't afford), finding career opportunities for a psychology major with no teaching certificate was as tricky as unearthing proof of alien life. Even psychology-related fields, like research and marketing, barred their gates when they learned I didn't have a graduate degree or experience. Still, my pride didn't allow me to apply for jobs for which I felt overqualified.

My sorority sister Sally, who faced a similar dilemma, hit on a possible solution while we enjoyed beers at a taproom near campus we frequented on Friday afternoons. "We need a job we can do for a couple of years while we save money for grad school. Something fun." She thought for a moment. "I know! We should apply to the airlines!"

I had just taken a swig from my bottle of the local brew when she revealed her brainstorm, and I nearly choked at the thought of my having anything to do with airplanes. "Just one tiny problem," I said. "I'm scared of flying."

"No kidding! Well, I'd love to be a stewardess. But maybe you could be a ticket agent instead. I've heard all the airlines are hiring right and left."

That could work! Feet firmly planted on the ground. Money rolling in.

She had mailing addresses for all the major airlines, including some I had never heard of, like Delta, National, and Northeast. We wrote for applications from all of them, and when we filled them out, I noticed some had special sections to be completed only by stewardess applicants. I saw no reason to fill them in, but Sally insisted, "Aren't you curious to know if they think you fit the bill to be a stewardess?" I scoffed at Sally's idea but went along with it to humor her.

Those extra questions were quite personal—hair and eye color, height, weight, and measurements; some even asked for wrist and ankle measurements. Every application had spaces to attach a head and shoulders and a full-length photograph. My friend Ann took pictures of me in a navy knit top and navy- and yellow-striped mini-skirt as I attempted a sophisticated pose, prompting us to burst out laughing.

TWA and Pan Am required fluency in a foreign language, but based on my limited conversational ability, even after many semesters of French, I tossed those applications in the trash. A section that popped up repeatedly convinced me this whole airline idea was futile: "Enter your uncorrected visual acuity in your left and right eyes; you must have a minimum of 20-40." Did this apply to agents, too? If so, I was out of luck. Although I had 20-20 vision with contacts, I couldn't see a foot in front of me without them. I could picture the hiring personnel having a good laugh when they read my dismal numbers, but I entered them anyway: 20-400. Sally and I dropped our fistfuls of applications in the mailbox and waited. She was optimistic, and I had considerable misgivings.

A month passed, during which I received numerous rejections for other jobs but still awaited responses from my potential airline employers. I told Sally, "I might as well sign up for summer school and pick up some education courses. That way, I can work as a substitute teacher until something else comes along."

Sally looked uncomfortable. "I have something to tell you. Promise you won't be upset. I just found out I got a teaching job near home, and I'm ditching the airline idea. Maybe you should have thought of a backup plan, too." It was nearly impossible to hide my anguish and jealousy. "But you'll hear from one of the airlines soon. I'm sure of it," she said in a less-than-convincing tone. At last, some of the highly anticipated mail arrived. I ripped open each envelope only to find an apologetic letter that the airline wasn't hiring at present (which made me wonder where Sally had obtained her information).

But one morning, I found a lone envelope in my mailbox, and it was from one of the airlines I knew very little about—Delta. The letter invited me to fly free of charge from the airport nearest my home to Atlanta for an interview. Oh, and while they understood I was interested in an agent position, they were only hiring stewardesses. *Maybe they feel desperate, too, if they want to talk to a semi-blind applicant whose ankles and wrists might be out of proportion.* But at that moment, I was ecstatic that someone, *anyone*, might want to hire me. I rushed to the hallway phone in my dorm to call Mom and tell her the good news, but I should have anticipated her astonished reply.

"I don't understand. You're going to interview for what?"

I approached the Delta counter and pulled out the letter that authorized my pass to Atlanta. The agent smiled and filled in the blanks on a ticket, leaving a smudge of red carbon paper on his fingers. After he wrote "H4" on the ticket folder with a black Sharpie, he said, "Flight 849 is leaving in an hour and a half from the second gate on the left down that concourse." I spotted a wide-open hallway behind him, thanked him, and turned to leave. "Good luck!" he called as I walked away. "Delta is a great company to work for."

My handful of flying experiences since my inaugural flight to Cuba had not eased my fear. My obvious discomfort elicited well-meaning comments from seatmates, "You shouldn't be afraid. Flying is much safer than driving." Logic told me that was probably true. But my emotions intruded and knocked logic to its knees. This flight could be *the* one that doesn't make it.

Waiting to board was a special little hell all its own. Residual symptoms from childhood, dry mouth and rapid heartbeat, returned with a vengeance. Searching for something to occupy my mind, I turned over my ticket repeatedly to read the "contract of carriage" in tiny print, even though the legalese made little sense. I organized and reorganized the contents of my purse and watched the minute hand of my watch rotate at a glacial pace. *I wish I hadn't gotten here so early.* A few other passengers straggled into the gate and entertained themselves with books and newspapers, totally at ease in their surroundings. To pass the time, I tried to guess why they were on the flight. *The woman in the yellow dress looks like she's been crying; she's either had a bad breakup or is on her way to a funeral. That older couple, smiling and holding hands, are celebrating their anniversary. I wonder where they're going.* I furtively watched them and others until an agent took his place behind the counter and arranged his paperwork. He was just as friendly as the first agent when I hurried to the desk. After he tore off one copy of my ticket, he asked, "Would you like a window seat?"

Sure. The better to see the ground disappear below me. I had never sat in a window seat for that reason, but I could tell the agent meant his offer to be kind, so I said in a near whisper, "Yes, please."

He turned to a prominent seat diagram on the wall behind him, pulled off a red sticker that read "4D," and stuck it on my folder. "Passengers will board in about twenty minutes. Have a nice flight." For me, boarding was the next worst thing to being in the air. My stomach fluttered when I faced the portable stairs and climbed toward the open door, realizing there was no turning around. I didn't feel as panicky when I returned home from a large city and was able to board the plane through a jetway, but I didn't know which option I faced on this flight. When the boarding door opened to a carpeted jetway, I relaxed slightly and stepped over the airplane's threshold without rubbery knees.

An attractive redhead in a pastel yellow short-sleeved dress, beige gloves, and a mod helmet-style hat with a stem on top greeted me with a bright smile. "Welcome aboard. May I see your ticket? Oh, wonderful, your seat is in Row 4 on the left next to the window."

I figured the agent had made a mistake and would soon come on the plane to scoot me past the curtain where the muted color of the narrow seats matched my ashen face. I wasn't supposed to sit in this plush purple and magenta seat. *Well, until someone tells me differently...*

On my past flights, I had checked my suitcase in the baggage compartment. However, a tote bag was adequate for the few things I would need on my overnight stay in Atlanta and a short visit with Sandy and her husband Paul when I returned to Chicago. As always on buses and trains, I stashed my bag on the open rack above my seat.

The redhead scurried over. "Let's put your carry-on under the seat in front of you. That way, it won't bounce off if we encounter choppy air." *Why did she have to say that?*

Over the years, I had shed most of my childhood phobias. I still didn't like high bridges, but I closed my eyes (if I wasn't driving!) rather than flinging myself to the floor where I would no longer fit anyway. I understood that turnpikes were just regular highways you paid a toll to use and that mountain roads curved gradually to the summit and back down like everyone had said. But fear of flying continued to plague me, probably because I had experienced actual terror, not imaginary scenarios, and I flew only when there was no alternative. As the plane accelerated down the runway, I was glad no one sat next to me or across the aisle to witness my ramrod-straight body and my death grip on the armrests.

There were only three or four other passengers in first class and two stewardesses to take care of us. The redhead and her partner, a dark-haired, brown-eyed woman who somehow reminded me of Snow White, gave us exceptional attention. An appetizing aroma filled the cabin, and the next thing I knew, the redhead placed a snack—a small salad and toasted turkey sandwich—on my tray table. Hunger took precedence over fear, so I released the armrests long enough to scarf down every bite.

When they finished their service duties, both stewardesses came to my seat, where one leaned over the headrest of the row in front of me and the other perched across the aisle.

"We saw in our paperwork that you're on a pass for an interview. What position are you applying for?'

"I wanted to be an agent, but they told me they only needed stewardesses."

"Oh, you will absolutely love it!" exclaimed Snow White. "It's the greatest job in the world."

"Oh, yes," agreed her partner. "I can't imagine doing anything else."

"I was wondering, do all Delta stewardesses have to live in Atlanta?"

"No, we're based in Chicago but spend lots of time in Atlanta. There's a standing joke that you can't get anywhere on Delta without going through the 'Big A'," the redhead laughed.

"Is there a base in Miami?"

"Sure is!" said Snow.

When they saw the happy look on my face, both grinned. "Someone has a boyfriend in Miami," said the redhead in a teasing singsong voice.

I blushed but felt a sudden intimacy with them and confided,

"I don't think they'll hire me. I'm probably not what they're looking for."

"Are you kidding?" said Snow. "You're cute as a bug. They'd be crazy not to hire you."

I wasn't sure she was right. It had been a long journey to feeling good about my looks, only to learn, contrary to what I once naively believed, that being attractive provided no guarantee of happiness.

Chapter Three

I was a cute, outgoing little girl, an uninhibited showoff, to tell the truth, until third grade when I became the one and only child in my elementary school to wear glasses, thick Coke bottle glasses. My teacher, Miss Reece, was concerned that I was falling behind in arithmetic and told my parents it might be because I couldn't see the blackboard clearly. "The school nurse is due to conduct eye tests next week," she said. "Let's see the results and then decide what to do."

The nurse arrived with her easel, and the chart with the letter E turned every which way on rows that descended into smaller and smaller sizes. I felt the stab of fear that arose whenever I confronted anything unfamiliar. *Please don't make me go first.*

"All right, class. Line up in alphabetical order," said Miss Reece. "Joey Adams, step over to the chart." *Whew!* Joey sauntered to the nurse with his thumbs dug into his pants pockets. Over his shoulder, he winked knowingly at the other kids. "I've got this," he seemed to say. My competitiveness overtook my worry. *If Joey can do it, so can I.*

"Cover your right eye, Joey," the nurse instructed. "Now point your fingers in the same direction the letter E faces. Excellent. Now cover your left eye, and we'll do the same thing."

When it was my turn, I stepped to the line the nurse had taped on the floor, and my confidence vanished. I could see the big E at the top of the chart, but all the others looked like curly noodles in chicken soup. Giggles from my classmates broke through my concentration, and my cheeks burned as I realized I was getting all of them wrong. What I *could* see was the writing on the wall. Glasses were in my future.

In the examination chair at the eye doctor's office the following week, I squinted as hard as I could to make the letters come into focus. Maybe the doctor would say, "Mrs. Davidson, I'm not sure why you brought Kathleen in. Her vision is perfect." But that didn't happen. The doctor ushered Mom and me into a brightly lit room where frames of all shapes and colors sat on mirrored shelves. There were hundreds of them, and I braced myself for what would most likely be a long and tedious process, given Mom's microscopic scrutiny and comparison before she bought anything.

"Which ones do you like, Honey?" Mom asked.

"None of them."

Ignoring my stubbornness, Mom made me try on a dozen styles and, after a half hour, narrowed the choices to two. ("Put these on; now try on the other pair; put the first ones on again"). Finally, she held up a pair of tortoiseshell browline frames, the ugliest ones I had tried on, and said, "We'll take these."

"Good choice," replied the optician. "They're very popular."

Sure, maybe with old people. They look like the ones the woman at the library wears. And she's as old as Mom.

I dreaded showing up at school with my new glasses, but it was even worse than I'd feared. The girls looked at me curiously. "How can she see through such thick glass?" they were thinking. But the teasing and taunts from the boys were relentless. "Hey, four-eyes" and "Where'd you get those ugly glasses?" along with exaggerated pantomimes of a blind person groping the air to find their way.

"Children, poor eyesight is not a laughing matter." Miss Reece declared sharply. But the snickers, now muffled, continued.

21

The bell that ended the school day finally rang, and I felt my brave front crumbling. I gathered my books, hurried past kids on the playground who looked poised to start teasing me again, and walked up the hill to my house. Mom greeted me guardedly. "How did school go today?" In response, the tears that had lurked all day came pouring out in convulsive sobs.

Mom hugged me tight, ignoring the wet marks on her dress, reached for a tissue, and wiped my eyes. "Honey, I know it's not easy being the first one. But your glasses are very nice and make you look like the smart girl you are. The kids will get tired of teasing you before long. You'll see."

I wasn't against being smart, but not at the cost of wearing this unwanted accessory. Since children with glasses were an unusual sight, I thought people on the street were staring at me or, worse, were laughing behind my back (although Mom assured me neither was the case). I never wanted *this* kind of attention and became painfully shy almost overnight.

Mom was right about one thing, though. The name-calling eventually stopped, and by the following year, a couple of my classmates needed glasses, too, so I was no longer a freakish outlier. Not having glasses caused me to fall behind in math, a problem that plagued me into adulthood, but having them severely damaged my self-image—a double whammy.

Even at a young age, I believed I knew all about romantic relationships and was sure that having glasses would exclude me from them when I got old enough. The third-grade boys were too busy being obnoxious to notice girls now, but Hollywood showed me how things would change. When Sandy and I went to the movies, we often sat through the film twice, especially musicals. But sometimes, if we saw a double feature, the second film was more adult-oriented— *Tammy and the Bachelor, Don't Go Near the Water, Pillow Talk,* and other movies Mom and Dad would have been displeased to know we'd watched even though much of the dialogue went over our heads. Yes, things would change, but sadly, when they did, boys would want Doris Day or Debbie Reynolds to be their girlfriends, not a shy, bespectacled wallflower with tight home-permed curls.

I furthered my education compliments of our neighbor Lucille, an avid reader of *True Story* magazine. I knew it was off limits, but I desperately wanted to read its seamy stories. One day, I returned a bowl Mom had borrowed and found Lucille occupied, stirring a pot on the stove. As I walked back to the front door, something in the dining room wastebasket caught my eye. It was the forbidden magazine, and it screamed, "Take me!"

In secret, I devoured the sordid content, the ink on the thin pages sometimes rubbing off on my sweaty hands. I read about women who married too young and ended up with drunk husbands who abused them. These stories were far from romantic—lessons about what not to do—and always insinuated that the woman probably deserved what she got by nagging her poor husband to death. Things like that didn't happen in my home or any of my friends' homes as far as I could tell, and they certainly wouldn't happen to me. I believed in the technicolor version. When I grew up, a handsome man would be out there waiting to take me in his arms and love me forever.

A few years later, I entered junior high, standing five feet six inches and towering over most of the boys in my class, a further barrier to approval by the opposite sex. However, I quickly made friends with a group of girls who had frequent slumber parties at one another's homes. We played records, danced, styled each other's hair, and giggled all night as we talked about boys while creating a mess of candy wrappers, potato chip crumbs, and spilled Cokes. At some point, the hostess would pull a Ouija board off the shelf (each of us had one) to discover what it might reveal about our futures. Someone would ask a question, and she and another girl would place their fingertips on the heart-shaped planchette. We collectively gasped as the device glided to various numbers and letters, most often those that spelled out the desired answer. "You pushed it!" one accused. "Did not! It moved on its own."

I thought a much more reliable blueprint for life and love came from the lyrics of fifties and sixties pop songs I listened to on Waterloo's radio station KWWL. The songs offered helpful advice—I'd better *Shop Around* even though *My Heart Has a Mind of Its Own. Johnny Angel* might be around the corner, but *Big Girls Don't Cry* if he's not. Although *True Love Never Runs Smooth, Breaking Up Is Hard to Do*. It all came down to this—*I Want to Be Wanted*. I fantasized about being beautiful and desirable. I was the girl who promised *We'll Sing in the Sunshine* until I chose to be on my way; I was *Runaround Sue* who broke the heart of every boy in town; I was the wise and experienced girl who counseled that the only way to know if he loves you is in his kiss. (Why did they call that one *The Shoop Shoop Song*?)

The songs depicted what I dreamed of becoming. I possessed some commendable qualities like intelligence, kindness, and a great sense of humor. But they weren't as crucial as good looks and popularity, which were synonymous with happiness in my teenage thesaurus. Someone had to notice me for serious romance to come into my life. I had to make changes.

From the time I got my first job at sixteen as a cashier at the downtown Rexall Drug Store, I had saved money. Still very shy, I blushed and averted my eyes when customers placed wart removal pads and hemorrhoid cream on the counter at my register. Now, it was time to cash in on that misery. Using convoluted logic as to how *they* would benefit, I convinced Mom and Dad to let me spend some of my savings on contact lenses.

What a difference! People made actual eye contact with *me*, not my glasses, and a few boys in my class smiled at me as though I was a new girl in class. So why stop here? Mom let me lighten my hair, and my mousey brown locks became strawberry blonde. I felt different inside—more confident, less shy—because, at last, I felt pretty. I lightened my hair more the summer after high school graduation. Gone was any hint of red; I was blonde with a capital B! And I knew from Miss Clairol ads that "Blondes have more fun."

Chapter Four

In 1966, I had mixed feelings about starting my first year at a small midwestern college. Dad had been diagnosed with Hodgkin's lymphoma a year earlier and lost his job when he no longer had the stamina to perform his duties. Although I broached the idea of sitting out of college, Mom and Dad insisted that I go ahead as planned with money they had saved and earmarked for that purpose. The selfish part of me looked forward to a fresh start. I had reinvented myself. No one knew I used to wear geeky glasses or that I had been on only a handful of dates. I had not felt such self-confidence since I was seven years old!

Classes had barely started when a drop-dead gorgeous guy appeared on my radar at dinnertime in the commons. I made casual inquiries and learned his name was Tom, a sophomore who several girls had unsuccessfully pursued the previous year. Realizing he was out of my league, I went to football games and Friday night dances in the student union with classmates eager for my company. And though I saw Tom everywhere, he never once looked my way.

I was shocked when, late one afternoon, I came downstairs to my dorm lobby to meet a date for pizza just as Tom suddenly appeared at the front door. Without a word, he took my arm and guided me outside, astounding me and leaving my date flabber-gasted. I sat in the front seat of his car in stunned silence, afraid to say a word, as he drove to a nearby cafe, where we sat in a snug booth, his leg touching mine. Electricity ran up my spine!

I turned to him, mystified. "What are we doing here? I didn't think you knew I was alive."

"Oh, I knew," he said, flashing the captivating smile I had admired for weeks. "I was just a little slow on the uptake that you were interested in me."

During our two-hour conversation, I learned about his family (he was an only child), prep school background, enthusiasm for cars and motorcycles, and love of the beach. I realized his family was in a much higher economic bracket than mine and felt some concern. But he checked all the boxes that were important to me—he laughed easily, was clearly intelligent, hung on my every word, and, of course, he was very handsome, which boosted my ego. When he dropped me off at the dorm, I was sure Tom was my long-standing dream come true.

Over the next several weeks, many issues arose that I had never dealt with before: How much time together was too much? How do we balance classes and studying with fun time? Were we ignoring our friends? Should we sleep together? This last one was particularly thorny. I knew that "nice girls" didn't have sex before they were married, but that might be eons from now. My pop song meter failed me—one saying, "Go to him, run to him" and another cautioning that he might not still love me tomorrow. One night, while we sat in his car in a secluded area, Tom said, "I love you and can't wait to marry you." The dilemma was over.

Tom went home with me sometimes when I checked on my parents, and his evident respect for them and for me eliminated their misgivings about my being in such a serious relationship. By the end of the school year, we couldn't imagine making it through the summer without each other. Waterloo was near my college, but Tom lived in New England, a galaxy away. Even though I received letters from him every day and a phone call every night, I was miserable during our separation.

"Mom, can a person actually die of loneliness?" I asked one night as she and I prepared dinner.

"I don't think that's ever happened. Can you set the table and pour milk for everyone?" Lost in my little world, I failed to recognize that taking care of Dad left her little patience for my romantic tragedies.

Tom's parents, whom I had met when they visited him on campus, came to the rescue when they invited me to visit for a week and, aware of my family's financial situation, offered to pay for an airline ticket. Mom and Dad exchanged worried looks when I pleaded to go.

I hadn't forgotten the torture of that flight to Havana many years before. But I was willing to suffer any amount of misery and distress in the name of love. On the day of my departure, Mom sat beside me inside the terminal, unsure I would go through with something I had vowed never to do. The Ozark plane that awaited no longer looked squatty like I remembered. It was sleek and modern.

Nevertheless, my heart pounded as I mounted the stairs and stepped inside the plane. The only stewardesses I had ever seen were on magazine pages, but the one on this flight perfectly brought the image to life. She wore a short, stylish A-line dress and greeted me with a friendly smile. "You can sit anywhere past the curtain." I chose a row about halfway back with no other passengers nearby and sat stiffly in the aisle seat.

The flight hopscotched across the Midwest, making four stops on the way to New York's LaGuardia Airport, during which I had to endure quadruple the agony of hearing the whirs, whines, bangs, hums, and screeches that accompanied each takeoff and landing. The stewardesses offered drinks on each segment, and, out of nervousness, I gulped down a Coke on each one and soon faced a problem. I desperately needed to use the bathroom, but I was too afraid to stand and walk to it, and I didn't think passengers were allowed to use the restroom when the plane was parked; you certainly couldn't do that when a train was at a station. Consequently, when I deplaned in New York and saw Tom waving at me, I quickly waved back and tore into the ladies' room.

I had a wonderful visit during which I also fell in love with Tom's parents. Their warm manner and concern for my dad's health helped me understand why Tom was so special. On the flight home, the unhappiness I felt at being apart from Tom for another month until school started again overrode my fear.

Back on campus that fall, I felt like the luckiest girl in the universe. I was in the best sorority with the most handsome guy on campus as my fiancé. Of course, this was unofficial—no ring—but we had an understanding. The band The Association released the song *Never My Love*, which immediately became our song. Every Friday night, at the dance in the student union, we held each other close, and Tom sang softly into my ear, "*You ask me if there'll come a time when I grow tired of you. Never, my love. Never, my love.*"

Even though my classes and relationship took up most of my time, Mom and Dad were never far from my thoughts. On my trips home, I didn't see their daily struggles; they always presented a brave front. Mom wrote newsy letters once a week, seldom mentioning Dad's condition. But one day in early April, she phoned my dorm floor, her voice uncharacteristically somber, to tell me Dad was in the VA hospital in Iowa City. A few days later, he passed away—only fifty-seven years old.

Tom drove me to Waterloo, and during the days before the funeral, I leaned on him like never before. He let me cry without saying, "There, there," or "Everything will be all right," like so many others did. He prepared light meals even though none of us felt much like eating, and he became part of the family despite not having a piece of paper to formalize the relationship. When we returned to campus, the remaining six weeks of the semester became increasingly hectic, and studying for upcoming final exams gave me something else to focus on. Both of us were tearful and miserable the day Tom drove home for summer break, but he felt sure his parents would invite me to visit again if it was OK with Mom. I returned home to face life without Dad.

I hadn't appreciated how strong Mom had been during Dad's three-year illness. She provided the bulk of his caregiving while holding down a full-time job, serving as a deacon at church, and hiding her worries from Sandy and me. Still, within a few days of being home, I recognized how emotionally fragile Mom was. I grieved for someone with whom I had recently established an adult-to-adult relationship, but Mom had lost her life-long companion, a boy she met in first grade to whom she would have been married for thirty-five years had he lived just two months longer. Neither of us had a clear idea of how to navigate through the summer that lay ahead.

I spotted a newspaper ad for a six-week position as a counselor at a sleepaway camp for Girl Scouts. This scenario amused Mom and Tom because I was not the least bit outdoorsy and had to rely on my nine-year-old charges to kill bugs and keep s'mores from falling apart. When the job ended, Mom allowed me to fly to see Tom. This time, in addition to the unpleasantness of being on an airplane, I felt self-recrimination about taking yet another respite from the sadness at home.

While our relationship remained healthy at the start of my junior year and Tom's final year, it took an upsetting turn when we returned from winter break. I wanted to be with him every waking moment as we had always been, but he did more and more things without me. When I asked him why I couldn't attend certain activities, he said, "None of the guys are bringing their girlfriends." Yet sometimes later, a female friend would say, "Why weren't you with Tom the other night? We had a blast." One thing stayed the same. Each Friday, he held me close as we danced. *"How can you think love will end when I've asked you to spend your whole life with me."*

Tom had packed his car two days before commencement as though he couldn't wait to get on the road. I felt adrift knowing we would not be together at school in the fall, especially since I didn't have an engagement ring to affirm that we would be married one day. Saying goodbye at the end of the school year had never been easy, but this time, a gnawing uncertainty about the future tinged my sadness. With little enthusiasm, he said, "Mom and Dad will send you a ticket to come out again. Just let us know when you can make it."

"You say you fear I'll change my mind. I won't require you. Never, my love, Never, my love."

I found a good summer job and tried not to focus on my worries about Tom. My neighbor Lucille worked at Asquith Jewelry Store downtown and recommended me to the owner for an opening. I knew the store's reputation as the most prestigious place in town for engaged couples to register their wedding gift choices, in addition to being the go-to for people seeking beautiful jewelry and unique gifts. An added service was complimentary gift wrapping, which I was dismayed to learn would be my primary duty.

"Tape shouldn't show anywhere on the package," Lucille instructed. "Double it over and hide it beneath the seam and the side flaps." She sighed, exasperated, as I tried to clamp my fingers down on layers of ribbon to secure them while I cut the anchor piece, only to see everything fly apart. But, over time, I became adept at controlling paper, tape, and ribbon, and I soon grew bored with the process. I paid close attention to how the salespeople worked with customers and summoned my courage to ask Mr. Asquith if I could help an engaged couple select china. He agreed and busied himself nearby, ready to step in if I stumbled. At the end of the appointment, the bride-to-be's praise was effusive. "We couldn't have made such an important decision without your help." Mr. Asquith was pleased, and I basked in the compliments from him and my coworkers. I thought with newfound pride, *I'm pretty good at working with people.*

Mr. Asquith gave me a week off in August to see Tom, and I departed with the hope that the problems we had experienced in the last months at school were transitory and caused by the stress of his impending graduation. But the disconnection was still there. He finally admitted he was depressed about the draft lottery looming ahead in December. With his college deferment gone and no plans for grad school, his fate rested on the whim of a blue plastic ball. *Maybe that's what's been wrong all along. Maybe it's not me.*

It was close to midnight when we watched Neil Armstrong and Buzz Aldrin take a stroll on the moon. However, what the rest of the world considered a historic accomplishment did nothing to cheer me up. I had an early morning flight but resisted saying goodnight. I had one last chance to say or do something that would make Tom look at me the way he used to, but he yawned, gave me a peck on the cheek, and headed upstairs to his room. I followed a few minutes later, knowing I was in for a sleepless night.

As we sped through light traffic toward the airport, Tom had little to say. "Don't expect a lot of letters and phone calls while I'm at the beach cottage for the rest of the summer. There's no phone or mail delivery." His goodbye kiss seemed loving and sincere, the sort someone would give if they didn't expect a reunion anytime soon. On the flight home, I didn't focus on my fear of flying but on my despair that something precious was ending.

After three weeks of hearing nothing, I was desperate to talk to him, but he hadn't yet returned home from the beach. Hearing my disappointment when I phoned, his mother remarked, "I'm not sure what's going on. I think he has a lot on his mind and needs time to sort some things out."

I returned to campus, where my friends were astonished that I had not heard from Tom in over a month. One night, after getting a little drunk, I phoned again. Tom's mother sounded exhausted when she called him to the phone. With no inhibitions to hide my sarcasm, I said, "Hi there, this is Kathi. Does my name ring a bell?"

His silence was terrifying. His monosyllabic responses to my questions made the blood pound in my head. At last, he produced a complete sentence. "I know I'll be going to Vietnam and coming home in a wooden box, so we should end things now."

"Don't say that! You don't know that!"

After I asked a few more questions that elicited curt responses, he said, "I have to go now." With that, the line went dead.

Tom couldn't break up with me! For three years, we had been as close as two people could be. I didn't know what to do. Maybe I could talk with his mom. Maybe I should write him a letter. A week or so later, one of his friends let it slip; Tom had gotten a girl from home pregnant and planned to marry her.

I lay on my bed and sobbed, yelling, "Go away" to anyone who knocked. I had been wrong all along. Good looks and happiness were not synonymous; being blonde and popular did not provide immunity to heartbreak and disillusionment. Worst of all, I pictured Tom holding a shadowy woman in his arms and singing, "*You wonder if this heart of mine will lose its desire for you. Never, my love. Never, my love.*"

Chapter Five

The Atlanta airport was gigantic! I hadn't expected that. I could see dozens of airplanes (mostly Delta) parked on either side of lengthy concourses, two of which ended in futuristic-looking circles of five or six gates. With their noses in proximity, the planes appeared to be holding a secret conference.

The red-haired stewardess waved a buoyant goodbye. "Good luck! I hope to see you on the line one day." *The "line"? Did she mean at a restaurant? In front of a firing squad?* I smiled and said, "I hope so, too," as I stepped back on *terra firma*. It had been hard to find any trace of Delta at O'Hare, but here, the red and blue triangle (which I later learned was called a "widget") popped up everywhere, from check-in desks to wheelchairs.

My first task was to find a hotel near Delta's headquarters at the airport. Mr. Asquith, an experienced traveler, had told me to go to the baggage claim area and find a wall display with direct-line phones mounted next to pictures of hotels. "Just pick up the phone on the one that looks best, and it will ring the reservation desk," he explained. I strode through the vast concourse as if I knew exactly where I was going and was relieved to see an arrow pointing to the down escalator. Long lines waited for their turns at the reservation board, but fifteen minutes later, I had booked a room and felt very proud of myself.

Outside, Georgia welcomed me with oppressive humidity. The courtesy car area offered only the scant shade of a slanted roof, and my skirt and blouse were damp when the Quality Inn van pulled up. When I unlocked the door to my room, a cold blast from the air conditioner made me shiver beneath my clammy clothes. I unpacked and hung up the outfit I'd brought for the interview. Against Mom's advice to choose a dress, hose, and high heels ("That's what the stewardesses wear," she observed), I brought a dressy pants ensemble instead. The soft lavender bell-bottom pants and knee-length button-front vest complimented the colors in a long-sleeved floral-print blouse. Never comfortable trying to balance in high heels, I brought cream-colored, flat-heeled Mary Janes. The result was a fashion-forward look that I hoped would create a great impression.

I skipped dinner. I was apprehensive about leaving the room (what if I locked myself out?) and didn't know I could call and have food delivered to my door. *It's better to settle in and get a good night's sleep.* While I didn't have a specific time for my interview (the letter said I could come on the designated day between nine and two o'clock), I wanted to complete the interview as early as possible so I could fly back to Chicago in the afternoon. I removed two small alarm clocks from my bag, made sure they were set on Eastern time, and placed them on the nightstand.

I had a disturbing dream during a fitful night of pillow punching and sheet wrestling. A half dozen men wearing identical navy suits and ties covered in Delta widgets sat behind a conference table.

"What's your name, and what are you doing here?" one shouted.

"I'm Kathi and I want to be a stewardess," I stammered.

Questions poured out of them all simultaneously, and I didn't know who to look at or what to say. Their crossed arms and sidelong glances at one another told the story—they would not hire me.

"Leave the room," one growled. "Next!"

I walked out feeling disheartened and relieved at the same time. The jangle of my first alarm clock vaporized the scene. I lay there wondering for the hundredth time what had made me pursue such a futile goal—one I would never have considered if Tom hadn't shattered my plans for a happily-ever-after life.

After I learned about Tom's impending fatherhood, my self-esteem plummeted to the lowest level I could remember. I emerged from my room only to go to classes and to bring back bird-sized portions of food from the commons. My friends were concerned. "You've got to put this behind you and move on. He's a jerk and you're better off without him." It was easy for them to dismiss it as though it was a blind date that went terribly wrong. They didn't understand how deep the hurt went, accompanied by the embarrassment that I hadn't known what was going on. "Rejoin humanity. Start socializing again," they insisted.

Reluctantly, I sat at a table in the union during a Friday night dance to sell raffle tickets for my sorority's fundraiser. Smiling couples strolled in holding hands, waved to friends across the room, and pulled up chairs to already overcrowded tables. I was dwelling on my sadness in a place with so many memories of happier times and didn't realize someone had spoken to me. The woman beside me tapped my elbow and nodded toward a tall guy with a deep suntan and longish dark hair wearing a tie-dyed T-shirt.

"Sorry. Did you say something?" I shouted above the music.

"Yeah. I asked if you'd like to dance," he said in a thick New York accent.

I protested that I couldn't leave the table, but my friend said, "Go ahead. It's OK." We joined a flood of dancers as The Rolling

Stones' *Jumpin' Jack Flash* blared from the sound system, but when the song ended, I couldn't believe my ears. A sadist must be in charge of the music. The unmistakable opening chords of *Never My Love* knocked the wind out of me. I left my partner standing alone in the crowd and rushed to the restroom. When I emerged ten minutes later, puffy-eyed, he stood a few feet from the door.

"So, why did you run out on me?" he asked. "I don't think I dance that badly."

"It's a long story."

He led me to a sofa in a quiet corner, sat down, and patted the space beside him. "I'm not going anywhere. Shoot."

Hardly taking a breath, I poured out the details of my broken relationship to this stranger, including why that song had caused my sudden exit. When I ended my drawn-out chronicle, to which he had listened patiently, he said, "Well, I never met the guy, but he sounds like an idiot." Why did I suddenly feel the need to defend Tom? "No, no! He was wonderful," I heard myself say. It was ridiculous! He extended his hand. "By the way, I'm Matt." I ran into Matt a lot after that night, and he asked me out several times, but I wasn't ready.

My friends had strong opinions about him. "He looks like a hippie." "He's only a sophomore." "God, that accent!" They felt I should find someone more suitable, meaning a member of Tom's circle. However, most of them already had girlfriends, and those who didn't might be reluctant to step into Tom's place out of an undeserved sense of loyalty to him. I finally agreed to go out with Matt when he scored tickets to a Blood, Sweat & Tears concert. They were one of my favorite bands, and I couldn't refuse an opportunity to see them in person. Besides, Matt seemed like a nice guy, despite what my friends thought.

From the beginning, Matt's and my relationship differed from the one I'd had with Tom, mainly because I never considered Matt a potential husband. He was just someone who would provide normalcy for my final year in college. There were better choices than self-imposed exile.

We were together a lot, but we also spent time with other friends, and I had no concerns about that arrangement when we were on campus. However, Matt had several buddies from home who attended the University of Wisconsin in Madison, and since it was an easy drive, he made occasional trips to visit them. Those weekends made me uncomfortable because I hadn't regained my trust in men. However, as our relationship progressed and deepened, and we promised not to date anyone else while we were a couple, I felt less concerned.

The night before I graduated, Matt and I talked about the future.

"How are we going to see each other with so many things undecided?" I asked. "You'll be on your way to the University of Miami, and I think Delta might have a base there, but what if they don't hire me? What if I have to live somewhere else? What if ..."

Matt put his finger on my lips. "Shh. Everything is going to work out."

I started to cry as I voiced my biggest concern. "What if I can't make it through training because I'm too afraid?"

"You'll stop being afraid when you start flying a lot. It will become second nature."

I wasn't as confident about that outcome as Matt was. Our only firm decision was that I would fly to visit him in New York in July, white knuckling it all the way.

The second alarm clock buzzed, and I returned to my present situation. Not only had the flight to Atlanta been as nerve-racking as all the others I'd been on, but here I was, alone in a strange room, getting ready to talk to someone about spending nearly every day on an airplane. *I don't want to do this. Maybe I can sneak back to the airport and tell everyone the interview didn't go well.* No, I couldn't lie to my family and friends. I was here, and I would go through with it.

Dressed in my brand-new outfit, I walked across the hotel parking lot to the Waffle House even though I felt too nervous to eat. I ordered orange juice and coffee, but each sip made the knot in my stomach worse. *What will happen at the interview?* My only experience in that department was a brief conversation with Mr. Asquith, who knew he would hire me on Lucille's recommendation. *Will they offer me a position on the spot or turn me down at the end of the meeting?* With my juice glass and coffee cup still half full, I returned to my room to retrieve my bag and check out at the front desk.

It was nine a.m. on the dot when I stepped out of the courtesy van and walked into the lobby of Delta's headquarters. "I'm here for an employment interview," I told the receptionist and handed her my letter. She skimmed it and then picked up the phone. After a brief murmured conversation, she handed the letter back to me.

"Have a seat. Someone will be with you soon. I can put your bag in here with me while you have your interview."

I sank into an avocado-green upholstered chair and tried not to fidget. I noticed the tendril of a potted philodendron on a stand next to the floor-to-ceiling window trailing toward the entrance as if it, too, wanted to escape. About ten minutes later, a striking blonde woman in a dark gray suit, hose, and high heels (yes, Mom, you were right) instructed me to follow her to a room with several long tables divided by partitions. "Here's your aptitude test," she said, handing me a booklet and pencil. "You have an hour and a half to complete it."

I didn't expect a test! As I opened the first page, I relaxed a little. Multiple choice was always better than having to come up with an answer. "What is the closest synonym for 'lethargy'?" "Which sentence best describes the theme of the paragraph?" *A walk in the park!* I paged further through the booklet, and my heart sank. "Solve: x + 5y = 3." "There are 38 dimes and quarters in a collection totaling $6.80. How many of each coin are there?" *Do you have to be a math scholar to be a stewardess?* When the time was almost up, I returned the booklet to the woman who had remained at the front of the room as I sweated through the exam. "Wait here while I grade your test."

What if I didn't pass? Now that I'd gotten this far, I would be humiliated to go home without even talking to someone. The woman returned, this time with a smile. "Come with me. Mr. Porter is waiting for you in his office." I was relieved I had successfully jumped the first hurdle, but little did I know I was about to engage in a friendly tennis match with a top-seeded player.

I entered a spacious wood-paneled office with plush beige carpeting where a gentleman rose from his chair and extended his hand across the desk. "Fred Porter," he said. "It's very nice to meet you, Miss Davidson. Please have a seat. Did you have a good flight from Chicago?"

"Yes, sir," I responded, a bit too high-pitched and enthusiastic. "Everyone was so nice."

"That's what I like to hear. We pride ourselves on providing outstanding hospitality, which is what you'll learn to do in training."

What? Does that mean I have the job? I must have done great on the test!

"What made you apply to Delta?" he asked.

Should I tell him Delta was the only airline that offered me an interview? No, that wouldn't be smart. "To be honest, I don't know much about Delta," I admitted, "but I'm so impressed with what I've seen that I'm glad I applied."

Mr. Porter smiled broadly. Nice opening volley! Kathi - 15, Mr. Porter - love.

"Well, we have a great many applicants. Unfortunately, we can't hire all the young ladies who want to join us. We're quite selective." Mr. Porter evened the score. He asked me about my educational background, work experience, and interests. He nodded with approval when I told him I had a degree in psychology (Yes!) and that I had learned customer service skills at the jewelry store. I was gaining confidence as I pulled ahead again. Kathi – 30, Mr. Porter - 15

He explained that Delta was in a growth cycle, adding new routes, airplanes, and personnel at a fast pace. "We are not the largest airline, but we know we're the best. Our people are the reason. We are all part of the Delta Family and work together to ensure every passenger has an excellent experience on every flight."

I want to be in this family!

"Our stewardesses will be getting new uniforms in November," he continued, "and for the first time, trousers are one of the options. That might appeal to you."

Is he saying I will be one of those trouser-wearing stewardesses, or is this a comment about my outfit? I ceded a point.

He mentioned one of the difficulties of frequent flying. "Not everyone can live out of a suitcase, which is what it will feel like at first. Have you traveled much?"

"Yes. My family took long summer vacations when I was a child. I loved the constant change of scenery." *True, but I was afraid to fly to our destinations. Is it wrong to withhold that little fact?*

About ten minutes later, Mr. Porter glanced at his watch and wrapped up the conversation. "Would you be available to train in July?" I nearly screamed, "Yes!" But then, Mr. Porter stroked his chin thoughtfully as he looked at the ceiling. "Hmm. That class may already be full. I'll have to check." I'd lost track of the score.

He stood, escorted me to the door, and shook my hand again. "Thank you so much for coming to Atlanta. We'll let you know something within a couple of weeks. The receptionist can have a cab take you to the airport."

On the short ride to the terminal, I replayed the conversation. While I didn't exactly nail it, I didn't think I had said anything that hurt my chances either. There was no point in worrying about it, as it was out of my hands now; however, I couldn't shake my self-doubt on the flight to Chicago. I had been determined to make a good impression, but had I? As I clung miserably to the armrest of my coach seat (no room in first class), I considered the possibility I would never again board an airplane with the red and blue Delta logo on its tail, and I decided that was OK. I had given it my best shot.

Sandy and Paul picked me up at O'Hare. On the two-and-a-half-hour drive south to their home in Normal, Illinois, I told them how the interview had kept me off balance. "They wanted to see if you could think on your feet," said Paul. The following two weeks would be agonizing as I waited to hear something. Except, as it turned out, they weren't.

Five days after I returned to Waterloo, an envelope arrived with the now-familiar logo on the upper left corner. I called Mom at work to tell her.

"Well, for goodness' sake, open it!"

"I'm scared."

"I know. Just take a deep breath and read it to me."

It said in part:

Dear Miss Davidson:

We are happy to offer you the position of Flight Stewardess to begin training August 3, 1970.

This offer of employment is conditioned upon your meeting all requirements for employment to the complete satisfaction of the company. These requirements include a physical examination, check on former employment, character references, etc. The four-week stewardess training program will be conducted at the Delta Training Center, located near the Atlanta airport.

Street clothes, including girdle and hose, are in order for classroom attire; however, you should also bring old slacks, socks, and low-heeled shoes. As emergency ditching procedures are included during training, you should also bring a bathing suit or old dress suitable for use in the swimming pool.

You should bring approximately $150 in traveler's checks to cover the purchase of uniform accessories, laundry, hair styling, and other miscellaneous expenses during training, as well as utility and rent deposits at your assigned base. Also, please bring an alarm clock and a sufficient number of clothes hangers for your own use.

We look forward to welcoming you into the Delta Family.

Very truly yours,
F.M. Porter
Personnel Representative

Note: Our offer of employment is also contingent upon your reporting for work at a weight not exceeding 130 pounds. This will be your maximum weight throughout your service with Delta.

Mom's reaction was subdued but congratulatory, and I was pleased despite myself. But now I had to make a choice—accept the offer or let the airline know this was all a big mistake. My ambivalence aside, two parts of the letter made me laugh out loud: What was a girdle supposed to do for a beanpole like me, and at a current weight of a hundred and ten pounds, I couldn't imagine ever weighing over a hundred and thirty!

Chapter Six

I don't know if anyone had placed a bet on which way I would go in my career pursuit, but I saw some raised eyebrows and astonished faces when I told my family and friends that I had accepted Delta's offer. Two days before my training began on August 3, Mom once again drove me to O'Hare; this time, she didn't pussyfoot around her concerns. "I'm worried that this is not a good decision for you. You complained about how awful your flights were when you visited Matt in July. Why put yourself through this?" Maybe I was just exhausted from the weight of indecision, but, at that moment, I felt confident about my choice.

When I arrived in Atlanta, I followed my instructions to call the Hangar Cab Company for a ride to the training center. An unexpected difficulty arose when the cab driver stashed my suitcase in the trunk, opened the back door for me, and said, "You gwine Delta trainin' cenna?" Until now, nothing about my conversations with Georgians had been unusual except their noticeable southern accents, but this sounded like a foreign language. Even though I didn't understand what he said, the word "Delta" gave me hope he knew where to take me, so I nodded and crossed my fingers that I would end up where I needed to be.

I entered the lobby of the training center, where a 50ish woman peered over her half-framed glasses and greeted me. Her remark sounded something like, "Ha dahlin.' Ahm Miz Downs, the howzmatha and you ahr...?"

The rise in her voice at the end of her utterance told me she'd asked a question, so I took a stab at the answer. "I'm Kathi Davidson."

"Oh sugah, arnt you jist the cutest little thang with yer accent?" she laughed. *I'm the one with the accent?* "You run on upstairs now and meet yer roommate. She's fixin' to git settled in. The second room on the raht. Ah'll see y'all later."

I needed both hands to pull my heavy suitcase up the curving staircase, and after catching my breath, I tapped lightly on the open door of Room 203 so as not to startle the statuesque blonde with her back to me. She turned and gazed at me with wide blue eyes.

"Hi, I'm Kathi. I guess we're roommates."

Her face broke into a dazzling smile. "Well, ha, ahm Betty Sue from Memphiz."

I relaxed, let her words wash over me, and found I had less difficulty understanding. But even though the accent had a certain charm, I hoped I wouldn't be the only Yankee in the class.

As the other stewardess hopefuls arrived, a few sounded like they could be from places other than the deep South. An ebullient Miss Downs confirmed this at our first meeting Sunday evening when she announced to seventy expectant faces, "Y'all are from evry parta the country."

The director of in-flight training, Miss Roberts, did not have Miss Downs's warm and fuzzy demeanor. In a stern, no-nonsense voice, she laid down the law. "Your training begins tomorrow at eight a.m. sharp. Do not be late. We will send you home if you are late for class three times. You will have to learn a great deal of material quickly, and we will test you daily. You will go home if you fail more than two exams. Each of you knows your maximum weight allowance. We will weigh you every morning, and if you exceed your maximum at any time, you will (*let me guess*) go home. You will receive your base assignments during the last week of training. Delta's stewardess bases are Atlanta, Chicago, Dallas, Houston, Miami, and New Orleans, but some may not be open to you. Many of you will go to a city you don't want to live in. If all of this is more than you bargained for, now is the time to speak up." The room was dead quiet, and I wondered if I was the only one who considered standing up and walking out the door.

On Monday, the first day of training, we trooped to the company doctor's office in groups of ten to receive our physicals. (If we failed, we would…go home.) My blood pressure, heart rate, hearing, and reflexes were normal. The doctor asked about my health history and if I had ever had any surgeries. "Only one," I replied. "An appendectomy when I was in high school."

"Any reason to think you might be pregnant?"

I stifled an embarrassed giggle. "No, I'm not."

My calm demeanor gave way to panic as I glimpsed a Snellen chart in the hallway and realized I'd be taking an eye test. When the nurse asked me to remove my contacts, that would end the shortest career on record. Fortunately, she only asked me to read the smallest line I could, and I quickly passed with 20/20 vision.

After returning to class, I introduced myself to the woman beside me who was leafing through her training manual, and we instantly bonded over being Midwesterners. "Are you having trouble understanding the instructor?" I whispered. She nodded vigorously and softly chuckled. Chris was from Wisconsin and looked like a walking advertisement for the state with her perfect skin and wholesome, outdoorsy looks. We made plans to study together that night in her room.

Following a dinner of dried-out ham and cheese sandwiches from a vending machine in the hall, we pored over our manuals and notes. So much to absorb already! Later, when we took a break to stand up, stretch, and chat, I learned she had graduated from the University of Wisconsin in Madison and hoped to be based in Miami, where one of her college classmates had an apartment she could move into.

"I want to go there, too, because my boyfriend transferred to the University of Miami to study oceanography," I told her.

"Where did you go to college?" she asked.

"It's a small school you've probably never heard of."

"Try me." When I told her the name, she looked surprised, and her face lit up. "I know that college. I went out a few times with a guy from that school when he came to visit his friends. You might know him." *Oh my God, could it be?*

"What's his name?" I asked, my heart pounding.

"Matt Nelson."

A tuxedoed Humphrey Bogart in the movie *Casablanca* popped into my head. Of all the gin joints in the world, Ilsa had walked into his. My astonishment matched Bogie's; the improbability of Chris's knowing Matt was astronomical! I couldn't find words as I stared at her, slack-jawed. "Are you OK?" she asked.

Still in shock, I muttered, "Just a minute. I'll be right back." I felt lightheaded as I walked away. Although Matt wasn't as big a part of my life as Tom had been, his betrayal hurt like hell. I had had opportunities to cheat on him, but I hadn't, and withholding details about his visits to Madison was equivalent to lying. How many other girls had he gone out with despite our promise? I went to my room and sat on the bed for a few minutes, feeling my anger rise.

"You awl raht?" asked Betty Sue. "You look like yer fixin' to swoon."

"Sure. I'm just great."

I rummaged in my dresser drawer and removed a small blue vinyl photo album that documented the past year of Matt and me as a couple—holding hands at a picnic with friends, dressed in formal attire for a college dance, posing together after my commencement ceremony. I returned to Chris's room and laid the album on her bed. "This Matt Nelson?"

As she turned the pages, her expression evolved from disbelief to denial to chagrin. At last, she looked up and said, "What a loser. I'm so sorry. I had no idea Matt had a girlfriend."

"Does he know Delta hired you?" It would be the ultimate insult if Matt considered that Chris's and my paths would likely cross and didn't care.

"No. I didn't decide to apply until early this summer." She paused. "If it's any consolation, I didn't sleep with him…"

"Even though he asked you to," I finished for her.

"He doesn't deserve either one of us."

Despite this revelation and the fresh batch of disillusionment it brought, I knew I had to concentrate on the task at hand—passing training to become a stewardess. I would find a way to deal with Matt—but that would have to wait.

The instructors quizzed us relentlessly on everything from interpreting weather forecasts (was there a concern that the pilots couldn't read?) to preparing for emergency landings. But at this point, it was all theoretical. Even if I aced every written exam, the question remained—will I be able to walk on a moving airplane, let alone help a hundred passengers escape down an emergency slide?

As we studied, we found that empty stomachs often undermined our concentration. It hadn't taken long to realize that we were on our own when hunger pangs struck. For breakfast, I kept a jar of Tang in my room and packets of Carnation Instant Breakfast. A vending machine in the classroom area produced weak instant coffee with a metallic taste. By lunchtime, my stomach roared in protest. The instructor's lips were moving, but I couldn't comprehend a single thing she said.

Fortunately, Morrison's Cafeteria was just two blocks away. With only a one-hour and fifteen-minute break, we were grateful for its proximity and reasonable prices that didn't deplete the $8.50 we earned daily. On the first Thursday of training, my new friends Jane and Sharon and I stood in the long lunch line that wound around the perimeter of Morrison's dining area, separated from it by a four-foot partition. We inched along until the line stopped across from a table of three young men finishing their meals. They were well dressed—one in a suit and tie, the other two in polo shirts and dress pants. The three of us stole glances at the trio while waiting for the line to move.

"Jane, is that you?" the man in the suit called across the partition. Jane's face was blank. "I know it's been a long time," he said with a tinge of disappointment, "but please tell me you remember me."

Sharon and I looked back and forth between Jane and the man, anticipating that a light bulb would come on and she would recognize him. How could she forget a handsome face like his? Then I noticed the other two men looking at the floor and trying to stifle laughter. I, too, had trouble keeping a straight face when I realized what was happening. Jane wrinkled her forehead, struggling to retrieve his face from her memory bank until she noticed my amusement.

"What's so funny?" she asked.

"You're wearing your name tag."

Sharon and I had remembered to remove our laminated badges that read "Delta Stewardess Trainee" across the top with our first name below. Even without our name tags, it was no secret who we were. Given the restaurant's location near the training center, who else could these numerous small groups of young women be?

Jane quickly removed her tag, her cheeks red with anger and embarrassment. The man said, "I'm sorry. I couldn't resist, but I didn't mean to upset you. Let me make it up by buying lunch for you and your friends." Sharon and I were all over this idea because it would save us a couple of bucks, and the other two guys were also good-looking. After some persuasion from us, Jane agreed. "My name is Alan," he said. "I'll wait for you at the cashier's stand."

Alan carried Jane's tray to a large table where Harry and Barry (I swear) had moved. We learned that the three of them were cousins who worked in the area at different companies and sometimes got together for lunch.

"I've never done that before, but you're so pretty, I had to get your attention somehow," Alan said apologetically, attempting to wriggle into Jane's good graces. By this time, Sharon and I were conversing with the other two men. I glanced at my watch. "Oh, my God, we'll be late for class!"

"Come on. Hop in my car. I can get you there faster than you can walk it," Alan said as he pulled out Jane's chair.

We waved goodbye to Barry while Alan opened the passenger door for Jane, and Harry helped Sharon and me into the back seat. In the short time it took to arrive at the training center, Jane and I had dates with Alan and Harry to go to Six Flags the following Sunday. The prospect of a change of scenery to have fun on our only day off was something to look forward to. And I took immense pleasure in accepting my first post-Matt date.

Our weekday classroom lectures and activities were devoted to the most important aspect of our job—ensuring our passengers' safety. But what about the other part—providing hospitality? Hadn't Mr. Porter told me at my interview that I would learn that skill in training? Observation flights on Saturdays helped fill in that gap. Our instructor explained that "observation" didn't necessarily mean we wouldn't participate. "Sometimes, the crew will expect you to help with the safety demonstration," she explained. "Let's all take a turn reading and performing it."

I felt awkward trying to keep up with the script a classmate read. I had pointed out the imaginary exits when I heard an unfamiliar phrase: "And remember, the closest exit may be behind you." *Maybe this is a good philosophy for life. Look behind you occasionally to see if you've missed anything important—like lessons from two failed relationships.* The instructor continued, "It's up to the senior stewardesses to decide if you'll help with the service or stay in your passenger seats and watch." *I hope the ones on my flights insist that I sit quietly in my seat and not make a peep.* If my first observation flight proved as disastrous as I feared it would be, there would be no Six Flags the next day because I'd be on my way home. I pictured Miss Roberts, arms crossed, a scowl on her face, tapping her toe impatiently and telling me to pack faster.

On Saturday, another trainee, Beth, and I boarded a flight to New Orleans. I wanted to stay under the radar, but Beth (the big blabbermouth) introduced us to the senior stewardess, who beamed joyfully to have two extra pairs of hands to help with the beverage service on a full flight.

"You two will work out of the back galley. One of you can take drink orders—maybe just two or three to start—and the other will make the drinks. Understand?" *Yes, I think she's saying one of us has to actually walk in the aisle and simultaneously balance a tray.* "Two of my crew will start at the front of coach and serve drinks from a cart until they meet you."

I had not divulged my fear of flying to anyone in my training class, and I didn't want this flight to provide the big reveal. If I could stay in the galley, I could brace against the counter and grab it if needed. I casually asked Beth if she'd mind being the order taker.

One of the stewardesses on the crew put a bag of ice in a bucket and set it on the counter. "Here's a couple of rolls of glasses and some cocktail napkins. You probably won't need any more than these," she said before she joined her partner on the cart and pushed it toward the front of the cabin. *There's no 'probably' about it. There's over fifty cups on the counter!.*

"Coke, orange juice, gin and tonic," said Beth, relaying her first passenger orders. "The gin guy gave me five bucks, so the stewardesses owe him change."

I located the beverage drawers and found the correct cans, but when I pulled out a long, narrow drawer from the liquor kit, all I saw were the unlabeled tops of thirty miniature bottles. And there were two more drawers just like it! Which one was the gin? As I pulled out bottle after bottle for inspection, Beth stood by, looking like her head would explode if she couldn't blurt out the next three orders before I made the first ones. We had served only four rows when the beverage cart stewardesses caught up to us. One stewardess stated the obvious. "You're going to have to work much faster to finish a service." I smiled apologetically at Beth because I knew I was responsible for our poor showing.

Despite our slow performance, I considered the flight a success because something unexpected happened. While concentrating on my work, I never once thought about my surroundings. I had a job to do, a puzzle to solve, and I was unaware I was soaring through the sky at thirty-five thousand feet as I completed my tasks. On the return flight, Beth asked to trade places. I nodded and hoped my expression didn't give away my panic. A little unsteadily at first, I walked with a small tray in one hand and grabbed seat backs with the other only once or twice, which mainly went unnoticed by the passengers.

My relief at the success of my first test made me babble on and on about the flight as Beth, and I rode back to the training center. She finally held up her hand to shush me. "I didn't think it was *that* much fun," she said.

The following morning, Alan and Harry picked up Jane and me for breakfast and a fun-filled day at Six Flags. Harry held my hand as we strolled on the grounds, and we shrieked with laughter when we came barreling down the water flume and felt icy cold splashes on our skin. *If this is life after Matt, I'll take it!*

Two more observation flights during the training period gave me additional perspectives on the nature of the job. A flight to Birmingham presented a high degree of difficulty because three stewardesses had to serve beverages in both first class and coach on a thirty-minute flight. "The flight's full today," said the senior stewardess, "so I think it would be best for you to stay in your seat rather than help. There's not much elbow room in the galley."

After takeoff, with the plane still at a steep climb, she rose from her jumpseat to prepare a tray of soft drinks. As she emerged from the galley, she lost her balance, and several plastic glasses flew off her tray into the aisle, nearly splattering passengers in the first two rows. Without a second thought, I sprang from my seat, grabbed some paper towels from the counter, and cleaned up the mess while she continued her service. When we landed, she said, "Thank you for helping. I don't think we would have finished if I'd had to stop to clean up. You can see how much effort we put into completing every service, no matter how hard it is."

On my final observation flight to San Diego, I sat in the coach cabin and watched a stewardess perform the safety demonstration in her short-sleeved pastel green dress. When she reached upward to indicate the oxygen mask panel, I stifled a gasp as the underarm seam of her dress ripped open, followed immediately by gales of laughter from some of the passengers. My face flushed with embarrassment for her, but she finished the demonstration with great poise, and I wondered if I could react with such composure. She instantly became a role model to guide my behavior as a professional stewardess (if I made it to graduation).

Chapter Seven

I wasn't the only one with an epiphany during my first observation flight. On Monday morning, at the encouragement
of our instructors, several trainees shared experiences ranging
from embarrassing to harmful. An airsick passenger had handed
a full barf bag to one of the trainees, and she nearly threw up,
too. Another spilled tomato juice on the white jacket of a woman
who would be rushing to a wedding when she landed, and a
third cut herself with the galley knife and spent several seconds
bleeding until one of the stewardesses handed her a Band-Aid.
Although I didn't share the epic news that I had walked during
a flight for the very first time (I could only imagine the stunned
silence if I had), their accounts made me realize I was not alone
in my struggle to become comfortable on an airplane, albeit for
different reasons.

As our training continued, we memorized the location of
every piece of emergency equipment on all five airplane types
in Delta's fleet. "Which fire extinguisher should you use on an
electrical fire? Anyone?" asked one instructor. "I'm shaky, sweaty,
dizzy, and confused. What's wrong with me?" asked another.
(This question caused some snickers in the back row because
the instructor herself was a little ditzy.) "There's a loud noise,
swooshing of air, and the cabin fogs up. What will probably
happen next?"

The lessons also covered passenger service issues, such as handling a meal shortage or assisting passengers who would miss their connecting flights. One instructor, lecturing in her southern vernacular on how to deal with unpleasant people, referred to such passengers as "ugly." My friend Debbie, who misinterpreted the usage of that term, was dismayed that Delta would discriminate against people who weren't good-looking!

We watched educational films that reminded me of *Molly Grows Up* in junior high and looked to be of about the same vintage. One film depicted an actual childbirth, during which a handful of trainees rushed from the room (probably not for a coffee break). Another addressed the effects of hypoxia (an insufficient oxygen level) during rapid or gradual decompression. The point of the film was to demonstrate TUC (time of useful consciousness), the maximum time one has at a given altitude for making rational, life-saving decisions and carrying them out without supplemental oxygen. Test subjects donned oxygen masks and entered an altitude chamber where they performed tasks such as a game of pat-a-cake or matching geometric wood blocks with shapes on a board. Their performance quickly deteriorated within a few seconds of removing their masks at a simulated altitude of 35,000 feet. While the subject was dead serious, we couldn't contain our laughter when a woman following instructions to apply lipstick smeared it all over her face.

Every morning, we had a make-or-break test on material we had learned the previous day. On Friday of our second week of training, one trainee bid us a tearful goodbye as she went home after failing three exams. Although I felt terrible for her, I was glad I had put in the effort necessary to stay on for another week.

One of the most challenging tasks was learning the airport codes for every city Delta flew to—all forty-five. These codes are the three-letter sequences airlines use as ticketing and baggage handling identifiers, among other functions. We didn't know why it was so important to memorize them. "You'll thank me when you start flying," one instructor assured us. She explained that our rotations (the itinerary for each trip in our base) would use these codes rather than spelling out the city names. "If you don't learn them, you might pack shorts and sandals for a layover in New Orleans (MSY) but end up knee-deep in snowdrifts in Kansas City (MCI)." Many were easy to remember because they were the first three letters of the city name: MIA for Miami and LIT for Little Rock. Some bore a resemblance to the city name: SFO for San Francisco, JAX for Jacksonville. However, some only made sense once I read the information sheet explaining their history. The Cincinnati airport is not in Ohio but Covington, Kentucky—CVG. When a plane lands in Orlando, it shares runways with McCoy Air Force Base—MCO. However, these nuggets of information weren't always helpful because now I had to remember additional facts. Is Standiford Field in Louisville or Lexington? Is TYS Knoxville or Nashville?

Hands-on training brought oral instruction to life and produced very realistic scenarios. One of the most nerve-racking exercises was an unanticipated emergency evacuation drill. In groups of twenty at a time, we entered a cabin mockup where trainees, two at a time, took roles as the stewardesses and the rest as passengers. I wished I hadn't been afraid to volunteer first because the exercise became more difficult with each run-through. A tape played the sounds of a plane on a routine flight, and then suddenly, we heard what sounded like the plane hitting the ground and skidding for several seconds. Having learned in the classroom what to do, the "stewardesses" yelled, "Grab ankles! Heads down! Stay low!" which was very hard to do since, contrary to their instructions to passengers, they had to sit bolt upright with their heads pushed against the jumpseat. It was a little like patting your head and rubbing your stomach at the same time. The tape went silent; the plane had come to a stop. The "flight attendants" continued their commands while they, themselves, unbuckled their seatbelts and harnesses and looked through the door's porthole to see if the exit was clear of obstacles and hazards. "Release seatbelts! Get up! Get out! Leave everything! Good exit! Come this way!" Once at the exit, the "passengers" heard, "Sit and Slide! Sit and Slide!" and pretended to do so by stepping through the door.

As subsequent "stewardesses" took their turns, conditions changed. Visual effects intensified the already disconcerting experience—smoke (water vapor) filled the cabin and obscured the exit, or a flashing red light outside the mockup indicated fire. In those situations, they redirected the "passengers". "Bad exit! Move away!"

We became experts at extinguishing fires (in an outdoor pit), bandaging one another's ankles, and administering CPR. Of course, these exercises occurred in a controlled setting with lots of elbow room, unlike actual conditions on a plane. "Don't worry," said one of our instructors. "You'll automatically adapt to the surroundings when your adrenaline kicks in."

As our final week began, the focus turned to life after training. Since we all had the same hire date, we would draw numbers to determine seniority within our class and, ultimately, in the system-wide seniority list. The person who drew number one might hold a regular schedule in a few weeks, while the person with a high number could languish on reserve status for months.

Our seniority numbers also determined the order in which Delta assigned base cities. Throughout training, rumors swirled about which of the six bases had openings. Most of my classmates had pinned their hopes on going to a particular base—some because they wanted to be near their families, some because they wanted to get as far away from home as possible. We listed our top three choices on the provided forms, handed them to the senior instructor, and crossed our fingers. I'd had my heart set on Miami for so long that, despite the disappointing news about Matt, I still wanted to go there. However, a budding romance with Harry, the man I met at Morrison's, prompted me to list Atlanta as my second choice. Chicago rounded out my top three because I would be nearer Mom, Sandy, and Paul.

On Monday afternoon, we gathered in the auditorium where the director of in-flight training, Miss Roberts, entered the room carrying a glass bowl in front of her at arm's length like a sacred relic. It contained folded pieces of paper, each with a number written on it, and in alphabetical order, we drew one. I opened mine, acutely aware that the next stage of my career rested on pure luck. Number two! That meant I would likely get Miami. I felt elated but squelched a "yahoo" when the woman beside me burst into tears upon seeing her number— sixty-six.

As it turned out, Delta needed stewardesses in all the bases, and everyone got one of her top three choices, including Matt's other "girlfriend," Chris, who was going to Miami, too. And it wasn't the end of the world for those who didn't get the base they wanted because they could apply for a transfer at the end of our six-month probation period.

That evening, we divided into groups according to base assignments. Those of us going to Miami had a vague idea of rents (much pricier than those in Atlanta), so we knew we would need more than one roommate and would have to double up in the bedrooms. We calculated our monthly income at $550 and didn't want to blow most of it on housing. Kelly, a woman two doors down from me in the dorm, asked if I'd like to share a two-bedroom apartment with her and ask two others to join us. Candy, a frequent study partner, was devastated that she wasn't moving to New Orleans, where her boyfriend lived, and Lucy, from Mesquite, Texas, was equally disappointed that she wasn't going to Dallas. But they gratefully accepted Kelly's and my invitation to move in with us. In the back of our minds, Kelly and I knew we would have to find new roommates in six months unless Candy and Lucy decided to stay in Miami.

The same day we learned our base assignments, a bug began to make the rounds, and over half the class got sick. It attacked the gastrointestinal system and made the victims miserable with fever and vomiting. For some, it was touch and go even to get out of bed and attend class. On the other hand, I felt fine and a little cocky about how I seemed to have a superior immune system. Fortunately, the symptoms only lasted about two days, so those afflicted felt much better by graduation on Friday.

Our instructors told us it was customary that each class choose a song to sing at their ceremony, so in our "spare time," we gathered in the auditorium to select a piece and rehearse. On August 28, 1970, in the banquet hall of a nearby hotel, we stood proudly in our new uniforms—wings pinned to our hatbands—and held gloved hands as we sang *Leaving on a Jet Plane*.

All but four of the seventy trainees who started had earned their wings. We had completed a grueling training regimen and, with the notable exception of one from Waterloo, Iowa, emerged as confident young women ready to conquer the world.

Chapter Eight

T he night before graduation, I realized I had a problem. I had arrived at training with a full suitcase, not an inch of room to spare. Lying on my bed were items I'd recently acquired—two uniform dresses, a serving apron, a handbag, a pair of shoes, and a bulky hat. How do I make the suitcase latches close?" It was a trick question—I don't. Nearly everyone faced this predicament and searched for a solution. So, we were surprised and grateful when we returned to our rooms after the graduation ceremony to find a beige Samsonite tote bag on each of our beds, a parting gift to get us off to a good start.

At the airport Saturday morning, I bid tearful goodbyes to women I had not even met a few weeks earlier. I thought about sorority hell week in college and how, by Friday, our pledge class had formed an unbreakable bond. Training was like that—there were more of us, and it was hell *month*, but our experience bound us together, even if we were never to meet again. I was simultaneously excited and apprehensive about beginning a new independent phase of my life. No more maid service, no more running to Miss Downs with a problem, and, most consequentially, no instructor to show me what to do if I was unsure.

When my group of ten newly minted stewardesses landed, the assistant base manager, Linda, met the flight, and we followed her down the stairs beneath Gate 3 to the stewardess lounge for orientation. Our application photos must have preceded us because she already knew our names—impressive and creepy at the same time.

The lounge bustled with activity as stewardesses hurried in and out. They chatted in small groups and checked themselves in the full-length mirror, exuding the confidence I didn't yet feel. Some smiled at us and said hello, while others didn't acknowledge our existence. Linda greeted every one of them by name, too.

"Gather 'round," she said. "Welcome to the Miami base. I look forward to getting to know you better in the weeks ahead. My job is to support you in performing your job professionally. So, let's go over some important rules to make that happen. Here is what you need to do when you report for a trip. First, sign in at least one hour before departure, and don't be late. Flying isn't like an office job where it's OK if you occasionally run behind. If you don't arrive at the airport on time, your office will leave without you." We chuckled nervously until her expression told us she didn't mean her comment to be amusing. "Next, go to the supervisor's office for a weight and appearance check (which we soon learned included a finger flick on the side of our hip to ensure we wore a girdle). Then, find the rest of your crew and listen carefully to the pre-flight briefing from the senior stewardess."

Several women clustered around a large round table and perused enormous sheets of paper ruled into grids, with names down the left side and dates across the top. "They're checking their schedules," said Linda. On closer inspection, we saw that each box held a penciled-in three-digit number. Our bewildered faces made Linda grin. "Here," she said, handing each of us a stapled sheaf of paper. "We call this the bid packet. It's a crucial tool that shows the details of each trip we fly out of Miami. Each trip has a number, and the packet helps you understand the details of each trip. Some, called turnarounds, are only one day, and some are two- and three-day trips." We smiled with relief as we grasped the importance of the bid packet in understanding our flight schedules.

We newbies were on reserve, which meant that on days we were on duty, we had to be ready—sometimes on short notice—to cover any flight that needed a replacement or additional staffing. The schedule sheets and the bid packets were our only means of knowing when and where we were going. Senior stewardesses knew their schedules for the entire month, but because we didn't, we had to go to the lounge when we returned from each trip to check for our next assignment.

"All of you are free from now through Tuesday to find living arrangements. Please find your name on the sheets and copy your September schedule. It's subject to change, but at least you'll see what you're doing for the next couple of weeks." My roommates each had an assignment on Wednesday—Kelly, a two-day trip, and Candy and Lucy, three-day trips. My first trip wouldn't be until Thursday. We eagerly checked our bid packets to see where we would be flying. "My trip has a layover in New Orleans," exclaimed Candy. "I'll get to see Jim!"

Linda introduced us to the crew schedulers, who ensured every trip had the correct staffing. "We must be able to reach you at any time of the day," one explained. "But since you don't have phone service yet, you need to call us every three hours from six a.m. to nine p.m. to see if we have a trip for you."

When Linda finished her briefing and excused us, we went to baggage claim to retrieve our luggage and catch a courtesy van to the Miami Skyways Motel, our temporary home across the road from the airport. Delta was paying for three nights, but if we had not found an apartment by Tuesday afternoon, we'd be footing the motel bill until we did. None of us liked the prospect of using some of our limited resources on interim lodging, making it critical to find a place as quickly as possible.

We were lucky that Kelly had a college friend (now flying for Delta) who was away on vacation and loaned us her car for our scouting expedition. When handing her keys to Kelly, she gave us tips about where to look. "Most of the girls live in Miami Springs, Hialeah, or Doral, and a few downtown. I'd start there," she advised. By Monday night, our search had left us worn out and desperate to find an apartment that we all liked and could afford before our deadline. Back at the Skyways, we ran into one of our classmates who told us about a new apartment complex she and her roommate were moving into. It was about ten minutes south of the airport, an area we had yet to investigate. "I think there may be a couple of two-bedroom units left," she said.

The following morning, we hurried to Le Chateau Beau to look. Among its amenities were furnished (including TV) one- and two-bedroom apartments with a pool between two three-story buildings. The resident leasing agent, Margie, said, "Almost everyone who lives here at the Chateau works for the airlines." We didn't necessarily consider that a plus. Kelly's friend told us that some places had earned the nickname "stew zoo," and it would be wise to avoid them due to their unsavory reputations, but we had to be out of the Skyways by four o'clock that afternoon. When we informed Margie of our tight deadline, she said, "No problem. You girls can move in today." So, we signed on the dotted line.

As we hauled our luggage up three flights of stairs to our new apartment, I suddenly felt queasy, and the second Kelly unlocked the door, I rushed into the bathroom to throw up. I had a fever, too, which mirrored the symptoms of the bug that had plagued the training center the week before. At least those women had had access to sheets and towels. I had nothing! I lay on the bare mattress of one of the twin beds, curled up in a ball.

Kelly hurried to a nearby K-Mart to buy linens and immediate necessities—toilet paper, paper towels, soap, and cleaning supplies. Candy and Lucy took a cab to a grocery store to stock up on the basics. We would figure out who owed what to whom at the end of the week. When Kelly returned, she made my bed while I sat in a pitiful heap in the corner of the room. The second she finished, I crawled under the sheets, shivering. After running back and forth to the bathroom all night, I was exhausted when morning finally came.

On Wednesday, my three roommates deserted me to fly their first trips. Miserable, with no sign of relief from my symptoms, I wished Mom was here to take care of me. "You're an adult," I scolded myself. "Stop acting like a baby." But I kept thinking about how sweet she was when I was sick. I didn't know what to do about my trip the next day. I might feel OK by then, but what if I didn't? Most of those stricken in training were sick for at least two full days. The last thing I wanted was to be ill and useless on the trip. I decided not to take a chance and summoned the energy to walk downstairs to a pay phone at the far end of my building to call Crew Scheduling.

"Hi. My name is Kathi Davidson, and I'm supposed to work Rotation 130 tomorrow, but I'm sick." The silence at the other end of the line made me wonder if anyone was still there.

"I see," said the scheduler, sounding slightly annoyed. "You're one of the new ones, aren't you?"

"Yes, this is my first trip. Several people in my training class were sick last week, and now I've caught what they had."

"OK, I'll mark you sick. Call as soon as you're well, understand?"

"Yes, ma'am," I murmured, trying not to make things worse by crying.

"Not such a good way to start, is it?" Then, more gently, she added, "I hope you feel better soon."

I trudged back upstairs, dispirited, and spent the rest of the day watching TV soap operas and game shows until I fell asleep on the couch. When the eleven o'clock news awakened me, I turned off the TV and dragged myself to bed.

On Thursday morning, I felt better and decided to do something useful. I unpacked, put away my belongings, and organized the kitchen and cleaning supplies Kelly had bought. It was too beautiful to stay inside, so I ventured to the pool, sat on the edge, and dangled my feet in the warm water. A couple of women lying on National Airlines beach towels were soaking up the sun in bikinis. Hungry for human contact, I started a conversation with them. They were amused when I told them I had called in sick for my first trip. "Well, it can only get better from here," one laughed.

The day dragged on as I awaited Kelly's return. In my excitement to see her, I nearly plowed her down when she walked through the door around eight o'clock in the evening, and I bombarded her with questions. "How was your layover in Chicago? Were the other stewardesses nice to you? Were the meal services difficult? Tell me everything!"

"Well, I laid over at a motel near the airport and heard planes take off and land all night long, and my roommate snored. The other girls were nice and showed me the ropes for doing a dinner service, so I feel a lot better now that I know what to do. The whole crew, including the pilots, ate together at an Italian place next to the motel, and I think I'm in love with the flight engineer. It was fun, but I'm exhausted! I'm going to take a shower and go to bed." I had several more questions, but she said, "We'll talk more tomorrow. By the way, how are you feeling? You look a lot better."

"I'm great!" After hearing Kelly's account, I couldn't wait to get into the game.

I anticipated receiving my first assignment, but my nine o'clock phone call took the wind out of my sails. "I'll mark you well," the scheduler said, "but I don't have anything for you now." I trudged back upstairs, turned the volume low on the TV, and watched reruns of *I Love Lucy* until I got sleepy.

After a weekend in which the four of us trekked to the pay phone every three hours only to learn there were no assignments for us, we were overjoyed when the phone installer showed up on Monday morning. Kelly called Crew Scheduling to provide our new number. "I need to speak with each of you," said the scheduler. Kelly, Candy, and Lucy each had assignments.

When my turn came, I eagerly grabbed the receiver from Lucy.

"This is Kathi," I said excitedly.

"I have nothing for you, but you're on call."

My roommates jetted away again, while I sat alone in the apartment and waited to lose my first flight virginity. By now, I'd met some other people in the complex, including two male Delta ticket agents across the hall and four Delta stewardesses who had been in the July training class and lived in the two-bedroom apartment at the other end of my floor. While all of them understood my frustration at being flightless, none of them shared my opinion that a conspiracy was afoot to keep me forever grounded in retribution for calling in sick. Finally, the following Wednesday evening, the phone rang, and it was for me. "I've got a trip for you," said the scheduler.

I felt like jumping up and down, but my enthusiasm quickly evaporated when I heard the details. A stewardess had become ill, and I would replace her for the final day of her trip. The scheduler instructed me to drop by Operations to pick up a pass and deadhead (ride as a passenger) on Flight 892, which departed Miami at ten o'clock p.m. and arrived in Detroit shortly after midnight (one a.m. my time since Detroit didn't observe Daylight Savings Time), where I would catch a limo to the Cadillac Sheraton Hotel downtown. I hadn't expected to be alone on my first assignment! What if I couldn't find Operations in Detroit to pick up the limo voucher? What if I got in the wrong limo? What if I wandered the concourses of the Detroit airport, never to be seen again? Even though I knew these worries were foolish and symptomatic of my pervasive anxiety, I was relieved to learn that the pilots' layover was at the Sheraton, too, and I could ride with them.

None of my roommates had mentioned this problem, so I was surprised at how difficult it was to juggle everything I had to carry. I had packed only a change of underwear, pajamas, and my cosmetics and toiletries in the tote bag, but because the bag itself was rather heavy, it felt like a lead weight when I picked it up with my right hand. It was unnecessary to bring a garment bag when there was no need for layover clothes, but I brought one anyway and put my extra dress in it as insurance (Ripped underarm seam? No, thank you) and draped it over my left arm. I tried to balance the weight distribution by placing my patent leather frame bag (a required but virtually useless accessory) on my left wrist. This arrangement didn't quite do the trick because I was wearing two-inch heels. I tottered along, looking positively "Chaplinesque" as I struggled to keep up with the pilots who strode purposefully to the limo pickup point.

When we arrived in the hotel lobby, I explained to the desk clerk that I was replacing someone on the crew for Flight 325 the following morning. Since stewardesses shared rooms, he checked the register, picked up the phone, and alerted my roommate that I was on my way up.

A very sleepy woman answered my soft knock. "Hi, I'm Kathi. Sorry to wake you up, but I just got here."

"That's OK. I'm Becky. I have my alarm set for seven thirty. See you in the morning."

On the ride to the airport, Penny, the senior stewardess said, "I know you're brand new, but I had planned to work with

Becky in coach today. Can you handle first class by yourself?" My dismayed expression answered her question. "Never mind. I'll work in the front, and you can work with Becky."

The first leg was a forty-five-minute flight to Cincinnati. While the full load of passengers boarded, Becky showed me how to stack ice-filled plastic glasses in ice buckets and stash them behind the last row of seats. I recalled a lesson during training about safety regulations that warned against such shortcuts.

"They told us in training not to do that."

Becky rolled her eyes and laughed. "They told you lots of things you need to forget. Everybody does this. It's the only way you can finish the service in time."

After takeoff, Becky filled six iced glasses on a small tray, half with Coke and half with Sprite, and sent me to the first row of coach to pass them out.

"What if they want something else?"

"Tell them we'll fix it after serving everyone if we have time." I didn't remember hearing that in training either, but I stifled a comment.

I expected that Becky would make drinks for the passengers in the back of the cabin near the galley while I started from the front, but she continued to send me back into the aisle with my replenished tray while serving no one herself. After I reached the last row, she made my special orders—two coffees, a ginger ale, and an orange juice (which I miraculously remembered)—and I relied on passengers to flag me down because I had no idea who had ordered what.

"OK, now you can pick up the trash," she instructed. *I made a mental note: It's good to be the galley girl. She must be so happy, evading work and letting the "new girl" do everything. I bet she wouldn't act this way if she were working with Penny.*

On my return trips to the galley, I noticed that Becky occupied her time chatting with three uniformed servicemen who sat in the last row. I couldn't believe it when I returned with my first load of empty glasses to find her perched in the lap of the one in the aisle seat, her legs dangling over the armrest. Becky and the three men were laughing and having a great time. Disapproving glances from nearby passengers embarrassed me because her behavior fed into the stereotype many had of stewardesses as women with questionable morals.

The dirty looks I gave Becky went unnoticed, and, as a newbie, I was too uncomfortable to say anything to her. She continued flirting and joking with the men, and I remained the sole worker in the cabin. She rose only to put things away in the galley when we got ready to land but not to help me check seatbelts and tray tables. The trip's second leg, from Cincinnati to Miami, didn't differ much in the teamwork department. I was still steaming when I returned to the apartment. "Wow," Kerry said, "that must have been awful! Did you say anything to Penny?"

"No, I didn't want to come off as a tattletale."

Lucy interjected, "I would have told Becky where to go." Lucy liked to think she was assertive but would have been as meek as I was.

A week later, my second trip—a turnaround to Chicago—was completely different. Peggy, the senior stewardess, was in her mid-thirties and belonged to a group known as the "senior mamas" who benefitted from a 1968 court ruling. Until that decision, stewardesses at most airlines were required to "retire" by age thirty-two, denying them the opportunity to make flying a long-term career.

During her pre-flight briefing, Peggy said, "I'll work in first class both ways. Can you two handle the breakfast service in coach?" The other stewardess nodded, and I looked at her with alarm. *Can we?* She had been flying for only three months but had done meal services on several flights. With her coaching and only a half-full passenger load, we efficiently completed our breakfast service from West Palm Beach to Chicago.

The return nonstop flight featured "Royal Service," a meal service that required two stewardesses in first class. A Chicago-based stewardess provided extra help for the flight to Miami. I surprised myself by asking, "Peggy, can I help you with the service? I want to learn how to do it." She seemed impressed and readily agreed.

Peggy had a professional yet friendly manner that I wanted to emulate. We enjoyed chatting with our half dozen passengers as we served them. A man in a business suit and tie inquired, "So, how long have you ladies been flying?"

"I've been on the job fifteen years," Peggy replied.

"And you?"

"Fifteen days," I laughed.

I was surprised two weeks later when my supervisor handed me a copy of a letter that Delta's corporate offices had forwarded to Miami. Our passenger had written it on the Delta stationery we had provided him, and it read:

> Dear Sir,
>
> Aboard flight 957, Chicago to Fort Lauderdale, this date, I have had the pleasure to experience the wonderful services of Miss Kathy Davidson and Miss Peggy P- - - -. My trip was made so much more enjoyable because of them. Thank you!

"Way to go!" said my supervisor. "You're the first of your cohort to get a 'good letter,' and you get a free pass as a reward." I felt good that this recognition helped compensate for my slow start out of the gate. By the end of September, I couldn't believe I had spent so much of my life as a scared wimp about flying. I still wasn't crazy about the minor bumps and bounces that sometimes occurred, but they no longer drained the blood out of my knuckles. But I didn't realize I had just been lucky up to then.

Delta's DC-8-51 airplane featured a lounge in first class with a permanently installed table on the right side where two seats faced forward and two aft. Two more passengers could sit on the left facing the stewardess jumpseat. Frequent travelers loved the wide-open space the lounge provided and preferred it to the regular first class cabin.

On a DC-8 flight from Atlanta to Miami, a senior mama named Patricia and I had finished serving drinks and were about to start our dinner service when I felt the plane dip a couple of times, just enough to make my stomach lurch. The captain spoke over the PA system. "Ladies and gentlemen, I'm turning on the Fasten Seatbelt sign and ask that you remain seated. We're getting reports of thunderstorm activity in the area, so we're altering our course, but we may encounter some moderately choppy air as we work our way around the system. I'm asking our stewardesses to take their seats as well."

No sooner had the captain finished the announcement than the plane began to pitch and sway, and I headed toward the jumpseat, overcome with fear. Patricia grabbed my arm. "We've got to put everything away in the galley before we can sit down."

The old fear returned as though it had never been absent. I clung to the counter as I shoved a tray of glass roly-polys into its storage space, returned the ice bucket to a floor-level bin, and latched all the compartments tight. When we were ready to take our seats, I braced against the wall in the narrow passageway between the galley and the lounge, Patricia behind me. The spot I was desperate to reach was a mile away across a cavernous space, with nothing to hold on to between it and where I stood. "Move!" said Patricia and gave me a little push.

I took several giant steps, dove into the jumpseat, buckled up, and clung to the edge of the seat. All my progress vanished into the angry nimbus clouds outside the window. I wanted to cry as I realized I couldn't continue doing a job that terrified me. If

I was going to have any chance of a career with Delta, I needed to figure out once and for all how to deal with my anxiety.

In my mind's eye, I saw a hoop-skirted Deborah Kerr in the movie *The King and I* as she whistled a happy tune on a dock in Siam to overcome her fear. I couldn't do that without looking unhinged, but that was when I discovered, quite accidentally, that I could mold my face into a calm expression that projected the opposite of what I felt inside. When I did this, it seemed to fool my body into relaxing. "Nothing to be concerned about here," my brain said. I loosened my grip on the edge of the jumpseat.

I didn't invent this simple technique, but adopting it changed everything by giving me a tool to use in all sorts of tense circumstances. I just didn't expect to have to use it again so soon. A few weeks later I answered the call bell of a man I found gasping for air and turning blue. My anxious thoughts were, *oh, my God, he's having a heart attack. I need to get an oxygen bottle and page for medical help and let the pilots know we have an emergency, and please, please, please don't die on me.* But my Stewardess Face allowed me to calm down, assess the crisis and realize I had a team of coworkers to help me. I rang his call button several times to alert the cabin crew, and they sprang into action. While I stayed at the passenger's side to reassure him, another stewardess arrived with a portable oxygen bottle, and I put the mask on his face. His color returned to normal and, after he took a missed dose of his heart medication, he said, "I was very scared, but I saw that you weren't (*oh yes, I was!*), and I knew I was going to be OK."

Chapter Nine

Telephone service is vastly underappreciated; you don't miss it until you don't have it. But now that we had a connection to the outside world, our phone rang off the hook. Usually, it was Crew Scheduling with a trip assignment for one of us or a family member or friend calling to chat. However, we didn't expect calls from women trying to book appointments at the hair salon of the famous Fontainebleau Hotel on Miami Beach. At first, we pleasantly informed the callers they had the wrong number, but when the calls continued, we checked the phonebook and discovered that the salon listing showed our phone number. A call to the directory assistance operator produced the same information with no resolution. The operator said, "I recommend you call the business office to see if they can help."

We followed her advice and spoke with a woman who had little sympathy for our plight. "The hair salon recently changed its number, and the business office reassigned it to you. There's nothing I can do about it," she curtly informed us. "You'll just have to wait until the new phonebooks come out next spring." When we asked her for the hair salon's new number, she confounded us by saying, "I don't have that information. Call directory assistance." (So that's where Lily Tomlin got the idea for her character, Ernestine, on Laugh-In! "We're the phone company. We don't have to care.")

We called the Fontainebleau Hotel and asked to speak to the hair salon manager who was unconcerned. "We've been notifying our regular clients of the phone number change when they come in. Most of our customers are walk-in hotel guests, so it isn't much of a problem." Maybe not for him. But at least he gave us the salon's direct number. We passed along the new number to callers, but even so, a few didn't believe us and insisted we make appointments for them. So, we did.

"A wash and set with Jeannie? OK, she can take you at one o'clock on Tuesday," I told a caller.

"Highlights with Sue? How about Thursday at nine a.m.?" said Lucy, covering her mouth to suppress her laughter.

We knew what we did was borderline evil, but we were at wit's end. Then, as suddenly as the calls started, they stopped, and we had no idea why. In retrospect, we were thankful we didn't have the reassigned number of a pizza place.

Our trip assignments tapered off, leaving my roommates and me with lots of time on our hands. But that didn't change the fact that we had to sit by the phone while on duty, and there was only so much TV and reading we could stand. Three stories below us, the siren song of the beautiful blue swimming pool wafted up to our balcony.

A clever Eastern reserve stewardess at the Chateau solved the problem, and the rest of us soon followed suit. Radio Shack (a now-extinct electronics store) stocked various lengths of telephone extension cords, and the 100-footer ideally suited our needs. One person dangled the phone over the balcony railing, ensuring it stayed plugged into the wall outlet. At the same time, another on the ground below grabbed the phone and stretched the line across the lawn to the poolside, where we had staked out chaises with our beach towels. On a busy day, as many as twenty phones might dot the deck, making it hard to determine which one was ringing. There was clarity about the music from the radios, though; everyone tuned into Miami's premiere pop station, WQAM. Slathered with suntan oil, we cranked up the volume to *Ain't No Mountain High Enough* and *Green-Eyed Lady* and hoped Crew Scheduling would let us continue to bake.

With this newfound freedom, I met more of my Chateau neighbors. While there were dozens of stewardesses from various airlines, our complex didn't rise (or was it "fall"?) to the definition of "stew zoo." Residents included an Eastern mechanic, two salesmen for Kimberly-Clark, several University of Miami medical students, a teacher or two, and a colorful character named Josh, a man in his mid-twenties who sold women's clothing out of his apartment. Overweight with a prematurely receding hairline, Josh was not exactly the most desirable man at the Chateau. But since he offered stewardesses discounts on his fashions, he always had a steady stream of us coming and going from his "store."

"Have you ever been to a kosher restaurant?" Josh asked one day as I tried to decide between two tunic tops I liked.

"No, I haven't. Is that a cuisine you like?"

"Yeah, not because it's kosher, it's just delicious, and I know the best place on Miami Beach. Do you want to have dinner with me?" A bit disinterested, I accepted anyway.

At that time, before South Beach became one of the trendiest places on the planet, Ocean Drive's miles of pastel Art Deco hotels and motels looked seedy and unkempt. They catered predominantly to older tourists and retirees from the New York/New Jersey area. As Josh drove slowly along the busy street, I saw women with compression stockings turned down below the knee and men inching along the sidewalk with grocery bags attached to the handles of their walkers. Various smells emanated from the structures—some mouth-watering, some vile.

Our destination was a stuffy hole-in-the-wall with about ten tables. A waiter brought us a large bottle of seltzer water, and Josh ordered for both of us since I had no idea what the Hebrew menu said. I agreed with Josh's assessment of the food; the braised short ribs in thick gravy and mashed sweet potatoes were outstanding. I had a couple of bites of his rugelach and sliced a sliver of my walnut honey cake for him. Suddenly, Josh took my hand and said, "I could fall in love with you." *Whoa!* I gently explained that I valued his friendship and didn't want to complicate things. He was disappointed, but I had told the truth—I already had enough relationship issues.

There was unfinished business with Matt, for one thing. I had fantasized about various ways to confront him—some positively wicked. When I learned of his deceit on the first day of training, I spent a half hour on an expensive, tearful phone conversation with Mom. She asked what she should do if he called, and I told her not to give away she knew I was on to him. Not long after we got phone service, Mom called to let me know she had given Matt my number.

"He said he's on his way to Miami and can't wait to see you."

My voice dripped with sarcasm. "Oh, Mom, I can't wait to see him, either."

Enough time had passed for Matt to arrive in Miami, but I had yet to hear from him. Obviously, I was not his top priority. My roommates and I had the following Saturday off and decided to throw a party and invite some of our neighbors. This occasion would be a perfect setting for the payback, and as luck would have it, Chris (the other woman) was off that night, too. We hatched a plan in hopes that Matt would call in time for me to invite him into my trap.

He finally phoned a couple of days before our party. "Hi, Babe," he said nonchalantly, as though it hadn't been two months since we spoke. "How was training? Can't wait to hear all about it." "Great! I made lots of friends, and they were from all over the country. There was even one from Wisconsin, and she's here in Miami, too. Hey, my roommates and I are having a party on Saturday night. Can you come?"

"Sounds great. My friends will be jealous when they hear I'm going to party with stews (cringe; I hated that word!). Just leave some time for us to have a private party."

"Oh, I don't think you need to worry about that," I said sweetly, suppressing anger at his "pick-up-where-we-left-off" assumption.

We had asked our guests to arrive at seven o'clock, but I told Matt to come at seven thirty to give Chris and me time to brief everyone on Matt's lies and our plan to confront him. When the doorbell rang, an expectant hush fell over the group, and Chris disappeared into my bedroom. "Keep talking," I said to the guests as I headed to the door. "Don't act weird, or he may be suspicious."

Matt gave me a long, passionate kiss before entering the apartment. "I've been so impatient to see you!" Another lie.

Once I introduced him to our twenty or so guests, he got into the swing of the party and chatted and joked with several people. I approached him as he basked in the attention of a cluster of my stewardess friends.

"Remember I told you about the girl from Wisconsin I met in training? We discovered we had much more in common than we could imagine. Can you believe it? You met her before I did!"

Conversations stopped. The color drained from Matt's face, and his beer bottle almost slipped from his hand as he scanned the living room frantically searching for someone he recognized. "Chris," I called. "Come on out."

When he saw her, he turned to me with a tortured look. "I swear, I just hung out with her a few times. I didn't care about her."

"You do realize I'm standing right here," said Chris, "and that's not exactly the impression I got when we were together."

Matt stammered for a few more seconds and gave up trying to compose a sentence. He looked from one guest to the next in search of an ally, but he was in enemy territory.

To end his nightmare, I said, "Relax, Matt. Neither of us cares."

His anger spilled out. "Then I guess you're OK if we don't see each other again."

"Pretty much."

With that, he headed to the door and slammed it so hard that the wine glasses on the table bounced and jingled. The room erupted in laughter and applause at the coup's success. But I didn't join in. Absent from the planning of the ambush was the sadness I would feel about the end of another relationship, another betrayal. I couldn't get back into the party mood.

I'd had almost two months to get over Matt before I faced him. Not long after discovering his breach of trust, I had my first date with Harry (of Morrison's fame). But when I learned I would be moving to Miami, we agreed that the distance made an exclusive relationship an unreasonable expectation. Even though we talked on the phone often and met in Atlanta a couple of times when I had layovers there, these infrequent occasions were not conducive to developing a deeper relationship. I considered a transfer to Atlanta when my six months in Miami were over to make it easier to see him, but the sacrifice would be to leave behind a new interest.

Mike was a first-year medical student who lived on the ground floor of the building across from mine. We met at the pool on one of his rare days off and immediately clicked, but our hectic schedules conflicted so often that it was hard to find time to spend together, even though we both wanted things to move forward. Other men at the Chateau asked me to go out, but I declined. Many seemed nice enough, but two men in my life were sufficient. Still, I couldn't help thinking that the gawky girl I was in seventh grade could never have envisioned a dilemma like this.

Chapter Ten

There was a phenomenon in the Miami base named Snookie, a stewardess known systemwide for her mischievous (but harmless) shenanigans. Kelly and Lucy had flown with her and related stories of her antics that made me howl. I couldn't wait for the chance to see her in action. She was from Red Oak, Iowa, home of the picture calendar (as she always added), and edged only a hair over the required minimum height of five feet, two inches. When asked about the origins of her unusual name, she explained that her mother had gone into labor in a pool hall and gave birth to her on a snooker table, a story that most of us regarded skeptically but accepted as part of Snookie's charm.

She used a variety of props to support her performances, including a fake desktop telephone she set on the beverage cart and controlled by pushing a button in her pocket. Every six rows or so, the phone rang, and she picked up the receiver.

"Hello. Yes, this is Snookie. Uh-huh. Uh-huh. Oh, OK, just a second." She handed the receiver to an unsuspecting passenger and said, "It's for you." Many passengers took the phone from her and hesitatingly said, "Hello?"

Passengers weren't the only ones on the receiving end of her pranks. Sometimes, newbie stewardesses would get a nudge from Snookie when they stood in the aisle in first class and prepared to do the safety demonstration. "Can you please step to one side?" she prompted, "The pilots are trying to back up the airplane and can't see around you." Some laughed at the joke, but others were flustered and complied with her instructions.

Another item in her bag of tricks was something that looked like a kitchen spigot. She stuck it to her forehead before she hopped on the beverage cart and addressed her passengers. "Good morning," she said, "I'm Farrah Faucet. What can I offer you to drink?"

One bit was a guaranteed crowd pleaser. Snookie removed the bin from inside the trash cart and contorted her small frame to fit inside. As another flight attendant rolled her down the aisle, passengers saw the bizarre spectacle of a human arm extending from the top of the cart to collect their used cups and napkins.

My first Snookie experience came in early January 1971. Crew Scheduling assigned me a two-day trip, and when I arrived in the stewardess lounge, I was excited to see Snookie's name on the crew list. The trip had a long layover in Manhattan at a hotel between West 55th and West 56th Streets, two blocks from Central Park and reasonable walking distance to shopping and the theater district. My excitement at laying over in New York doubled when Snookie shared her plans for the following day. On her flight from New York to Atlanta the week before, Doc Severinsen, the flamboyant bandleader on Johnny Carson's *The Tonight Show*, was one of her passengers. Like everyone else, he found Snookie's infectious humor and zany personality irresistible, maybe recognizing a kindred spirit. Before deplaning, he handed her his card. "Here's my number. Call me next week when you're in New York again, and I'll get tickets to *The Tonight Show* for you and the other ladies." And tomorrow was the day. I couldn't believe my luck!

When we returned to the hotel after breakfast on the morning of the show, we huddled around Snookie as she dialed Doc's number. "Yes, I'd like to speak to Doc, please. Oh, he's in rehearsal? Well, he's expecting my call. Sure. Just tell him it's Snookie. OK, I'll hold." Less than fifteen seconds later, Doc came on the line to give her instructions on how to pick up the tickets.

We had only a short window after the five thirty p.m. taping to return to the hotel in time for our ride to the airport at eight, so to save as much time as possible, we wore our uniforms and checked our luggage in the hotel lobby. After a brisk walk to a coffee shop to grab a quick dinner, we arrived at the studio in Rockefeller Center just as the doors opened to let in the audience. A page ushered us to seats in the middle of the studio, about halfway up, where the camera couldn't miss us as it panned the audience at the beginning and end of each segment. Snookie had written "Hi Red Oak, Iowa" on the back of the paper placemat she saved from dinner and held it up each time the camera swept by.

We were disappointed that Johnny was off that night, but David Steinberg, the substitute host, was a favorite of mine and did a killer monologue. Helen Gurley Brown, editor of *Cosmopolitan* magazine, and actor Richard Chamberlain were guests, along with a singer I'd never heard of. She blew me away with her powerhouse voice, charisma, and over-the-top outfit, resplendent in fringe and sequins. Her name was Bette Midler.

Around 1975, Delta launched a no-frills option on some Florida to New York flights in response to competitors' leads. In exchange for a sizeable cut in the price of their tickets, no-frills passengers were entitled to only a seat, a seatbelt, and, presumably, an oxygen mask in case there was a decompression. They had to pay for every amenity offered free of charge to the rest of the passengers. "Do you want a glass of Coke? A deck of cards? One dollar, please." And no food whatsoever, not even a bag of peanuts.

On these flights, we usually served a hot meal to regular coach passengers. However, sometimes a no-frills passenger, lured by the aroma of bacon and eggs or barbequed chicken, sneaked into the regular coach section. If none of us noticed, a freeloader might eat a meal intended for a full-fare passenger, and we'd be short. The L-1011 was the plane best suited to keep the "riffraff" in their place. The forty-seat aft-most cabin, known as D Zone, had a bulkhead separating it from the rest of the coach cabin, so we could more easily detect "Sneaky Petes." Snookie loved to work in the no-frills section because it provided a perfect platform for her crème de la crème of pranks. Once the plane took off, she would put on a ratty bathrobe, furry slippers, and a rubber mask resembling an old hag with stringy gray hair. Around her neck, she wore a sign reading "No Frills Flight Attendant." The passengers loved it!

After several months of flying over and over to the same places—Atlanta, Chicago, Detroit, Cincinnati—Crew Scheduling called me with a much-anticipated assignment. I would work the most senior trip in the base to a city I couldn't wait to visit.

San Francisco had fascinated me ever since, as a child, I scoured travel magazines and clipped photos of its iconic landmarks—Fisherman's Wharf, the Golden Gate Bridge, Coit Tower, and crazy crooked Lombard Street. I never dreamed I would visit these places in person; they might as well have been on another planet. Back then, I knew traveling there required either a plane ride or a dangerous car trip through the pointy mountains, neither of which I would do. But now here I was, on my way, and I couldn't wait for the senior mamas to give me a grand tour of the city.

After a long and busy flight, we began our descent into San Francisco International Airport, and I could no longer contain my excitement. "What are we going to do on the layover?" I asked the woman I worked with in coach.

She gave me an odd look, probably thinking, "We?"

"I may run down to Cost Plus to pick up a few things and come back to the room to finish my book."

She had to be joking! Was she choosing to spend most of a twenty-hour layover in a hotel room? With great disappointment, I learned the other two stewardesses had equally exciting plans: shopping, an early dinner, and bed. Then it occurred to me—they had been to San Francisco hundreds of times and were no longer enchanted by it like I was.

As we rode into the city, I caught my first glimpse of the steep hills, and I stifled an excited "Look!" when I spotted a cable car. As we checked in at the Canterbury Hotel on Sutter Street, I noticed a stack of Gray Line city tour brochures on the desk and picked one up.

"How far is Union Square from here?" I asked the desk clerk.

She responded, "Four blocks. Turn left when you go out the door, walk two blocks, and turn right. You'll see it straight ahead."

Although I wasn't usually comfortable venturing out alone in an unfamiliar place, I glanced at my watch and made what, for me, was a bold decision. "Can you make a reservation for me on the city tour, leaving in twenty minutes?"

The other three stewardesses leisurely strolled to the elevator, and I nearly knocked them down in my haste to get to the room and change clothes. "Have fun," my roommate said, covering a yawn as I dashed out the door.

Passengers were boarding the bus when I arrived, so I hurriedly paid for my ticket and chose a window seat in front of two men about my age. The three-hour tour covered an extensive area. We swept past Seal Rock and the famous Cliff House restaurant, Mt. Davidson, with its iconic cross, Golden Gate Park, and Haight Ashbury, where hundreds of flower children in tie-dyed shirts, bell bottoms, and beads roamed the sidewalks.

I learned that the two guys behind me were on leave from their army base and exploring various places in Northern California. Coincidentally, one came from Evansdale, Iowa, near my hometown, and we discovered we had some acquaintances in common.

When the tour ended at Fisherman's Wharf, the driver announced we could either return to Union Square on the bus or disembark and find our way back on our own. "We're getting off. Why don't you come with us," urged one of the men, and without hesitation, I hopped off with them. The three of us roamed the wharf, ducking into the occasional gift shop, and eventually wound up at Ghirardelli Square. I had heard of the nearby Buena Vista Café and its famous Irish coffee, so we sat at the long wooden bar and sipped pure heaven from heated glass mugs.

"Do you know how to get back to your hotel?" asked one of my companions.

"No clue," I responded nonchalantly (courtesy of the Irish coffee).

"We can hail a cab for you, or you could take the cable car. I'm not sure how close that would get you, though."

"The cable car would be great!"

The white-jacketed bartender, overhearing our conversation, gave me instructions on navigating back to Union Square. "Take the Powell-Hyde right outside. Tell the conductor you want to go to Union Square when you get on, and he'll tell you when to get off and switch lines."

After exchanging contact information with me, the men waved goodbye as I hopped on the cable car for a thrilling ride up the hill. It was dusk when I returned to the hotel and found my roommate asleep with her open book on her chest. No novel in the world could be more exciting than the adventure I'd been on, and I made a promise to myself. In the future, when I flew with new hires, I would show them around a city that excited them, even if I had been to it dozens of times and never become so jaded that I couldn't enjoy an adventure with them.

Fortunately, stewardesses weren't limited to the whims of Crew Scheduling for opportunities to explore new places. Nearly every airline worldwide had reciprocal travel agreements with Delta—discounted fares, tour packages, flat rates—that included immediate family members. I knew where I wanted to go first. I had been fascinated by Greek mythology ever since my fourth-grade teacher read aloud the stories of the fickle gods intervening in the lives of hapless mortals. So, I invited Mom to go to Greece with me. If only Dad could have shared our adventure. I imagined that he would have worn out his pass card if he were still alive and had recovered from the shock that I was a stewardess.

The nine-and-a-half-hour TWA flight from New York to Athens was exhausting, but after a nap at our hotel, we felt ready to see the famous sights. Our travel package included an afternoon bus tour of the city where we met fellow travelers, including an Atlanta-based Delta stewardess, Colleen, and her mother. The four of us enjoyed each other's company throughout the week.

Colleen and I unwillingly became part of the entertainment after the welcome dinner at a taverna the night of our arrival. "Come, come," a dancer coerced, so we joined a dozen other diners in a traditional *Kalamatianos*, a dance I'd seen in *Zorba the Greek*. The costumed professional dancers led us in a circle that moved to our right (although I kept wanting to go left) as we tried to follow the leader's steps. The tempo increased, and I felt the ouzo I'd been drinking kick in. Amid laughter and applause, I collapsed in my chair, vowing never again to combine that particular spirit with strenuous dancing.

I was in awe of the ancient sites we visited, from the lofty structures on the Acropolis to the Temple of Poseidon on Cape Sounion. One excursion brought us to Delphi, the site of the Temple of Apollo. Dad's comments many years ago about our footprints at Morro Castle in Havana came back to me as I trudged the rocky path past small treasury buildings where dignitaries placed offerings in hopes that Apollo would speak to them through the Oracle. Centuries older, this path had been trodden by even more humanity than I could imagine, and now I added my mark.

Dining in Greece was a mixed experience for me. Always a somewhat picky eater, I was reluctant to try some of the dishes, especially lamb, and I didn't care for the taste of olive oil. But Mom loved everything she tried. However, by the end of the trip, she had reached her limit for Greek food. On our last day in Athens, we spotted a restaurant boasting "American Food" in flashing red neon lights, and we ordered hamburgers and fries. The waiter delivered limp fries and soppy buns drenched in olive oil, and we realized that the Greek definition of "American Food" was, in fact, still Greek food. We laughed as we courageously took bites and raised our wine glasses to toast the unexpected delights of international travel.

Chapter Eleven

The most predictable aspect of flying was that it was unpredictable, which made it both challenging and fun. I never knew what awaited me on the next flight, but I developed skills to handle various situations.

Last Call for Alcohol

As a college student who never went to bars and clubs without a fake ID, I understood the desire of some underage passengers to have a beer or a sophisticated highball like vodka and Sprite during the flight. However, my math skills were not quick enough to determine someone's age when they showed me their driver's license. And sometimes, when I did card them, low lighting and tiny print made it too hard to see, so I gave them the benefit of the doubt. But I came up with a solution that worked most of the time.

"I'll have a Bud," a teenager said to me.

"Are you eighteen?" I asked skeptically.

"I'm twenty," he replied, reaching into his pocket for the proof.

"Then I'm afraid you're out of luck. You have to be twenty-one to drink on an airplane."

If looks could kill!

The Club

Sex in the sky—now, that's something we never learned about in training, but it was hardly rare. I couldn't understand why anyone would want to join the mile high club in a lavatory's small, smelly confines. In fact, I found the idea of doing the deed in such unsanitary quarters disgusting. Yet, some passengers felt compelled to become members. It was entertaining to watch a couple try to disguise what they were up to. They walked to the galley together and waited for a vacant lavatory. First, the woman went in and "forgot" to lock the door. The man hung out until the stewardesses didn't seem to be paying attention and stepped inside.

The trickier part was the exit. In a typical scenario, another passenger waited impatiently to use the lavatory and tried to enter when the man came out. "Sorry," the man said, "my wife is still in there. She's not feeling well."

I oozed sympathy. "Oh, no! Is there anything I can get for her?"

He knocked on the door and said, "Are you OK, Honey? Someone wants to use the bathroom."

She opened the door, hair messy and clothes wrinkled, and responded, "Oh yes, I'm much better now." Which was probably true.

And You Are?

Sex didn't always occur in the privacy of the lavatory, as I learned on a half-full all-nighter from Atlanta to San Diego. In the early 1970s, it was a good bet that servicemen on flights to cities with military bases were headed to Vietnam before long, and my heart always went out to them.

A young man in a navy uniform boarded with a pretty woman barely out of her teens. "Do we have to sit in our assigned seats?" he asked.

"You can sit anywhere you like once everyone is on board. We have a very light load tonight."

The plane had sets of three seats on either side of the aisle, and the couple selected the next-to-the-last row on the left side, well away from other passengers. They grabbed several pillows and blankets from the overhead rack and settled in. I told the other stewardesses my guess that the sailor's girlfriend was seeing him off, and these might be their last hours together for a very long time, if ever again.

After the snack service, we dimmed the cabin lights low so that passengers could sleep, and the couple lay down across the seats and covered themselves with blankets. We weren't voyeuristic but couldn't help noticing the telltale signs of lovemaking as we made periodic walkthroughs. At last, they fell asleep.

As we approached San Diego, I gently tapped the young woman on the shoulder. "We'll be landing soon," I whispered. "You'll need to put on your seatbelts."

She looked disoriented, noticed her sleeping boyfriend, and remembered where she was. "Thanks," she said, giving the young man a rough nudge. He looked at her through bleary eyes. "Wake up. We're going to land," she said matter-of-factly.

When the plane arrived at the gate, the couple searched through the blankets to ensure they had everything. They were the last two passengers, and, waiting to exit the aircraft myself, I stood nearby as they retrieved their luggage from under the seats. The sailor started to say something to me but turned to the woman instead. "What's your name again?"

"Wendy," she said in an irritated tone.

He looked back at me. "Wendy here has to make a connection to Sacramento. Where does she go?"

I realized their passionate love affair had blossomed in the gatehouse in Atlanta. At least he had a nice sendoff, and she had a good story to tell her friends.

Lone Suspect

Then, there was solo sex. I worked in first class on a late-night flight from Atlanta to Houston. There were only two passengers in my section: a man in the aisle seat of Row 2 on the plane's left side and a woman in the aisle seat across and one row behind him. I finished my service quickly and had little to do but check on them every ten minutes or so. The man unnerved me with an inappropriate grin whenever I walked by his seat.

An interphone chime rang. It was the captain. "Hey, Darlin', Jim and I could sure use a cup of that excellent coffee you make. I like sugar in mine, but if you stir it with your finger, it'll be sweet enough."

There were two types of pilots. Most were friendly and professional and valued the stewardesses as part of their team. Some even became good friends with whom I enjoyed flying. The other group was the good ol' boys. Misogynistic and crude, they loved to tell dirty jokes and make stewardesses as uncomfortable as possible. The captain on this flight fell into the latter group.

I entered the cockpit with the coffee on a small tray and a stir stick in the one with sugar and handed the captain his cup. But instead of taking it, he said, "Gee, I wonder what we have in here." He lifted a small round metal cover in the middle of the yoke to reveal a nude photo of a woman with huge breasts. The copilot squirmed, but the captain got quite a chuckle from my disgusted expression. "Take your coffee," I said, eying the captain with loathing. "I have to get back to my passengers."

As I entered the cabin, I heard a call bell and approached the woman passenger in Row 3. She subtly gestured toward the man who had made me so uncomfortable and whispered that he had been exposing himself. I cautiously turned my head to look at him. Whatever he had been doing before, he now sat with his hands folded in his lap and displayed no other anatomical parts.

"He seems to be behaving himself now. Why don't you slide over to the window seat so you can't see him? I'll keep an eye on him."

I walked to the back of coach to tell the other two stewardesses what had happened, and the three of us stood in the aisle between coach and first class, two rows behind him, to observe. I'm unsure if he knew he had an audience, but he unzipped his pants and gave his private parts some fresh air and stimulation. I was irate! I grabbed a blanket from the overhead rack and threw it in his lap. "Keep it in your pants!" I snapped at the startled exhibitionist.

I needed to report the incident so that, if necessary, the agent could have the police meet the flight. Still fuming, I went into the cockpit and told the pilots what I had witnessed. Even though the captain was reprehensible, I expected him to support me and maybe even have the copilot go into the cabin to talk to the man. But instead, he looked over his shoulder and appraised me from head to foot. "Well, Darlin'," he said. "I guess he looked at you and couldn't help himself." That was it. With no repercussions for his behavior, I'm sure the passenger performed encores on other flights.

Acting 101

Sometimes, I wished I could speak a dozen languages because that skill would have been useful in countless situations. I could convey basic requests such as pointing to a passenger's reclined seat and motioning them to return it upright. But one day, I witnessed a talented co-worker demonstrate an extensive repertoire of communication skills.

We were working on either end of a meal cart in coach when we came to a row of passengers who spoke what sounded like an Eastern European language. My partner asked them if they would like chicken or fish, and they looked at one another, puzzled. Unfazed, my partner pointed to her meal cart and "clucked" while she tucked her hands under her armpits, elbows flapping. The passengers broke into smiles. She raised her finger. "Wait." Next, she moved her arms as if swimming and puffed her cheeks in and out. The passengers laughed with appreciation and, one by one, imitated her actions to convey their meal preferences.

Occasionally, pantomiming didn't produce the desired result. My friend Nancy's plane was at a gate in Dallas/Ft. Worth, an intermediate stop on her flight. She was tidying the cabin the inbound passengers had left in a mess. On such flights, we always encouraged the passengers continuing to the next stop to deplane and stretch their legs in the gate area instead of blocking the aisles while we tried to clean. A tour group of around twenty non-English speakers remained on board and strolled up and down the aisle, impeding progress.

Nancy located the group leader, who had only a tiny command of English himself. "We must clean the cabin," she said and demonstrated by picking up a crumpled napkin from the floor, pointing to her trash bag, and dropping it in. "Could you please ask your group to sit down?" She made a sweeping motion to include everyone who stood nearby. The leader understood perfectly. After speaking to his charges for a few seconds, they all began to pick up trash and bring it to Nancy.

The cabin was spotless in no time.

Nowhere to Hide

I was working on a very unpopular turnaround that reported at two forty-five a.m. in Miami, made stops in Atlanta, Dayton, and Detroit, and then returned nonstop to Miami. One winter morning, after completing the first leg, we were ready to push back from the gate in Atlanta with a full load of passengers when the captain announced that Dayton had zero visibility due to fog, and we couldn't leave the gate.

Loudly groaning and complaining, many passengers wanted to get off to make phone calls (no cell phones in the 1970s), but the agent discouraged them. "The minute we get clearance, we'll have to leave, even if you aren't back on the plane."

My crew and I had a dilemma, too. The leg from Atlanta to Dayton had a fast breakfast service, so we had already cooked the meals on the ground (a practice discouraged by the company for this very reason) before we learned of the delay. Passengers were hungry and crabby, and the aroma of food denied them added to the ugly mood. I conferred with the captain and decided we would complete as much of the breakfast service as possible before leaving the gate and then finish once we took off. As it turned out, we served everyone because the delay crept on and on.

We continued to offer coffee and juice, even to those who opted to wait in the gate area, and we made the passengers as comfortable as possible. There were plenty of pillows and blankets to go around, and having satisfied their stomach rumblings, many passengers slept.

We were "off the clock" when we did all this. Our hourly rate didn't begin until the door closed and the plane pushed away from the gate. A much less generous "duty rig" system sometimes compensated for time between flights, preflight preparations, boarding, and delays at the gate. But, the passengers did not see any trace of irritation on our faces; Delta was consistently number one in customer satisfaction for a reason.

At last, the pilots received clearance to depart. We were over two hours behind schedule, inconveniencing both north- and south-bound passengers. It also meant my crew and I would be lucky to return to Miami by three o'clock instead of twelve thirty. Several passengers made comments that lifted our spirits when they deplaned in Dayton: "Nice job." "Thanks for getting us here safely." "You gals were a great crew." Nearly everyone got off in Dayton, and with no local passengers to board, we quickly departed for the short hop to Detroit.

When our remaining passengers deplaned in Detroit, we had made up a little time, now running ninety minutes behind schedule. However, we would likely lose that if it took too long to service the airplane and board passengers for the return flight. The quicker we could accomplish those tasks, the better. When this trip ran on schedule, the stewardesses often used the ground time in Detroit to take a catnap while the consistently efficient Detroit cabin cleaners accomplished their work. This time, however, we pitched in by folding blankets and picking up trash, and we were quickly ready to board the passengers.

Whenever I was the Flight Attendant in Charge (a designation that replaced "senior stewardess"), I stood next to the cockpit door to greet passengers and direct them to their seats. But on this flight, the captain stood there. Some captains went above and beyond in delay situations by talking with passengers and heading off flak the cabin crew might otherwise get. This one, fresh from a restful layover, did a great job answering questions and keeping the mood light. With my usual post occupied, I stood in the first class galley and faced the stream of passengers in the aisle. Most were happy to finally be on their way and responded pleasantly to my greeting.

However, boarding moved at a snail's pace on this full flight as passengers arranged and rearranged their carry-on luggage and bulky coats in the overhead bins, blocking the aisle from others. A rotund, balding man waiting in the aisle next to me shook his head in irritation at the chaos that prevented him from proceeding to his seat.

I gave it my best shot. "Good morning, sir. I'll bet you're glad to be heading to Miami on such a gloomy day." He looked at me as if I were a pesky fly buzzing around his head. His response was simple and to the point. "This is a real horseshit airline."

With that, he faced the plane's rear again and waited to move along. Only the line didn't move. Disconcerted, I glanced toward the cockpit door to see if the captain had heard the man's remark, but he was engaged in conversation. However, the passengers in front of and behind the man had heard. Some of them looked at me with a mixture of sympathy and amusement.

"Why do you say that, sir?"

"You're always late. I've never once been on a Delta flight that wasn't late."

I attempted to lighten the mood with my perky stewardess voice. "Well, today, the weather didn't cooperate with us, but we worked hard so you would have as short a delay as possible."

Inside, I was angry. We *had* worked hard, and this rude passenger didn't appreciate the extra effort we expended so that he could jet to Miami and lay his pasty body on a beach towel. *Why isn't the line moving?*

"And that's another thing. You always have some horseshit excuse."

Now, I had an audience. "I'm sorry we've disappointed you today, sir." There was no appeasing this man and nothing more to say. Or was there? I glanced at the boarding pass in his chapped hand and added, "By the way, you're in Stall 18."

I wanted to stuff my words back in my mouth. But there they were, wafting around like smoke rings. In a second or two, the corners of the man's lips curved upward, the lines around his eyes crinkled, and he burst out laughing just as the line finally moved.

As he inched toward the back of the plane, he looked over his shoulder at me. "You still have a horseshit airline, but I like your sense of humor."

Chapter Twelve

I wasn't the only one in my circle of college friends to chase an unlikely career after we graduated. Ann, a theater major, moved to New York City to pursue acting as a livelihood; however, like thousands of other dreamers, she quickly became disillusioned about the probability of success. After hundreds of open auditions, she finally got a callback. She was optimistic and excited about possibly landing a part in the road show of *Fiddler on the Roof*, but the director shattered her hopes when he said, "Your singing and dancing are fine, but you don't look Jewish enough." She was exhausted from working from three p.m. until eleven o'clock at an ice cream parlor and rushing to her second job as a hat check girl at a midtown nightclub until three in the morning. I hated hearing the unhappiness in her voice during our occasional phone conversations, and I thought I could boost her spirits with a visit.

One of many perks offered to new hires was a reserved seat pass to any city in the system. I used mine to fly to New York and stay with Ann for two days in her rented room at the Spencer Arms on West 69th Street. She liked living there and considered it one of the few positive things about Manhattan. Another was that she met her soulmate, Dave, who bartended at the club where she worked.

As Ann and I discussed our respective living situations, the idea of moving to Atlanta took shape. She lamented, "Dave and I are barely making ends meet. We're ready for a change."

I chimed in with my tale of woe. "I love my roommate Kelly, but with four people living together in a small apartment, there's constant bickering. Candy complains that Lucy doesn't pick up her clothes. We all get on Kelly's case for playing the TV too loudly. And I admit I sometimes leave dirty dishes in the sink, but they act like I should be thrown in jail."

I would be eligible for a transfer at the end of February, but I dreaded telling Kelly my plans. My announcement came as a one-two punch after Candy and Lucy told us they were transferring to their preferred base cities. Fortunately, Kelly lined up new living arrangements quickly, which somewhat assuaged my guilt.

Even though the move to Atlanta would make home life less stressful, I wasn't sure how my decision would impact my relationships. I hadn't seen Harry often since I moved to Miami, so I didn't know if we could resume our relationship or if he even wanted to. In the meantime, my ties to Mike, the medical student, had deepened as we spent more time together. But it was too late to change plans; I had already put a deposit on a townhouse in Atlanta in a complex where several friends from training lived.

Ann and I arrived in Atlanta on the same day, March 3rd. We had barely finished hauling in the last of our belongings from our respective rental cars when there was a knock on the door. Two men stood on our doorstep, one juggling four glasses and the other carrying a pitcher of margaritas. "Welcome, neighbors," said the redhaired one. "Hope we're not intruding, but we thought you could use a break." *Where were you when we were sweating our rear ends off carrying boxes upstairs?* With no furniture, we sat on the floor and cooled off with their icy drinks. Several hours and many limes and salted rims later, we knew the highlights of each other's histories. Both men were copilots for Southern

Airways, a small regional carrier, and had recently transferred to Atlanta from Memphis. Both drove flashy, expensive cars. Russ (the redhead) had an orange Porsche Targa, and Bill had a yellow Datsun 240Z. I thought how risky it was to leave cars like those parked in the open—an invitation for someone to steal them—but maybe I was just jealous. I couldn't afford even a Ford Pinto.

A week and a half later, Dave arrived in Atlanta, and we started our *Three's Company* arrangement. While he immediately found lucrative work in construction, Ann went on several employment interviews without committing to any offers because the jobs lacked the creative element she craved. In New York, she had learned from a friend how to make unique leather fashion belts—a blend of hippy, boho, and Peter Maxx-like designs—and had made a decent supplemental income selling them. "If I can devote all my time to making belts, I should be able to earn enough for my share of the living expenses," Ann reasoned. After visiting the local Tandy Leather Company, where she purchased belt blanks, buckles, leather dyes, and tools to add to those she'd brought from New York, she got to work. Her small enterprise appropriated every square inch of our living room, but her efforts paid off. Sales soared as word spread through the large apartment complex about her trendy creations, and she secured consignment deals with Rich's and J.P. Allen department stores and several upscale boutiques.

Now that I had comfortably settled into my new digs, I wanted Mom to come for a visit. I invited her to use my pass benefit to fly to Atlanta for Easter, never considering this was a terrible idea. Holidays always saw a high volume of air travel, making it difficult for non-revs (passengers riding standby on a free pass) to get on a flight. Unfortunately, that's what happened to Mom. She stood by for three flights from Chicago to Atlanta and watched the last one push back from the gate without her. With no idea what to do, she must have looked like a lost soul when a young woman approached her.

"Are you, by any chance, a Delta employee's mom?"

How did she know? "Yes, I am, and it looks like I'm stranded."

"My name is Sheila, and I'm a Delta stewardess here in Chicago. My mom and I are trying to get to Los Angeles through Atlanta, and I noticed you were standing by, too. Why don't you come to my place for the night, and we can all try again in the morning?" Mom was overwhelmed by Sheila's kindness. The three took a bus downtown and walked a short distance to Sheila's apartment, where they ordered pizza, played cards, and enjoyed Sheila's airline stories. The following morning, after only a few hours of sleep but full of good cheer, they took the bus back to O'Hare, where each got a seat on the first flight. I had told Mom about the Delta Family, but she had now experienced it firsthand.

After enjoying Mom's visit and having someone to talk to all the time, I felt lonely after she left. Ann and Dave had the freedom to come and go as they wished; I continued to be a reserve and was stuck in the apartment waiting for the phone to ring (or not). It was a classic "the grass is always greener" scenario. My highly anticipated quieter living arrangements that replaced the frequent squabbles with my roommates in Miami turned into a feeling of isolation. Bill, one of the pilots who lived next door, kept me company sometimes when he wasn't flying and occasionally taxied me to the grocery store or to run errands. Occasionally, we'd grab dinner or go to a movie when we both had a night off.

In the meantime, my relationship with Harry became just as geographically challenging as with Mike in Miami. Harry had moved to Albany, Georgia, three hours south of Atlanta, for a new job, so I saw him only once or twice a month when he rode his motorcycle to town.

From our first date at Six Flags, Harry had been honest with me (a refreshing change) and told me he was married but separated and had a three-year-old son. Although he still loved his wife, their differences were so profound that he couldn't see a path to reconciliation. I continued the relationship, fully aware it had an uncertain future and could end anytime. Late one afternoon, he unexpectedly knocked on my door, and I saw camping equipment loaded on the back of his motorcycle. The look on his face told me something was about to change. "My wife has agreed to try counseling to see if we can salvage our marriage. I've been up in the mountains all weekend trying to figure out what to do."

"And what did you decide?' I asked quietly, unable to meet his eyes.

He held my hand. "It's so hard to say this because I love you, too, but for the sake of my son, I have to try to make the marriage work."

I kissed him on his cheek. "Yes, you do."

We held a lengthy embrace and cried as we said goodbye for the last time.

A few minutes after Harry's motorcycle roared away, I heard another knock on the door. "Is everything OK?" asked Bill. "He sure didn't stay very long."

"We broke up," I said, suppressing more tears.

"I'm sorry," he said, a bit insincerely. "But you're still seeing what's his name in Florida, right?" Then, with unexpected bluntness, "Are you in love with him?"

That was a good question. Mike and I always had a good time together, but managing the relationship was difficult. It would only become more so as he entered his second year of medical school with years more of education ahead of him.

"No, I like him a lot, but I'm not in love with him."

"Good. Because I want to convince you I'm the guy you should be with."

I had not seen that coming.

I wasn't physically attracted to Bill. He was not much taller than I, round-faced and slightly paunchy. Did that make me shallow? Yes, and I knew that. Even if my high school campaign for self-improvement had not turned me into a beauty queen, I tended to put a premium on the good looks of others. However, as the months went by and we spent time together in a variety of settings, I was drawn to his decisiveness (he knew what he wanted in life), his intelligence (we had interesting discussions on all kinds of topics), and his social ease in groups (it compensated for my lingering shyness). But he seemed to have been born without a funny bone, maintaining a humorless demeanor most of the time. I laughed quickly and often, and it was disconcerting when he did not react to things I found hilarious.

Still, my circumstances gnawed at me. Here I was, twenty-three years old and still single, in danger of becoming an old maid. And even though the social norms and expectations of the early 1970s were evolving, my socialization made marriage a milestone I didn't want to miss. Most of my high school and college friends had already tied the knot; some even had kids. Convinced that Bill might provide my only chance of having a husband, I broached the topic after we had dated for about eight months. But even though he professed to love me, he vetoed the idea of marriage, at least for the time being. He liked things fine the way they were.

I hadn't forgotten how Tom had strung me along when it came to getting married or even engaged, and I was determined not to allow Bill to do the same thing. But when he decided to buy a house, he felt ready to take the next step and asked me to move in with him. A marriage proposal would surely follow, so I saw this as an invitation to start planning the wedding I had always dreamed of.

"Whoa! Not so fast," he declared. "We can get married eventually, but not in a big ceremony."

Clearly, Bill's decisiveness had a downside. If I had been honest with myself, I would have ended things right there. Why would I want to be with someone who refused to show his commitment to me in the presence of family and friends and, in the meantime, shatter my dreams of a beautiful wedding? On the other hand, I wasn't getting any younger. Other opportunities would dwindle. I suppressed my desires and held on to the man I had.

Chapter Thirteen

Service! That was the primary directive for stewardesses (and all other Delta employees), and it set us apart from our competitors. The CAB (Civil Aeronautics Board) governed airlines' business practices until 1978. It regulated to which cities airlines could fly, their frequency of service, and how much they could charge on any given route. If passengers wanted to fly from New York to Miami, they paid the same fare whether they flew on Eastern, Northeast, or National. So, how did airlines distinguish themselves? With on-time departures, accurate baggage handling, helpful ground personnel, and attractive and friendly stewardesses.

Amenities played an essential role in staying on top. Delta provided an array of pastimes in an era before inflight entertainment systems. There were magazines in sturdy leatherette binders to satisfy every interest—*Time, Forbes, Sports Illustrated, Ebony, Popular Mechanics, Better Homes and Gardens*—to name a few. And they weren't issues from two years ago like those at the dentist's office. Cabin service crews changed the magazines weekly or monthly, as the case might be.

There were other options, too. If passengers were behind in their correspondence, they could request picture postcards of Delta aircraft flying in cloudless blue skies or stationery with the Delta logo at the top. Many passengers enjoyed a game of gin rummy or solitaire with a deck of playing cards featuring one of twenty-five different travel posters on the backs. Some passengers aspired to collect the whole set. ("I already have Nashville. Do you have San Francisco?") And some boldly asked for two decks "so we can play canasta." There were activity books to keep restless kids occupied. And, if passengers forgot to bring their lighters, no problem. Stewardesses were happy to furnish souvenir books of matches so smokers could puff to their hearts' content between Point A and Point B.

But the most important amenity of all was food. Delta provided food on almost every flight regardless of length or time of day. I never knew there was a meal called "munch," but learned it was the afternoon equivalent of brunch. One evening, my crew and I unexpectedly faced a challenging fast dinner service from Raleigh-Durham to Chicago when severe weather caused massive reroutes across the system. Each of us had worked many such services, but we were dismayed to learn that this one was in a category of its own.

As we waited for the inbound plane, Emily, the Flight Attendant in Charge, asked the captain, "How much time will we have for our service?"

"Oh, about fifty minutes, give or take. Lots of the girls don't finish. I've had to circle to give them time to pick up all the meal trays and put them in the galley, and the company sure gets upset about that."

Then why do they make us do this ridiculous service?

Fifty minutes to serve beverages and hot meals to twenty first class and forty-five coach passengers! Even my poor math skills told me that meant we could devote less than one minute per passenger. If this wasn't demanding enough, we had to perform this feat on an aircraft we detested. Most of our DC-9s had two galleys—one in front and one in the back—making it straightforward to do separate first class and coach services. But, this rogue airplane, inherited from another airline, had only one galley at the front, forcing us to work the service as one big cabin.

The three of us agreed—we would finish the service no matter what. None of us wanted to submit a flight report with this shameful entry: "Unable to serve everyone because we ran out of time." We carefully mapped our game plan (praying that turbulence wouldn't throw it into chaos). Having seniority on the crew, Emily took what she must have considered the plum position. "I'll work in the galley." I was happy to hear that because the galley was a claustrophobic space overflowing with equipment and supplies that I avoided whenever possible. Emily would be confined to that spot for the entire flight and place everything Judy and I needed for the service on a hinged shelf between the galley and the aisle.

Judy looked at me. "I'd like to do beverages if that's OK with you."

By default, that made me the meal runner, and when I say "runner," I mean that literally—no wheeled meal cart on this airplane. Emily would set up the meal trays two at a time, and I would hand-deliver each. "Fine," I said. "I guess I'm going to get my exercise tonight."

After takeoff, once the airplane's angle made it minimally safe to stand up, we put on our red paisley aprons and flat-heeled shoes and began our mission. The service in first class required precise ballet-like choreography; one misstep threw the whole thing off. Judy offered a hot towel to each passenger while, right behind her, I placed a white linen tablecloth on each tray table. Judy hurried to the front again and, row by row, took the passengers' drink orders, which Emily made and put on the shelf. The second I finished placing tablecloths, I rushed to the front of the cabin to pick up the used hot towels and help Judy complete the beverage service.

By this time, the passengers in the first few rows were ready for their meals. I noticed on our paperwork that the two passengers in the first row on the right side of the aisle were a Delta employee and his wife; their two teenage kids sat directly across the aisle. While I always kept a low profile when I traveled on a free pass, some non-revs could be more demanding than paying passengers, and this family struck me as the type who would be a nuisance. The kids had already asked for refills on their Cokes twice, and the wife stared at the meal tray I put on her table, frowned, and whined, "Don't you have some other kind of salad dressing?" We didn't. Yup, they were likely to slow us down. As I served meals, Judy followed me with a wine bottle in each hand. "Would you care for wine? Red or white? Would you care for wine? Red or white?" Sure, it sounded robotic, but she didn't have time to explain that the chardonnay had a rich buttery finish, and the cabernet was complex and full-bodied. After serving two rows of meals, I picked up a basket of warm dinner rolls from the shelf and put one on each tray. This fancy footwork continued with split-second timing until we had served everyone in first class.

Next, we began the coach service, which was less a dance and more an endurance race. There were two seats on one side of the aisle and three on the other, and behind the last row sat a fully stocked drink cart in an enclosed cubicle. I began serving meals in the back row, and Judy followed me from back to front with the cart.

The aroma of barbequed chicken wafted from the galley as I picked up the first two coach trays. Nestled next to the chicken breast were green beans and cheesy mashed potatoes and, on the edge of each tray sat a dessert I had never seen before, a luscious-looking key lime tart with a graham cracker crust and a big dollop of whipped cream on top.

A faster meal runner had never been born! I had wings on my feet as I returned to the front galley, grabbed two more trays, pivoted, power-walked through the narrow aisle, and set the meals on two more passengers' tables. It was hard to maneuver in the close quarters between sets of seats, but I made my tight pivot again and sped back to the galley. I found myself in a Zen-like state and heard a voice inside my head say, "Be one with the meals."

Around the time I finished serving the fourth row, something intruded on my concentration as I picked up the next two trays. I tried to ignore it, but there it was—a slight movement in my peripheral vision—and I realized the non-rev who sat in the aisle seat of the first row was trying to catch my eye. I ignored him, grabbed two trays, turned, sailed past him into the coach cabin, made my crisp pivot, and charged back to the front.

As I reached the galley again, I couldn't believe it. From the corner of my eye, I saw the man make a slight movement that could have been a wave if I had turned to look. "No," said my Zen master. "Pay no attention. You must be one with the meals."

But my inner voice took over. *What a jerk! He can see how busy I am. He'll have to wait for more wine or to have me pick up his tray or whatever he wants.* With gritty determination, I grasped two more trays, sped even faster down the aisle, made my tight turn, and flew back to the front.

"Miss," he said, too loudly to pretend I hadn't heard.

I turned to him with a forced smile. "Yes, sir?"

He beckoned with his forefinger for me to bend down to his level. With cupped hands, he whispered, "I just want to tell you that every time you come up the aisle, you have more and more whipped cream on your rear end."

I thought about the stewardess with the ripped seam and the one who nearly spilled the tray of drinks on her passengers. What would they do in this situation? Somehow, I maintained my poise and thanked the passenger for letting me know that I had, indeed, become one with the meals.

But, by God, we finished the service without having to circle!

The Raleigh-Durham dinner service was far from the only mission impossible. A hot breakfast from Philadelphia to Boston on a single-aisle 727 was just as daunting. Crew schedulers sneakily hid this flight in various rotations from month to month. Unsuspecting senior stewardesses when deciding which trip they wanted, would look at a beautiful rotation, spot the dreaded Flight 580, and recoil as if encountering a scorpion. That's the reason I could usually hold the trip. And for the price of one hour of torture, I could fly a trip that was, otherwise, a cakewalk.

The logic of this breakfast service escaped us. The flight left at seven o'clock, five minutes earlier than a USAir flight that was also going to Boston. It offered only a cellophane-wrapped cold Danish, and both flights were always full.

The Dobbs House catering supervisor who checked that we'd received the correct number of meals shook her head, perplexed. She couldn't understand why Delta went to the expense of serving hot food when it was unnecessary from a competitive standpoint. "Oh well," she joked, "job security for me."

It was difficult enough to serve one hundred thirty-six passengers in forty minutes under ideal circumstances, but specific menus made it nearly impossible. Of all the breakfasts on the rotating schedule, the worst was cheesy scrambled eggs that had a paper cover over them so they wouldn't burn while they cooked. We had to remove this doohickey from each casserole before we served it, and it notoriously stuck to the cheese and took half the eggs with it as we pried it off with a swizzle stick. Tick-tock.

The only salvation on this flight was the Row 48 Club. Behind the emergency exit door at the rear of the plane on the right side were two rows of passenger seats. The first of these, Row 48, sat directly across from the galley and was popular with passengers in the know because of its immense amount of legroom. We got annoyed when passengers sat in Row 48 on a light flight because it deprived us of a great place to take a break. But on the full Philly-Boston flight, we couldn't manage without the help of the

Row 48ers, commuters who knew one another and got to know us. They were well-versed in their "duties." In exchange for a couple of liquor miniatures, they would skip breakfast and help stuff dirty meal trays into the carriers if it looked like we wouldn't finish before we landed. Some even poured coffee for the last few rows of coach. I'm sure it made for amusing conversation at their offices when they talked about being "crew members," but those of us who benefitted from their help thought they should have worn superhero capes instead of suits and ties.

Chapter Fourteen

I remembered the adage, "Why buy the cow if the milk is free?" If I decided to live with Bill, I would likely remove any incentive he might have to get married. But, despite my reservations, I bid goodbye to Ann and Dave and moved into a newly constructed house south of the airport in College Park, Georgia. It was a lovely ranch on a secluded cul-de-sac with only three other homes. Beyond the large backyard were woods that extended about a quarter of a mile until they reached a seldom-used gravel road. Jack and Mildred Kraft, a retired couple who lived across the street, welcomed us warmly. Mildred loved to cook and often brought us delicious casseroles that we appreciated because my efforts in the kitchen produced the utilitarian food you might find in a school cafeteria. Jack's constant companions were two good-natured but ferocious-sounding German shepherds, Oscar and Elsa, who immediately accepted me as a friend, especially since I would play endless rounds of "fetch the stick" with them. The Kraft's thirty-five-year-old son, Rick, frequently stopped by to help with odd jobs and to enjoy his mother's culinary skills. But, despite his good nature and kind heart, he sometimes acted impulsively. He once dug up Mildred's prized rosebushes to make room for some azaleas he'd bought on sale; another time, he changed the oil in his car, leaving unsightly stains on Jack's pristine driveway. His parents, as patiently as they could, often admonished him to think before he acted.

While the house improved living conditions, work remained stubbornly unchanged. If I were still in Miami, I'd have been holding a decent schedule by now, but Atlanta was a far more senior base. I seesawed between being on reserve and flying a regular schedule of genuinely awful trips—awful in that I could imagine a band of nefarious crew schedulers, perhaps back from the dead, convening in a cobwebbed dungeon and cackling as they created them. But after several months of being chained to the phone on reserve (beepers didn't come along until much later), I subjected myself to a torturous month of one of their evil itineraries—an all-night turnaround which I flew three times in a row with three days off between sets.

My sleep patterns went haywire. I reported to the airport at ten thirty p.m. for a short hop to Augusta that continued to Savannah on what Delta's marketing department coined an "Owly Bird" flight. What a cute image he made in advertising—a sleepy little owl snoozing under a warm blanket in his cozy seat. However, since each leg was barely thirty minutes long, most passengers didn't get a wink of sleep before they shuffled to the door and down the portable stairs into the terminal building.

Once the last passenger left the airplane in Savannah, the pilots and stewardesses made a beeline to a circle of black Naugahyde recliners in the crew lounge. Each of us did our best to create our own little Owly Bird nest with wadded-up blankets that had probably never seen the inside of a dry-cleaning establishment and miniature pillows from the plane. Even in this less-than-ideal environment, I fell asleep. That is, until light pouring in from the hallway blinded me as the Operations agent opened the door to tell us we had to board the plane for our three a.m. return trip to Augusta and Atlanta. The same creative team responsible for the Owly Bird christened flights like this one, "Early Birds."

The Early Bird was a perky, wide-awake rooster that in no way whatsoever mirrored the way the crew and passengers felt about this ungodly hour.

When we arrived in Atlanta from Augusta, we had to rush to another plane to take us to Washington, D.C., and back to Atlanta for the second half of our turnaround. Most of the passengers on the Washington flight were well-rested, alert, and ready for the breakfast we served them. On the other hand, we looked like we'd slept in our uniforms. Oh, yes, that's because we had. The merciful end to this trip occurred at around ten a.m. as I headed home for much-needed sleep. But the cycle repeated when I got up around eight p.m. to shower, eat dinner, and leave for the airport again.

One of these turnarounds was doable. Two in a row were terrible, but three were borderline inhumane. On one of the coldest nights of January, I drove to the airport to face my third consecutive night of self-inflicted misery. I had not felt well before leaving home but told myself to shake off the aches and fatigue. Feeling even worse when I arrived in the crew lounge, I desperately wanted to go home, but the penalty for claiming illness this close to departure was severe—maybe resulting in a suspension. I would have to hang on until I could collapse into the recliner in Savannah. As I stood in the airplane's rear galley and checked supplies for the flight, the combined smells of instant coffee, lavatory cleaner, and the jet fuel fumes coming from the open back door made my stomach churn.

By the time we reached Savannah, I knew it would be impossible for me to continue the trip past Atlanta, so I asked Operations to call ahead and inform Crew Scheduling that I was sick. With three hours' notice, they could easily replace me on the Washington segments.

When we landed in Atlanta at five a.m., all I could think about was curling up under the covers and sleeping until I felt better. Outside, a cold, biting wind lent credence to the forecast of an ice storm. Even though I had been hot and sweaty earlier, I shivered as I drove home in the darkness. But as awful as I felt, I was slightly cheered by the thought that my illness might be a blessing in disguise by allowing me to avoid a weather-related reroute or delay. I was irritated when I had to stop the car at the top of our steep driveway and get out to open the garage door. For over a month, Bill's to-do list had included installing an automatic garage door opener, but he still hadn't done it. After I succeeded in lifting the heavy door, my headlights projected a harsh glare on the white back wall of the garage. Back inside the car, I saw a shadow flicker on the wall that I attributed to the blowing branches of one of the tall pine trees in the yard.

Easing into the garage next to Bill's Datsun, I opened the door to get out. Suddenly, a pair of hands reached inside the car grabbed my left arm and roughly pulled on it while I instinctively grabbed the steering wheel with my right hand to resist. When my heart started beating again, I focused on a man dressed entirely in black—pants, peacoat, knit hat—even eye black beneath his eyes and on his cheeks. "Get out of the car and don't scream," he growled. "I have a knife."

I had always heard that in a life-or-death situation, the brain provides a signal to fight, flee, or go into paralysis, which was the option I experienced. It was as if I were an outside observer watching a disturbing *National Geographic* film of a lion holding a motionless antelope in its jaws. My throat burned as I tried to scream, but the only thing that came out was a muffled whimper. It must have been louder than it sounded because the man tightened his grip on my arm and hissed another warning.

In hindsight, I know I had options. The keys were still in the ignition, so I could have started the car, thrown it in reverse, and dragged him until he released me, or I could have honked the horn. Of course, neither of these actions guaranteed my safety and could just as easily have backfired. He could see from the presence of the other car that someone else was in the house and might come out at any moment, so he held my arm tightly and wrenched it backward, trying to get me out of the car quickly. I knew if he succeeded in overpowering me and forcing me into the dense woods or a waiting car, I would most certainly be raped or killed. Although I was using all my strength to remain in the car, I still couldn't scream, and it was doubtful I would have awakened Bill anyway. Not only was our bedroom at the far end of the house, but Bill was a very sound sleeper. My attacker had a secure grip on my left arm, but as my adrenalin kicked in, I reached across with my right hand and shoved him as hard as I could. Caught off guard, he lost his balance momentarily but recovered quickly and scowled as he reached into his pocket. I heard blood rushing through my head. In seconds, he would gain complete control.

But, as suddenly as it had started, the attack ended when he released me and vanished into the darkness. I was numb and in shock, my hands shaking so badly that I struggled to pull my key ring from the ignition. I unlocked the door to the kitchen—foolishly leaving it wide open—and, on rubbery legs, wobbled through the house to the bedroom. At last, I found my voice. "Bill, wake up!" I shouted frantically. "There was a man in the garage who attacked me!"

Groggy and disoriented, Bill grabbed a baseball bat propped up in the corner, stumbled through the house to the open doorway, flipped on the garage light switch, and raced to the driveway with me close behind. Only then did I hear Oscar and Elsa's frenzied barking across the street.

As the pink edges of dawn appeared, Jack Kraft materialized at the foot of our driveway. "Morning. Just checking things out. The dogs have been restless all night like something was prowling the neighborhood. They started barking up a storm a few minutes ago, so I came out front to look around and noticed your garage door open. Is everything OK?" Just before I collapsed into Bill's arms in convulsive sobs, I felt sure I saw gauzy wings sprout from Jack's shoulders.

We took a cue from how well Oscar and Elsa warned of abnormal sounds and activity. However, the wire-haired fox terrier we adopted and named Zach was a far cry from the size of the German shepherds, and his presence, although comforting, did not make me feel safe enough to spend the night alone in the house on nights that Bill was away. I expressed my misgivings to Mildred, which prompted her quick response, "Then you must spend the night at our house." My half-hearted protests went unheard as she ended the conversation with a firm "I insist."

One night, several weeks after the attack, Bill was on a trip, and as I prepared to go to Mildred and Jack's, Zach pricked up his ears in alert and growled near the back door. Anxious, I went to the kitchen phone to call Mildred and tell her I was coming over immediately when two gunshots exploded behind the house. Before I could lift the receiver, the phone rang, and I jumped what seemed like several inches into the air.

Mildred was on the line. "It's OK! Rick is shooting in the air. He saw someone lurking to the side of your house and chased him into the woods. I told him to wait until I called you, but you know how he is. Come on over; we can both use a glass of wine. I'll stand at the front door and watch as you cross the street."

Immediately after the original assault, I provided the police with a detailed description of the attacker. Though they hadn't found any suspects, Mildred convinced me to file a second report and have the police check things out. When he returned the following day, Bill was incensed. "Since the police don't seem to be any help, you need to learn to protect yourself. I'm going to teach you to shoot."

I feared guns. Nevertheless, the following afternoon, we drove down the gravel road on the back side of our woods and searched for a secluded area where we could target shoot. As we rounded a curve, I gasped. My attacker stood in front of a makeshift shack, axe in hand, cutting firewood. "That's him!"

"You sure?" asked Bill as he slowed down. I nodded mutely, feeling my limbs begin to shake. To my shock, Bill idled the car, got out, and approached the man. "You selling that firewood?" he asked.

The man did not look at Bill but glared straight into the car at me and replied, "No. Chopping it for myself." His menacing expression made me turn my head away. I was sure he recognized the yellow sports car from the garage and knew who he was talking to.

"OK, thanks," said Bill and returned to the car.

"We should call the police," I pleaded, still trying to control my shaking body.

Bill ignored my obvious distress. "No, I have a better idea. We'll let him know what's in store for him if he ever comes around again."

A few yards further down the road, out of sight of the shack, we found a clearing and fired the revolver for thirty minutes. When we passed the shack to return home, the man was no longer in the yard. We reported his whereabouts to the police, but not surprisingly, given the delay in notifying them, they didn't find a trace of him. Fortunately, I never saw him again.

Even though the threat seemed to have disappeared, we wanted to strengthen our defenses. The next day, Bill installed a garage door opener, and the following week, we fenced in the property. We also adopted a new member for our security team, a German shepherd puppy we named Manfred von Waldmeister, Fred for short. What Zach lacked in intimidation power, Fred made up for in spades. Because of his ferocious bark, strangers gave him a wide berth, but he had a gentle disposition with people who weren't threatening, a trait he inherited from his parents, Oscar and Elsa.

Chapter Fifteen

Bill announced he was ready to get married. But I wasn't as happy as I would have been if this meant a real wedding. To make the occasion even less momentous, we pigeonholed our service into a Wednesday evening in March, one of the few days neither of us was flying. Another reason for my lack of enthusiasm was that Bill and I had had sporadic heated arguments since moving in together, usually when I had to defend myself against something I didn't find important, like letting the ironing pile up. "You have two good hands; iron your own shirt," I'd say. But Bill subscribed to a traditionalist's view of the division of household labor and insisted it was my job. "I do the yard work and house maintenance; you do the cooking, cleaning, and laundry." I couldn't recall agreeing to this, but the arrangement fit the norms of the time, so I grudgingly accepted it.

The day before the wedding, we had one of these blowups (I think it was about something stupid like the color of the drapes I wanted to put in the bedroom), and it intensified into a shouting match about whether we would go through with our plans. These episodes should have been a warning sign, as obvious as Wile E. Coyote standing next to a bundle of Acme dynamite tied to a red flag with a skull and crossbones, but denial is a powerful thing. We calmed down and proceeded with the ceremony the next evening with Ann and Dave as our only witnesses.

We settled into married life, which was not notably different from living together. I had always dreamed of spending my honeymoon in a tropical paradise, and this time, Bill didn't ruin my fantasy. We decided on Hawaii. Bill loved the islands when he spent his R&R there during his tours in Vietnam, and I looked forward to seeing in person some of the scenes I had clipped from travel magazines as a child. In May, we finally packed our bags for a week-long getaway.

Delta and Southern offered generous pass privileges to their employees, but this trip allowed us to combine them for the first time. We flew from Atlanta to Los Angeles in first class on a Delta 747, where a friend of mine on the crew kept our champagne glasses full. Southern had an interline agreement with United that allowed us to reserve coach seats from L.A. to Honolulu and upgrade to first class at the gate if seats were available.

The Delta flight landed late in Los Angeles, forcing us to race to the United gate in another terminal. After drinking champagne for over four hours, running wasn't easy, and we arrived at the Honolulu gate with only a few minutes to spare. As we had hoped, there were open first-class seats, so the agent gave us boarding passes, shooed us down the jetway onto the plane, and closed the door behind us.

After being on the enormous 747, I felt a little claustrophobic walking into a single-aisle DC-8. Our seats were in the first row on the right side of the aircraft, and as I observed our surroundings, I noticed only a few other passengers in our cabin. An older couple sat across the aisle two rows behind us, and four or five people were chatting in the aisle. I was overheated from the sprint and relieved to have made the flight, so I happily settled in and fastened my seatbelt as I heard the stewardess asked the group of folks who stood to take their seats.

The service in first class was, well, first-class. Bill started with scotch on the rocks before dinner while I sipped United's signature mai tai. There were hot and cold hors d'oeuvres, salad, bread, and a main course of prime rib from a roast the stewardess carved in front of us. The wine flowed freely—every time my glass went below the halfway mark, a flight attendant filled it again. When we thought we couldn't eat another bite, a serving cart displaying a sinful chocolate torte appeared, and we each indulged in a slice along with coffee and amaretto. Then, to top it all off, we "forced" ourselves to sample a selection of cheeses served with port. I felt like a slug when this gastronomic orgy was over, but my bladder insisted I get up. I crawled over a dozing Bill and walked (actually, staggered) to the lavatory a few feet in front of our seats. When I returned, I realized it felt good to stand, so I braced myself against the bulkhead next to our seats and performed what I thought were subtle stretches—a few calf raises and a couple of shoulder rolls. My attempts to be inconspicuous had failed. I saw that a passenger a few rows back, apparently one of the ones standing in the aisle when we boarded, was looking at me and smiling.

An internal conversation began. *You're drunker than you realize because you're seeing things. This guy has private jets, so why would he be on a United flight? It's probably just someone who* looks *like him. There's no way it's him.* I realized I was telegraphing my thoughts with facial expressions because he chuckled and waved. After a tentative, embarrassed wave back, I scrambled over Bill to my seat.

"What's going on?" he said, annoyed that I had awakened him.

"Elvis Presley is sitting four rows behind us," I whispered.

Bill looked at me indulgently as he would a small child announcing she saw Santa Claus on the rooftop across the street. "And just how many drinks have you had?"

"I don't know. A vast number. What's your point?"

Suddenly, the man I'd been staring at perched on the armrest of the seat across the aisle from Bill. "How are you folks doin' tonight? "His distinctive Mississippi accent left no doubt. I poked Bill and gave him an I-told-you-so look.

"Well, hi there," Bill replied, seemingly unintimidated that he was speaking to the King of Rock and Roll. "We're just fine. How are you doing?"

"Oh, just wishin' this flight would be over. I hope you don't mind me botherin' you, but I'm not a very good flier, and it helps pass the time to talk." I hoped Bill wouldn't make a smart-assed remark like, "Why yes, you are bothering us. Please go back to your seat and leave us alone." But he said, "Oh, no problem at all."

I leaned forward in my seat and turned my head toward Elvis, intending to tell him I was also a fearful flyer, but no words came out. Bill was far from speechless. Elvis listened as Bill related that he was a Southern Airways pilot who had lived in Memphis for a while and used to ride Harleys with some people Elvis might know.

For the next ten minutes, I listened to a surreal conversation. "Oh sure, I know that ole boy. I used to ride bikes with him some. Haven't seen him in a good while, though," said Elvis.

"That's because he moved to Atlanta. I still see him some."

"Is that right? Well, I'll be. Whatever happened to ole so-and-so? Wasn't he in a wreck over on Winchester?"

I sat silently, still trying to wrap my head around the fact that this was Elvis Presley, *the* Elvis Presley, the one on my 45 records, the one who sang *Love Me Tender* from a colossal movie screen. It seemed impossible that he was chatting with my husband as though they were old drinking buddies who hadn't run into one another for a while.

After a few more minutes, Elvis said, "Well, it's sure been nice talkin' to you. I'm gonna go back to my seat now and see if I can sleep a little."

I could have kicked Bill when he boldly asked, "Say, are you performing somewhere this week? We'd sure love to catch your show (hint-hint)."

"No, this trip is strictly for rest. I need a little break."

With that, he stood up, walked toward the back of the cabin, and left me wondering if I had just awakened from a crazy dream. With all the food and drink I'd consumed, I drifted off but woke up, unaware of how long I had slept, to find that Bill wasn't next to me. I craned my neck and saw him standing near the galley at the back of first class. Curious, I dragged myself out of my seat to see what he was doing. As I passed Elvis's row, I noticed his eyes were closed, and I felt glad that we might have helped him relax somehow. In the galley, one of Elvis's bodyguards, a muscular, good-looking-but-not-truly-handsome man, was trying to get something going with the stewardess as Bill waited for her to ask him if he needed something.

"I never know when I ask a girl out if she says 'yes' because she likes me or if she's just trying to get close to him."

Out of patience, Bill cut in. "Well, here's an idea. Maybe you should look for another line of work to be sure. Can I have a beer, please?" The bodyguard glared at him.

As we returned to our seats, I shook my head. "Bill, that wasn't a smart thing to say to someone who's half a foot taller than you and outweighs you by a hundred pounds."

"Aw, he wouldn't do anything to me. Elvis and I are tight."

Even without the privilege of seeing Elvis perform, we had a magical week. We checked into our hotel at nine p.m. and, exhausted, fell into a refreshing sleep. When I walked out on the balcony the following morning, I saw Diamond Head perfectly centered on my very own postcard. We did all the touristy things—visits to Pearl Harbor and the Polynesian Cultural Center, an excursion to the north shore to see the surfers on Waimea Beach, and, of course, the mandatory luau (which we attended in our newly purchased Hawaiian clothing). The only thing we did that was off the beaten path, literally, was to take a wrong turn in our rental car and end up in the middle of a sugar cane field. For the entire week, there were no quarrels.

The afterglow of the honeymoon continued when we got back to Atlanta. Tensions that previously existed seemed to have been exorcised by the change of scenery. But about six months later, Bill began a pattern of gaslighting and belittling that shocked me. He accused me of various transgressions I had no memory of committing—making a guest feel unwelcome, saying something inappropriate at a party, or making derogatory remarks about one of his friends. Added to these tactics were inferences that I wasn't very intelligent. Sometimes, when a group of friends discussed a topic of interest, and I dared to chime in, he said snidely, "Better listen to her. She has a college degree." These incidents didn't happen frequently, and I could never determine what prompted them. I only knew they were hurtful.

As sometimes happens in a marriage, the qualities that attracted me to Bill gradually turned into negatives. His decisiveness became dictatorial; his intelligence became a weapon to demonstrate my comparative denseness; and his ease in social situations became an uncomfortable contrast to my shyness and discomfort.

Even though his behavior sent a clear message not to start a family, I wanted to have a baby because...wasn't that what you were supposed to do? Bill agreed, motivated by his competitiveness and a certain macho desire to prove his manhood; his younger brother already had two boys, and Bill needed to catch up. But after eight months with no success, I went to my doctor for an exam and tests. His diagnosis was blunt, "It will be difficult, if not impossible, for you to conceive. Surgery might help, but it could also be risky." At that time, there were no alternatives other than adoption (which Bill refused to consider).

Bill was enormously disappointed, but seeing my devastated reaction, he appeared upbeat about the idea that we would be unencumbered by children and free to travel to our hearts' content. However, he couldn't conceal his true feelings when, during one of his episodes of verbally attacking me, he remarked that he wished he'd married someone who could have a baby. Stinging from the remark, I was glad I would not bring a child into this turbulent relationship.

I don't remember which of us brought up the subject of divorce the first time. Initially, it was a tool to inflict as much hurt as possible on the other. Angry silence ensued for a few days, accompanied by my departure to the guest room. But the D word began to lose its power the more times we said it, and neither of us followed through. There had been only one divorce in my extended family, and as miserable as I was at times, I didn't want to be the second casualty. It seemed easier to accept that we were unsuited for one another, but to shamble through the marriage anyway rather than take steps to end it. And, when it came down to it, we enjoyed many of the same things despite our divergent attitudes and methods of communication. A factor contributing to our ability to keep going was that our schedules often kept us apart. On the other hand, that could have been part of the problem; I was never sure.

There was no doubt about one thing. Our lives revolved around what was most expedient for Bill's career, and he usually made unilateral decisions regarding his work life. The opportunity arose for him to check out as a DC-9 captain if he transferred back to Memphis, where he was based when he got hired. Unfortunately, Delta did not have a base there; one of us would have to commute, and I had no illusions about which of us it would be.

In the spring of 1974, we moved to Memphis, and I reluctantly joined the ranks of stewardesses who had to fly to another city to go to work. Twenty or more Delta stewardesses chose to remain in Memphis after Delta closed it as a stewardess base in 1970. Most of them commuted to Atlanta, so I knew there would be a lot of competition for non-rev seats. To make my experience more manageable, I transferred to Chicago, where there were fewer Memphis commuters and my seniority in the smaller Chicago base would improve my trip-bidding options.

Even so, I was nervous before every trip. After carefully checking flights to see which had available seats, I might find my plans thrown into chaos by a flight cancellation, bad weather, or some other negative occurrence. One time, I boarded an aircraft, stowed my luggage, and buckled my seatbelt only to have the agent come on board and tell me a late passenger had shown up and I had to get off. I breathed easily only after the plane took off, ironically, the opposite of my pre-stewardess pattern of anxiety.

I had a better situation than many commuters because I could also non-rev on Southern. Between the two airlines, eleven daily flights connected Memphis and Chicago. The problem was that Southern flew into Midway Airport while Delta used O'Hare. If I arrived at Midway, I had to take a bus to the Loop and wait in front of the Palmer House Hotel for a transfer to O'Hare, a route that often took three hours or longer. I discovered I could get an interline fare on Chicago Helicopter Airways, which shuttled between the two airports and cost less than the bus. I had never ridden in a helicopter, and despite my progress on keeping aerophobia at bay, the wrap-around windows that afforded a panoramic view of the city resurrected many of the same stomach-clenching fears I'd had as a child. However, the time savings in getting between airports made me continue to use the service even though the helicopter had only six seats, and I could never count on getting on the flight. Sometimes, I bypassed a bus to stand by for the chopper, only to be bumped and forced to wait an hour or more for the next bus. Misery!

Although not as nerve-racking as getting to work, coming home was also stressful. I often flew on a trip that returned to O'Hare around seven p.m. With only two later flights to Memphis on Delta—one at ten o'clock and another at eleven thirty—I often arrived home in the early morning hours, exhausted after working a twelve-hour day. If neither flight had seats, I either spent the night in a recliner in the crew lounge (which the base manager discouraged) or found a motel room and tried again the next day. I was always tired and harbored a grudge against Bill for putting me in this situation. My life was far from the happy one I had hoped for. What if things had worked out with Tom, Matt, or Mike? It was anyone's guess, but I couldn't help feeling anything would be better than this.

Chapter Sixteen

Sharing a hotel room with a stranger was unthinkable to most people, but that's just how it was for Delta stewardesses until the mid-1970s. We learned to accept this right from the beginning in training while sharing a dorm room with someone we didn't know. This shared-room policy saved the company money, but there might have been other, more nuanced reasons for the arrangement. Pilots didn't share rooms and, in fact, often laid over at a different hotel than the stewardesses. This practice led me to suspect that Delta wanted to promote the morality of its sky angels. Sure, the company also had safety in mind. If a crazed killer broke into the room, it was better to have two delicate flowers pummel him with their handbags instead of just one! But I think the main reason was to put the kibosh on fraternization and prevent the repercussions it might have on a pilot's marriage and a stewardess's (as well as Delta's) reputation. In practice, no one who wanted to have a fling (or participate in any other shenanigans, for that matter) was the least bit constrained by a roommate as a guardian. Sometimes, that person became a partner in crime; sometimes, roommates just went their separate ways, as happened on my first San Francisco layover.

From the crews' perspectives, the setup had a few significant drawbacks regarding personal preferences. A non-smoker might get stuck with a smoker; a night owl might bother an early-to-bed adherent with a flickering TV screen into the wee hours; some liked it hot, and some liked it cold. Who would get up first to take a shower? Maybe a roommate brought a stinky takeout meal into the room, making it smell like a garlic patch. The only deviation from sharing a room was in the case of an odd number of stewardesses. When that happened, the one with the highest seniority claimed the single room. But not always.

The Bare Facts

I was a reserve on a trip with two women I'd never met, and we'd had a pleasant time working together. I was surprised when we checked into the hotel in the late afternoon, and the most senior stewardess said to the other woman on our crew, "You can have the single. I'll share with Kathi."

We picked up our keys, headed to the elevator, and rode to our floor. My roommate unlocked the door, threw her coat and purse on the bed nearest the window, and entered the bathroom. I quickly changed into my "civvies" and flipped on the TV. When my roommate emerged from the bathroom—STARK NAKED—she strolled across the room to her bed with her uniform and underwear draped across one arm. I'm not a goody-two-shoes, but I was dumbfounded! I didn't know where to look, so I turned my back to her and arranged my uniform for the next day. I heard hangers rattle and a riffling sound from her tote bag as I hoped she would fish out something to put on.

Several minutes passed, and I heard no sounds other than the canned laugh track from the sitcom on TV, so I slowly turned toward her. She was still nude and sat cross-legged on the bedspread (eeew!) reading a magazine. She looked up with a big smile and said, "So, where do you want to go for dinner?" I wondered if she knew of a clothing-optional restaurant.

Why had she not taken the single room if this was her pre-ferred state? The answer was as evident as (what's the correct analogy here? Not "nose on your face." Hmm.) She enjoyed my discomfort.

Stranger in the Night

My worst nightmare with a roommate occurred on an otherwise great layover. Chicago Crew Scheduling was experimenting to see if it was more practical for pilots and stewardesses to work identical DC-9 trips, quite a departure from the painstaking way Delta had always tried to keep us apart on layovers.

I was excited to learn that I would fly with a captain named Sam for the month. All the Chicago stewardesses liked him, a fun-loving guy who, although not handsome, was incredibly sexy. I didn't know how he had managed to stay single. While I didn't appreciate hearing off-color jokes from pilots, Sam could do it without offending me. In response to sometimes shocked reactions from other stewardesses, he feigned innocence with a surprised look and a "Did I say something wrong?" It was fun to banter with him, exchanging double entendres. He was "safe," and I was never concerned that he would take our rep-artee seriously.

For the Crew Scheduling experiment, we flew on a two-day trip that laid over in a town everyone made jokes about as the most podunky of "Podunks." What many stewardesses didn't know (and those who did know kept it secret) was that it had one of the best hotels in the system, with mini suites instead of standard rooms. Each had a small sitting area with a sofa and TV, a separate bedroom, and a bathroom off the hallway between them. The hotel amenities were outstanding—a beautiful indoor swimming pool, complimentary hors d'oeuvres with happy hour, and free admission to the hotel's nightclub. Granted, the performers were mainly on the downhill side of their careers, but they were fun to see. These extras offered a break from the typical bare-bones accommodations we usually encountered. On this trip, we arrived at three p.m. and had a seven a.m. pick up the following morning, so we could take advantage of everything the hotel offered.

A fellow commuter, Melissa, had swapped with another stewardess and would only be on this first trip of the month. We had never worked together but had chatted in the crew lounge once or twice about the trials of commuting. She was the senior stewardess, and I looked forward to getting to know her better. When we arrived at the hotel, Melissa offered the third stewardess, Brandy, the single room. While we all waited for the elevator, Sam suggested, tongue-in-cheek, that Melissa, Brandy, and I come to his room for a "ménage a quatre" to get the month off to a good start.

"In your dreams," we laughed. "Now Pete, on the other hand…" Pete, the first officer, reddened a little, but he knew we were joking. The young married pilots like Pete, either of their own accord or under strict prohibitions from their wives, often didn't mingle with stewardesses on layovers. But Pete enthusiastically agreed to meet us in an hour for a swim.

When I strolled into the pool area in my favorite bikini, Sam was already in the water and gave a low whistle. I had never cheated on Bill and wouldn't, but it felt good when another man looked at me like that. Sam and I swam a few laps, then hung onto the side of the pool and talked as we waited for the others. Pete was next to arrive and looked slightly incongruous in his surfer jams with snowdrifts piled up outside the glassed-in room. Next came Melissa in a sleek yellow tank-style suit, which generated stares from Sam and Pete as she slowly immersed herself. Missing was Brandy, who felt like she was coming down with a cold and decided not to join us. We lingered in the pool for a while and then returned to our rooms to change clothes for happy hour and dinner.

After we ate, we discussed whether to see the nightclub show that starred the Coasters, but Sam didn't think it was the original group, so we decided to go back to the bar for a nightcap instead. The FAA rule was that pilots could not drink alcohol within eight hours of flying. Delta had stricter regulations for stewardesses— no drinking within twelve hours of flight. A glance at my watch told me it was time to stop. I was ready to call it a night anyway, but Melissa showed no indication of being prepared to leave. Sam took out his key as I stood up and said, "OK, Darling, let's go back to the honeymoon suite."

"No, Honey," I replied, "You stay here and have fun, but be a good boy."

Sam pouted. "Those two instructions are incompatible."

"Whatever." I laughed and waved goodnight to the three of them.

Back in the room, I took a shower, watched a little TV, and fell deeply asleep in the comfy bed, only to be awakened sometime later by laughter from the hallway and someone bumping up against the door of my room. I looked over at the other bed to see if Melissa was awake, but she wasn't there. Confused, I turned the clock toward me and saw the illuminated blue numerals: 2:15.

I could distinguish Melissa's voice but couldn't make out her words. I also heard a male voice that sounded like Sam's. Goofing around was one thing, but I was furious that Sam and Melissa were still up at this hour and, more seriously, had probably been drinking the whole time.

The hallway door opened, followed by a loud thud and then laughter and exaggerated shushes from Melissa. Even though I was angry, I felt frozen in place. *You've got to put a stop to this!* I had almost summoned the courage to confront them when the laughter suddenly stopped.

Pants and rhythmic moans came from the sitting room. They were having sex! I froze again; how could I go out there now? Even though I had lost all respect for the two of them, it would be a humiliating encounter for all of us. Later, a flash of light told me that one or both had left the room, and the sitting room was silent. I tossed and turned and caught only intermittent periods of sleep as I worried about what might happen in the morning. *We'll have to cancel the flight if two crew members are drunk!* The alarm clock shrilled; it was five thirty, time to get up.

I moved stealthily to the hall and peered into the sitting room. Melissa was alone, sprawled on the sofa with nothing on, her bra and underwear lying on the floor. I was scared and enraged at the same time. I called her name, but she didn't respond. I tapped her arm. Nothing. I shook her, and she was like a Raggedy Ann doll, but she murmured something incoherent, so I knew she wasn't dead. The clock in the sitting room kept ticking, and we had to be ready to leave the hotel in an hour. I knocked on Brandy's adjoining door, and when she opened it, her eyes widened in shock at the scene.

"What happened? Is she OK?"

"It looks like Sam and Melissa made quite a night of it. They came in here around two o'clock and proceeded to go at it on the sofa, complete with sound effects."

Brandy was horrified. "Sam?"

"Yup."

"That's unbelievable. Why didn't she and Sam go to his room if they wanted to have sex? He knew you were in here, too."

"Because he's a scumbag. And you know what? He can damn well come and take care of his little girlfriend because I won't do it."

With that, I picked up the phone and dialed Sam's room.

A chipper voice answered. "Joe's Bar and Grill."

"Sam, I'm not in the mood for your stupid humor. You need to get over here right now and do something with Melissa."

"What's wrong?" He sounded concerned.

"Oh, I think you know very well what's wrong. Melissa's out cold on the sofa where you left her last night."

"Kathi, what the hell are you talking about? Pete and I left the bar at ten o'clock, and she was still there. I tried to get her to go to her room, but she told me to fuck off. Is she hurt?" I felt nauseous as reality sank in. The idea of Sam and her was bad enough, but now I knew a stranger had been in my room within a few feet of my bed.

Sam's voice yanked me back to the present. "I'm getting dressed. I'll be there in a few minutes."

Thankful that I had showered the night before, I put on my uniform, did a quick makeup job, and zipped my bag. There was a knock on the door, and when I opened it, I saw that Sam wasn't in a joking mood now. "Pull the bedspread off one of the beds," he ordered, taking charge. He draped it around her, carried her to the bathtub, and turned on the shower. She sputtered and flailed her arms as she yelled every cuss word she could manage, but within a few seconds, she was lucid and appalled that Sam and I were, for some reason, staring at her naked body. Sam turned away as he realized she was now fully conscious. I tossed her a towel and put her underwear on the bathroom counter. To Melissa, "Put these on." To Sam, who waited outside the bathroom, "I'm sorry, but I can't deal with this."

"It's OK," he said. "Go downstairs. I'll make sure we're there in time for pickup."

Brandy, Pete, and I stood in the lobby with numerous businessmen who would undoubtedly be passengers on our flight. We filled Pete in on the details, and he shook his head. "Sam tried his darndest to get her to leave the bar when we did, but I never dreamed she would do something like this."

The shuttle driver had just called for passengers to board the bus when the elevator doors opened, and Sam and Melissa, in full uniform, stepped out. Well, Melissa's uniform wasn't quite complete; she was in her stocking feet. Sam approached me and whispered, "I can't find her shoes." As the businessmen folded their newspapers and picked up their briefcases to head to the airport and entrust their lives to us, the desk clerk came out from behind the counter waving a pair of size seven navy heels. "Are these yours?" he asked our little group as all heads turned to see what he held. "We found them in the bar last night."

It was a very long day. Melissa performed her duties flawlessly as though nothing had happened. She didn't smell of alcohol, and no one would ever have guessed she had been drinking all night. She tried apologizing several times, but I was not ready to forgive.

When I went to the cockpit to deliver snacks, Sam said, "How could you think I would do what you thought I did?"

I shrugged. "I don't know. Alcohol makes people do crazy things."

"There's not enough alcohol in the world to make me do that."

"I'm sorry, Sam, I'm just so angry at her."

"Believe it or not, that's what Melissa is most upset about."

I should have reported the incident immediately, but I didn't, and neither did Sam or the others. I kept my distance from Melissa and even swapped off a trip I was supposed to fly with her. I couldn't get past the idea that she had put me in such an appalling position, both safety- and responsibility-wise.

A few months later, I flew with someone fuming about a trip she had worked on with Melissa, during which a similar situation occurred. This stewardess was brave enough to report the incident. Shortly afterward, I heard Melissa lost her job due to excessive no-shows. She truly needed help, but I wonder if she ever got it.

Let's Hear It for the Boys

I was ecstatic when the shared room policy ended. Many of us looked back on it as a weird practice and wondered how we had ever considered it normal. And who did we have to thank for this welcome change? Male flight attendants.

As a child, I didn't understand why anyone would want to do such a dangerous job, but I knew women worked on airplanes and were called "stewardesses." Little did I know that women were the Jenny-Come-Latelies of the occupation. Men filled those roles at the outset of commercial aviation in the 1920s and 1930s. The public associated airplanes with war and engineering, a natural fit for "masculine" men who wore military-inspired uniforms and performed such tasks as loading luggage and rowing passengers to shore from Pan American seaplanes, in addition to tending to passengers' needs during the flight (Wickman, 2013).

In 1930, Ellen Church, a registered nurse who had also earned a private pilot's license, applied to be a pilot with Boeing Air Transport Office (a forerunner of United Airlines), but the company employed only males for that position. Boeing had planned to add male stewards to the cabin but changed this strategy when Ms. Church promoted the benefits of having onboard nurses to tend to sick or frightened passengers. After a successful three-month trial, the company asked Ms. Church to recruit seven more nurses (Krause). In addition to their medical training, the women had to be young, single, and weigh no more than 115 pounds, supposedly to avoid the expense of extra fuel, but, in practice, to appropriate the women's sex appeal as a marketing tool (Wickman, 2013).

The pendulum swung again in 1936 when Eastern Airlines and a few others hired all-male flight attendant cadres. Pan Am featured life-size cardboard cutouts of Rodney, the Smiling Steward, in its advertising. Dashing and elegantly uniformed, he was both good-looking and approachable. However, Eddie Rickenbacker, the CEO of Eastern, faced backlash from the macho pilot corps and the businessmen who were his core customers (Tiemeyer, 2013, p. 45). When the United States entered World War II, the nurses and stewards left in droves to join the military service, and airlines, for the first time, began to hire women who were not nurses. There was no change, however, in the required attributes for women, which continued to focus on appearance rather than medical knowledge.

Although some stewards returned to their jobs after the war, the public's perception had changed to view the occupation as "women's work." Many people felt that men who wished to pursue this career were effeminate and probably homosexual, a perception that gained credibility due to a sensational murder case in Miami in 1954 involving a gay steward. In response, many airlines backed away from hiring stewards, both gay and straight (Wickman, 2013). In the following decade, finding a male in an aircraft cabin crew (other than those in purser positions) was almost as rare as sighting Bigfoot.

Meanwhile, on the women's front, most airlines compelled stewardesses to sign an agreement that they would quit their jobs when they turned thirty-two and, presumably, were no longer presentable to the flying public. The objectification of steward-esses as eye candy took off in the 60s and continued into the 70s. The 1967 publication of Coffee, Tea or Me, the purported memoir of two stewardesses (later discovered to have been written by a man), intimated that stewardesses were available to provide more than just beverage service. Advertising slogans such as "Fly me", "Mix business with pleasure", and "We really move our tail for you" did nothing to discourage this impression. A tasteless joke asked, "Would you like some TWA coffee or some TWAT?"

And then, Celio Diaz, Jr. forever changed what a cabin crew looks like today. Title VII of the Civil Rights Act of 1964 laid the groundwork for Diaz's lawsuit against Pan Am when he was denied employment based on gender. Pan Am initially won the case in a federal district court in Miami, claiming that femininity was a "bona fide occupational qualification." Not to be deterred, Diaz appealed the verdict to the U.S. Court of Appeals in New Orleans, which reversed the decision. However, it was not over yet. Pan Am (with support from other airlines) took the case to the U.S. Supreme Court, hoping to end this nonsense once and for all. However, when presented with the case in 1971, the high court declined to hear it, so the lower court's decision stood, and airlines reluctantly made plans to open their inflight training programs to men.

In January 1973, Delta's "stewardess" training class included four men. These brave souls were the vanguard of increased numbers of "stewards" until the gender-neutral term "flight attendant" took hold, and they faced discrimination on multiple fronts. In late 1973, I witnessed this bias on my first trip with a male coworker. When I called the cockpit to ask if the pilots wanted dinner, the captain replied, "Yes, but you need to bring them up here—*not anyone else!*"

Not all stewardesses were thrilled with the change. Some resented that one of the few exclusively female careers now allowed men; others fumed that the men didn't do their share of the work; and a few complained of being hit on by their male coworkers. Just as often, I heard men complain about being hit on by the women.

A major source of contention was the hotel room situation. Because Delta contracted with hotels across the system to provide a specific number of rooms each month based on operational needs, it upset the apple cart when a male flight attendant was part of the crew. He always got a single room, which caused resentment from some of his female coworkers, especially if this situation required the most senior flight attendant to share a room. Sometimes, the hotel didn't have extra space, so he had to stay elsewhere, and since layovers provided our social time, splitting off these male attendants meant all of us missed the critical opportunity to bond as a crew.

One of my friends told me that because crew schedulers wished to avoid the room problem, they assigned him and other male reserves more turnarounds than two- or three-day trips, denying them the opportunity to explore new cities. Eventually, it became logistically too complicated, and the situation forced Delta to change its policy to one that provided a single room for everyone. For those who had come through the system with the requirement to share accommodations, it was a tremendous relief to have privacy and no longer worry about anyone else's behavior.

Inventing the Wheel

Not only did cabin personnel look different, but so did luggage. Traversing airport concourses became much more manageable, and I finally found relief from juggling multiple items while walking from plane to plane.

Anita Willets-Burnham, the innovator of the rolling suitcase, fashioned one in 1928 for her family's travels using baby buggy wheels and featuring a retractable wooden handle (Winnetka Historical Society, 2017). However, Bernard D. Sadow was the first to file a patent in 1970. Sadow removed the casters from a wardrobe trunk, mounted them on a suitcase, and attached a five-foot strap to the front, allowing the traveler to pull the bag behind them (Goldstein, 2019). Unfortunately, the suitcase often behaved like a naughty puppy; sometimes, it refused to come when tugged by its leash and often rolled over and played dead.

While skycaps were the experts at transporting luggage, dollies were far too large to take aboard an airplane. Innovative manufacturers developed wheeled, slim metal carts large enough to hold a good-sized suitcase secured with bungee cords but which could fold up compactly once the passenger removed the bag. Passengers and crews were thrilled with this innovation, and the carts became ubiquitous. But, their arrival marked the beginning of the eternal boarding process as inexperienced flyers stood in the aisle puzzling about how to stow the darn thing. "Oh, I guess I need to take the bag off the cart first. Now, let me figure out how to do that." Flight attendants loved the cart. Among other conveniences, the cart allowed them to bring home from West Coast layovers the ultimate status symbol, a case of Coors beer, which they strapped onto the cart beneath their suitcase. Since Coors was unavailable east of the Mississippi River, they delighted in casually offering a can of the rare brew to their super-impressed friends.

However, it wasn't until 1989 that the perfect suitcase rolled down a concourse for the first time. Bob Plath, a Northwest Airlines pilot, invented wheeled luggage as we know it today and manufactured it at his company Travel-Pro™. Today, nearly every luggage company in the world has a version, with the added innovation of independent wheels allowing the bag to coast next to you. No more straggling, obstinate puppies!

Chapter Seventeen

I kept hoping to wake up to find that commuting had been just a bad dream. Unfortunately, that was not the case, but there was one upside to living in Memphis—my beautiful house. It was a two-story brick with four bedrooms, three-and-a-half baths, formal living and dining rooms, a huge eat-in kitchen, and my favorite feature, a family room with a fireplace and a view of the back porch and fenced-in backyard. Its only drawback was proximity to a few acres of undeveloped land overgrown with weeds and tall grass. Concerned neighbors cautioned their children to stay clear of the wild kingdom that resided there—raccoons, possums, skunks, foxes, and even a pack of wild dogs.

The backyard had enough room for a vegetable garden, and even though I had never grown anything outdoors, I wanted to try it. Soon, radishes and scallions poked their heads out of the soil, and tiny green spheres promised future plump tomatoes. Due to inexperience, I planted six mounds each of yellow squash and zucchini, unprepared for the massive output of even one hill. The proliferation of produce soon became a problem. At first, neighbors up and down my street accepted the bounty with appreciation, but by the third time I made the rounds, I don't think I imagined that they pulled down their shades and pretended not to be home when I came up the walk with the latest harvest. Fortunately, a local food bank gratefully accepted my garden's seemingly never-ending output.

While gardening was a pleasant new diversion, our move to Memphis didn't change the ongoing relationship problems in our marriage. I had hoped Bill would be happier and less prone to verbal and emotional abuse when he became a captain, but his pattern didn't change. He began to talk about a Southern Airways flight attendant, Karen, with whom he often worked. At first, it was an occasional reference, but then it became, "Karen said the funniest thing" and "Karen agrees with me that (fill in the blank)." I didn't think he was having an affair. If he were, he wouldn't mention her. He just wanted me to be upset that he *might* be. Typical of his modus operandi, he intended these comments to demonstrate his dominance in the relationship. His disparaging remarks would fire up for a period and then stop completely, replaced with compliments and thoughtfulness. I rode a rollercoaster, worried I'd do or say something to set him off.

Then, an experience changed the focus of our lives for several months. During the last week of April 1975, the nation watched its TV screens in disbelief as a long line of people stood on a narrow stairway to the roof of a building near the U.S. embassy in Saigon, South Vietnam, where a helicopter hovered to evacuate them. Other images showed hundreds more trying desperately to scale the walls of the embassy to escape the invading North Vietnamese troops. Bill, who had served in Vietnam as an army reconnaissance pilot, was irate. Even though President Ford and Congress soon authorized the evacuation and resettlement of thousands of Vietnamese and Cambodian refugees in the United States, Bill knew that thousands more who had worked for the U.S. government and military were left behind to suffer whatever punishment awaited them under the North Vietnamese regime.

Public service ads on TV asked Americans to sponsor Vietnamese refugees currently housed at various military bases nationwide. We looked at our spacious house and, with next to no discussion and perfect agreement, called the toll-free number. After we provided all the requested information and agreed to sponsor two people, the operator said someone would contact us with details in a week or two. Three days later, our phone rang. A man with an Asian accent was on the line and said, "Is this the home of Bill and Kathi? I am at a place called Fort Chaffee, and I found a card on a desk with your telephone number on it. My cousin and I need a place to go. Can you help us?"

Before Bill could reply, someone snatched the phone from the caller, and another voice (American) came on the line. "I sincerely apologize for this phone call. We have a protocol for placing refugees, and this young man should not have called you directly."

Impressed by the caller's boldness and initiative, Bill said. "Actually, my wife and I would happily sponsor him and his cousin if possible."

We never dreamed the process would take so little time, so a week later we were caught off guard when we got a phone call that our two men, Giang and Khan, would arrive in an hour. I was painting the walls of our living room when the call came, so Bill went alone to pick them up at the airport.

When the two men walked through the door, each carrying a small cardboard box that contained his only possessions, they took in the house's interior with wide-eyed wonder. Giang spoke fluent English, while Khan had a limited speaking vocabulary but seemed to understand more words than he could say. Kahn gestured for me to get off the ladder. Puzzled, I complied, and he immediately assumed my place and started to roll paint on the walls. I guessed he wanted to express his gratitude, but I hoped he knew we didn't expect his help. We weren't housing the two of them to be indentured servants.

I showed them their bedrooms; again, they seemed stunned that each had so much space. (As it turned out, they preferred to sleep in the same room.) I explained that we would help them find employment, and to that end, we needed to get some clothes for them to wear to job interviews. Catholic Charities gave sponsors a small sum for this purpose (which we far exceeded), regardless of whether the refugees were Buddhist, like our two men, or another non-Catholic religion.

On our shopping trip, we purchased toiletries, underwear, pants, shirts, shoes, and socks. I encouraged each of them to choose a pair of solid-color pants, a solid-color shirt, a pair of color-coordinated plaid pants (this was the 1970s!), and a striped shirt that would go with the solid-color pants. These selections allowed them to have three combinations from four items. The following day, when they came downstairs for breakfast, ready for their first round of interviews, both wore a fourth combination—plaid pants with striped shirts. I didn't have the heart to ask them to change.

Because the two had been helicopter mechanics in the South Vietnamese Army, I thought their skills might transfer to other types of machinery, so I took them to Baptist Memorial Hospital, which had advertised for help in its power plant. An HR representative seemed interested in hiring Giang because of his technical background and fluency in English and took him on a hospital tour while Khan and I stayed in the waiting area. Kahn looked sad, almost as if he were in pain, and I attempted to cheer him up.

"Don't worry, Khan. We'll find a job for you, too."

He turned to me with a pitiful expression and said, "Bathroom?" I smiled to myself as I realized my misreading of his feelings, and from that point, I tried not to project my emotions on either man.

Giang didn't get the job, so the search continued. In the meantime, our domestic life became quite interesting. After he watched me test the soil of my houseplants to see if it was moist,

Khan began to do this. He walked from room to room, stuck his finger into the pots, and gave the plants the water they needed. One morning, at the risk of insulting him, I invited Khan to watch Sesame Street because I thought it might help his English. Far from being offended, he tuned in every morning.

One night, Giang volunteered to cook Vietnamese food for us, and he prepared chicken cooked with ginger and fish sauce. "Cooked" is probably the wrong word, as the chicken had only a passing acquaintance with flame and was essentially raw. With some trepidation, Bill and I eyed one another after the first bite but continued to eat and suffered no adverse consequences.

Giang told us there were two wishes at the top of his list now that he was in the United States—to change his name to an American one and to earn money to buy a car. I tried to convince him that his name was part of his heritage and that it wasn't necessary to change it. "You don't look like a 'John Smith,'" I said, although he didn't appear to get the joke.

His questions were incessant as he tried to understand as much as he could about American culture, and he sometimes awakened us to inconsistencies in our behavior. After he watched Bill mow the lawn, Giang asked, "Why do you cut the grass?"

"So that it won't get too tall."

When Bill fertilized the lawn the following week, "What did you spread on the grass?"

"Fertilizer. It makes the grass grow."

"Then why do you cut it?"

What an interesting question!

The cousins wanted to work together, which limited their opportunities, but ultimately, they found custodial jobs at a downtown business. After three months of living with us, we helped them find an apartment near their work, and they began to make friends in the Vietnamese expatriate community. We saw them less frequently, but I felt good that we had helped them gain their footing and independence. Several months after they moved out, the phone rang early one morning after I had come home late from Chicago, and Bill was on a trip. Bleary-eyed, I picked up the receiver. I always knew the call was from Khan when there was a pause after I said "hello."

"I am Khan."

"Yes, Khan, is everything OK?"

"Giang buy car, must chonge nom."

I was exasperated. Bill had wanted to help choose a car to protect Giang from an unscrupulous salesperson. However, Giang was headstrong and, wanting to assert his independence, had purchased a car alone.

"So, Giang bought a car? What does that have to do with changing his name?"

"No, no." Khan's frustration was almost palpable. "Must chonge nom!"

I gave up. "Khan, Bill will be home tomorrow afternoon at about two o'clock. Can you call back and talk to him about this?"

"OK. I call tomorrow."

When I told Bill about the strange phone call, he, too, was unhappy about Giang's decision. "But why does he insist on changing his name?" I asked.

"I think he just needs to change the title on the car."

I hated it when he was right.

When Giang and Khan moved out, our lives quickly returned to normal, my hating to commute, Bill loving to criticize me. After a particularly strenuous two-day trip, I was elated to be headed home to Memphis on a flight I usually couldn't get on. *Thank goodness for no-show passengers.* I hoped there was something for dinner in the fridge so I wouldn't have to cook. I nodded off for a few minutes until I felt my head tilt sideways toward my seatmate and jerked awake to avoid plopping it on his shoulder.

When I landed in Memphis and rolled my suitcase out of the terminal, there was a pleasant lack of humidity as the sun sank low in the sky. I couldn't wait to change out of my uniform and pour a glass of wine. Bill wasn't flying that week, so he'd be home with Zach and Fred. *Please don't let him be in one of his carping moods. I don't think I can stand it.* As I entered the kitchen from the garage, there was no welcome committee to greet me, and I didn't hear a sound in the dimly lit house.

"Hello," I called out.

Bill emerged from the darkened family room, holding a cup of coffee. "Hi," he said, "you made your flight home. That's great. How was your trip?"

He was never this chatty, and it made me uneasy. "Where are the dogs?" I asked.

"Oh, they're in the family room. Come on, I'll take your suitcase upstairs, and you can have a nice shower, and we'll go get some pizza."

I brushed past him into the family room and saw Zach and Fred with their foreheads pressed against the glass of the back porch door. "Hey boys, what are you looking at?" I asked. They glanced at me with disinterest and went back to their vigil. "What's going on, Bill?" With a sheepish look, he turned on the porch light.

Near the door, lying on its side, sat the big cardboard box that had contained our recently delivered TV. I was startled to see it move a little, and three pairs of dark eyes gazing out from the opening. "What the hell? What's in there?"

As we all stared at the container, Bill related what had happened. When he came home from running some errands earlier in the day and pulled into the garage, which, like many in the neighborhood, lacked a door, he braked sharply to avoid hitting three puppies curled up on the floor. As he approached them, they fearfully plastered themselves against the back wall. He

146

tried to pick up one of them, but it snapped at him, and the other two growled. He threw an old car wax towel over them, gathered them in one squirming mass, and deposited them in the cardboard box he'd intended to put in the trash. After carrying them to the back porch, he put down bowls of dog food and water, which they greedily ate and drank once he backed away. After that, they retreated into the box and hadn't emerged since.

"I guess their mother must have abandoned them or got killed, and they found their way here. I knew I should have called animal control, but I couldn't do it. I was kind of worried about what you'd think of this sudden increase in our pack size." I hugged him tightly and kissed him. He was generally not so soft-hearted.

Over the next few weeks, we earned the puppies' trust. Two females with Collie coloring and a solid black male romped happily with Zach and Fred in the backyard. I invited the woman next door and her little girl to come over to see them. Christie squealed with delight when all three puppies simultaneously licked her face. Her mother, Amy, smiled ruefully and said, "She wants a dog so badly, but we don't think she's ready yet. We'll start with a goldfish and see how it goes."

I laughed. "Sounds like a good plan. You won't end up having to take a fish for walks."

"By the way," said Amy, "I'm glad I caught you. Judy decided to have a last-minute shower for her niece next Tuesday because it looks like the baby will be early. She couldn't contact you, so I told her I'd ask if I saw you. Can you come?"

Judy was an across-the-street neighbor who was the self-appointed monitor of all comings and goings on our block. She loved to gossip and, more than once, she had crossed the street to relate a lengthy account of a neighborhood happening while I held heavy bags of groceries. But I liked Judy's niece Joannie, a friendly woman who had attended neighborhood gatherings, so I called Judy to tell her I'd be there.

On the afternoon of the shower, I sat in Judy's living room with a few other neighbors and six or seven women I didn't recognize but decided were most likely relatives and in-laws of the mother-to-be. The guests balanced cake slices on paper plates patterned in pink and blue baby footprints. Dabbing her lips with a similarly patterned napkin, Judy said, "You're a hard one to track down, Kathi. I was afraid I couldn't tell you about the shower in time." All eyes turned to me. "She's a stewardess for Delta based in Chicago," Judy explained, "and she's gone several days a week."

What followed were the usual comments from people outside of the airline business. "Oh, how exciting!" and "You must see so many interesting places."

I thought of my current trip. *Only if you consider taking off and landing in five cities in one day and ending up on a ten-hour Shreveport layover exciting. But I didn't want to burst their bubbles.* "Yes, it's a great job," I responded.

"Oh, did you hear that accent?" laughed one of the guests, a plump woman whose shoes and purse matched perfectly. "There's no doubt you're from Chicago."

This comment interested me for two reasons. First, I was *not* from Chicago, and second, when I mentioned to fellow Chicago flight attendants that I lived in Memphis, many would say, "I knew you were from someplace in the South because of your twang."

"Her husband's a pilot for Southern Airways, so he's gone a lot, too," Judy continued in a confidential tone. Again, their eyes turned to me, and I prepared for the next round of predictable questions and comments. "Oh my, do you ever see each other?" and "I'd love it if my husband would go away for a few days a week. Ha-ha."

"I saw your car in the driveway last Wednesday morning," Judy continued, "and I thought, 'I must run over and catch Kathi.'

But you were gone by the time I put on my face and changed into decent clothes."

"Last Wednesday morning?" I asked. "I was off that day, but what did I do?" After a few seconds, it came to me. "Oh, I remember. I flew to New Orleans to have lunch with Bill. He had a six-hour break in his trip and asked me to meet him."

There was silence, and a noticeably cool vibe permeated the chintz chairs and drapes as I realized, too late, how pretentious I sounded to them. I might as well have said, "How lucky for you that you scheduled your little gathering on a day when I wasn't dining at Delmonico's or shopping on Fifth Avenue." I made a mental note to be more careful in the future about my references to spur-of-the-moment travel. Airline people understood how mundane my outing was, but not those outside of the biz.

Chapter Eighteen

Out of the blue, Bill informed me we were going to learn to scuba dive, a decision he made unilaterally over my objections that I felt uncomfortable underwater and was not a strong swimmer. "That's the reason you take lessons, so you get comfortable," he retorted as if my response was an unreasonable denial of his all-knowing authority. Southern had recently added flights from Ft. Lauderdale to Grand Cayman in the Caribbean. "It'll be an ideal spot to do our first open-water dive once we earn our scuba certification. Everybody says the diving there is unbelievable." In contrast, what *was* believable was that despite my apprehensions, I gave in to avoid an argument.

One of Bill's fellow pilots had an in-ground pool on his property and invited a small group to take scuba lessons from a certified YMCA instructor. Bill dragged me to Oshman's Sporting Goods to buy masks, fins, and snorkels, the minimum equipment necessary to participate, and while we shopped, he gazed longingly at the items that would, no doubt, be next on the list—dive watches, BCDs (buoyancy control devices), and numerous gauges. Fortunately, for the duration of the classes, the instructor provided pricey regulators and scuba tanks.

After passing written exams on the physics of diving, we entered the pool to learn how to snorkel, which would give us the rudiments of breathing in the water. "Surface dive to the bottom of the pool, and when you come back up, blow forcefully into the mouthpiece to expel water from the tube," our teacher instructed. So far, so good. The next step proved more difficult. When the instructor hooked up my tank and regulator, I couldn't clear my facemask when it flooded, and I repeatedly choked when the water went up my nose.

"You're way too tense," observed the instructor. "Relax."

That wasn't the most helpful advice since I was uncomfortable with the entire endeavor. "I can't control my breathing, and then I feel panicked," I explained.

Bill looked embarrassed at my inability to master the task and swam away to another area of the pool. The instructor worked with me and one other person with the same problem.

"Stand in the shallow end and practice deep, slow breaths. This alone will help calm you down. When the mask floods, you want to inhale a good bit of air through the regulator, put one finger on the top of the mask, look up and exhale slowly through your nose so the water gets pushed out of the bottom. Practice, practice, practice. It will soon become second nature."

And it did. But I had another concern. I removed my contacts before I got in the water so I wouldn't lose them, but this rendered me essentially blind. While this wasn't a big deal in the pool, I worried about being unable to see clearly in unfamiliar surroundings. I was relieved when the instructor told me I could order a mask with a prescription lens.

The swimming pool dives were only the first step. Bill and I had to complete some dives in open water to become fully certified. With our preliminary certificates and gear (which included newly purchased regulators, booties, and gloves) tucked into our luggage, we headed to our island destination to complete this final step. I loved Grand Cayman's beautiful beaches and warm, friendly people, and, to my surprise, I enjoyed my first dive to a depth of forty feet. A menacing-looking barracuda checked out our group, but for better or worse, I could see it! On a two-tank dive the following day, we reached a depth of seventy feet with the first tank and emerged thirty-five minutes later. When we reboarded the boat to change tanks, the water's choppiness caused a bobbing motion on the boat that made me seasick. "Just get back in the water," Bill said impatiently, again more concerned about the reaction of other divers than to my discomfort. "The nausea will go away once you're below the surface."

The divemaster agreed and put me at the head of the line to re-enter the water, but I felt acid in my throat as I suppressed vomiting. "I can't. I'll stay here with the boat captain."

"That doesn't make sense," Bill snapped. "You'd rather be seasick for another hour than to dive under the surface and feel better?"

I knew it sounded stupid to him, but I couldn't force myself to get in the water again. Even though I couldn't see it through his face mask, I knew Bill had an expression of displeasure, as he disappeared below the surface with the other divers.

There was little shade from the blazing sun, and I could only make the nausea subside by lying flat on my back on the deck with my eyes tightly shut, covered by sunglasses. I was relieved when Bill and the other divers finally emerged from the water, and we headed back to the dock at the dive shop. Fortunately, I felt better as the boat picked up speed and skimmed the waves; unfortunately, I didn't realize my forced sunbathing on deck would lead to further discomfort on shore.

The stupidity of what I had done became apparent later that afternoon. I had a horrible sunburn, which forced me to stay in the shade for the last two days of our vacation rather than explore more of the island. I sat dejectedly on the hotel's patio reading a book under an umbrella while Bill went on a solo visit to Pedro's Castle and the iconic Hell, Grand Cayman post office.

On the morning of our departure, the sunburn had turned into a deep tan on the fronts of my arms and legs (while the backs remained a paler shade), but my face was still painful and looked hideous. I had huge blisters except where large white circles ringed my eyes, and I looked like a freakish monkey-lizard creature that couldn't entirely shed its skin. When I bent over the sink to wash my hair, the slightest touch of water on my face was so unbearable that I had to let my hair, stringy from the saltwater still in it, hang limp on my shoulders. As we went up the steps to board the Southern DC-9, Bill exclaimed, "Karen! I didn't know you were working this flight." As an afterthought, "This is my wife, Kathi."

Karen, a petite blue-eyed blonde with a perfect figure— everything I had feared she would be—smiled. "I'm happy to finally meet you. Bill has told me so much about you."

I wanted to scramble back down the stairs and crawl into the cargo bin. "Likewise," I replied. "I'm afraid I don't look my best today."

"Oh, my goodness. That sunburn looks very painful. I'll bring you some cool towels for your face when you get in your seat." It wasn't fair; besides being beautiful, she was friendly and thoughtful. (I ran into Karen many times after that day, and our conversations convinced me that any relationship she had with Bill, other than friendship, existed only in his imagination.)

Unfortunately, scuba diving triggered a latent longing in Bill. This time, he announced, again out of nowhere, that he had a big dream—he wanted to sail around the world. I was dumbfounded! He had never even mentioned boats, let alone a colossal revelation like this. But now he talked incessantly about how much he had enjoyed sailing in his youth (never heard about it), how similar sailing and flying were (didn't know that), and how he'd like to someday live on a sailboat (yikes!). He subscribed to three sailing magazines and joined a book-of-the-month club specializing in nautical subjects.

I had some questions. For starters, we lived in Memphis—not exactly a sailing mecca—and where did I fit into his plans, given our marital ups and downs? I had been roped into scuba diving and felt this new activity would entail similar coercion.

He had quick answers. "We won't live in Memphis forever. We'll move somewhere where we can sail all the time." And, "Of course, you're included in these plans. I want you to love sailing as much as I do. You got sick in Grand Cayman because the boat was anchored and bobbing around. When it was underway, you were OK." Maybe so, but I was still apprehensive about his new obsession.

One afternoon, after I'd gotten home late the previous night, he excitedly interrupted my peaceful nap on the sofa in the family room.

"Look at this ad!"

I opened my eyes to see a magazine page three inches from my nose. "This kit's got everything I need to build an eighteen-foot boat."

As I cleared the cobwebs from my brain, I saw the ad as a warning. This was the beginning of a new phase of our relationship, one in which *Bill's* dreams would come true at the expense of any I might have.

"The kit's got the hull, superstructure, and all the hardware and fiberglass lath I need. It's pricey, but we can save a lot of money if we pick it up at the factory instead of having a freight company deliver it." There was that "we" again that took my buy-in for granted.

The factory was in Marion, Virginia, an eight-hour drive from Memphis. I couldn't think of anything I wanted to do less. But, at daybreak on the day of our expedition, I climbed into our pickup truck with a boat trailer hitched to its rear and squinted at the rising sun as we headed toward his fondest desire.

After spending the night at a motel near the factory, we picked up the kit components and headed back to Memphis. However, the boat made its maiden voyage prematurely when a problem with the trailer hitch nearly caused the hull to plow into the pickup bed. Was this an omen?

Bill spent every minute of his free time constructing the boat in the backyard. Zach, Fred, and the puppies made wide arcs around the project to avoid the burnt cotton candy smell of fiberglass. I sympathized with them because this odor became Bill's signature scent, and he sometimes tracked strands of the smelly stuff into the house, causing my skin to itch when I came in contact with it.

A couple of months into construction, Bill phoned me from his layover hotel room in Atlanta. "You're not going to believe this," he said excitedly. He seldom called while away, so it must be big news. "Southern just announced they're opening a crew base in Ft. Lauderdale. Isn't that great? I'm putting in my bid right now." Although he had, once again, made a major decision without discussing it with me, I felt happy from one standpoint. I would no longer have to commute to Chicago because Delta had made Ft. Lauderdale a co-base with Miami, and I could quickly transfer.

We sold our house for top dollar in the Memphis market, stored most of our belongings, packed up the five dogs, and moved in temporarily with Bill's parents in their rural Alabama home. The unfinished boat sat on its trailer next to a half-acre catfish pond on the property, and passersby chuckled at the incongruous sight. One of my father-in-law's friends asked, "Is that boat going in the pond, or is the pond going in the boat?"

Country living was a departure from everything I was used to. No running to the grocery store on a whim; it was fifteen miles away. And no pop music radio stations, my preferred genre. The only stations with a clear signal played country, and my father-in-law blasted his radio as he worked on outdoor projects from early morning until he went to bed. Some of the songs became earworms that drove me crazy. The rhythm of brushing my teeth became Dolly Parton's plea to Jolene not to take her man. Or a pulsing quick waltz tempo would wake me up in the middle of the night, and, suddenly, Roy Clark would be singing *Thank God and Greyhound You're Gone*. I felt like I had undergone brainwashing because, after a while, I truly liked certain artists and songs—*Blue Eyes Crying in the Rain, Behind Closed Doors*. Some of the songs about troubled relationships hit a little too close to home, but before long, I could correctly identify the singer of each song blaring out of the radio just as quickly as I could with pop songs from the fifties, sixties, and seventies.

Our base transfers came through, and we managed to hold parallel schedules for the next few months, allowing us time to house hunt. To make this easier, Bill drove our car from Alabama to the employee parking lot in Ft. Lauderdale and left it there to use on our search. On workdays, we drove the pickup truck an hour and a half to the airport in Birmingham, caught a flight to Ft. Lauderdale, and met after our respective trips. Commuting wasn't so bad when I knew it was temporary.

We chose a real estate agency in Pompano Beach and met with Mr. Solomon, a deeply tanned, white-haired gentleman with years of experience. "So, what are you looking for?" he asked.

"We want a house on a deep-water canal with a boat dock. I want to get my sailboat out in the ocean without having any fixed bridges."

"How many bedrooms?"

"Two or three. It's just the two of us."

Mr. Solomon probably pictured a big commission until he asked, "And what's your budget?"

When Bill proudly told him the amount we had from the sale of our Memphis house, Mr. Solomon looked like he needed to go to the ER.

"It doesn't sound like you did much research on South Florida prices. It's doubtful I can find anything close to what you're looking for with that sum."

Bill always resented being called out if he was wrong about something, so it was a hard pill to swallow. "Well, see if you can come close, and we'll try to find additional money." Mr. Solomon eventually found a small two-bedroom ranch in Lighthouse Point, a community on the Intercoastal Waterway surrounded by Pompano Beach. The house didn't fulfill everything on Bill's wish list, but even so, it forced us to dig into reserves we were hoping to save for a rainy day.

The house seemed like a shack compared to our luxurious home in Memphis. While only twenty years old, it looked dated and a bit rundown, with its terrazzo floors in the kitchen, small family room, jalousie windows, and a pool deck in need of repair. Its best feature was a Florida room, which I planned to fill with potted plants to enhance the view of the pool and canal.

The day arrived to hitch the boat and trailer to the pickup and drive to Florida with Zach and Fred. Lighthouse Point restricted each house to two dogs. We were grateful that Bill's mom and dad had grown attached to our three orphaned puppies (now happy, friendly young dogs) and allowed them to stay behind.

Although the boat was still unfinished, the hull was complete and able to go into the water, so when we arrived at Lighthouse Point, Bill launched the boat at a public boat ramp and motored to the dock behind our house. At the same time, I drove the truck and trailer to our new home. When I opened the truck bed canopy for the dogs, they tore out, headed to the back of the house, and, to their surprise, plunged head-first into the pool. Welcome to Florida, boys!

Bill continued to work tirelessly on the boat, stimulated by the prospect of taking her out for a sail. From the start, I felt skeptical of Bill's ability to build a seaworthy vessel and condescendingly christened her *LeakiTiki*. Bill was amused, so the name stuck. My only contribution to the project was to paint the name on the transom while balancing on my knees in our brand-new rubber dinghy.

The first time we took *LeakiTiki* onto open water, the wind and tide conditions created closely-spaced choppy two-foot waves, like those I had encountered in Grand Cayman. And just as it had then, nausea reared its ugly head. When the boat heeled sharply, I became terrified despite Bill's assurance that the keel prevented the vessel from capsizing. It did not bode well in maintaining a marriage when one partner could, literally, not stomach the other's passion.

As I clung to the rail of the boat, I remembered a similar grip on airplane armrests that gradually loosened when I became more comfortable on a plane, even in rough air. I needed to overcome seasickness, too, since the only alternative seemed to be walking away from our marriage. I recognized a familiar feedback loop— fear caused nausea, and nausea caused fear. But just as with my childhood anxieties, I couldn't pinpoint the exact reason. Maybe I feared I would go overboard and drown, perhaps that the boat would capsize and sink. I had made strides in overcoming aerophobia only to unwillingly host a new intruder—thalasso-phobia—an intense and persistent fear of the sea.

Chapter Nineteen

It wasn't all work and no play for Bill. As focused as he was on the boat project, we did take occasional travel breaks. In 1977, Sam, an old army friend who was based in Frankfurt, extended an exciting invitation. If we flew to Munich, we could attend Oktoberfest and stay with him and his family in their guest quarters. On the agenda was a VIP event at one of the enormous beer tents. We flew into Zurich the day before we planned to meet Sam and rented a car. Bill wanted to take the scenic route to Munich, which would add almost four hours to the drive, but first, we drove to a small village near Lake Constance, where we checked into a guesthouse near the railway station to get a little sleep before continuing. I had trouble waking up after the two hours Bill had allocated to recharge our batteries. He impatiently threw back the warm quilt I nestled under and tapped his watch.

"We need to get on the road. We'll stop in Innsbruck for lunch."

We reached Munich (with no hotel reservation) in heavy late afternoon traffic. The map we had purchased was a complicated affair, unlike anything I had ever used, with folding strips that refused to match up.

"Where are we?" Bill asked over and over.

"I didn't know when you asked me two minutes ago, and I still don't know. Even if I did, there are no hotel symbols on the map. Maybe we should pull into a gas station and ask."

Bill's disparaging glance told me he would prefer driving aimlessly around the city. When we finally spotted a hotel on a wide boulevard where Opels, VWs, and Mercedes sped by, Bill pulled up to the curb, and I ran inside to inquire about a room.

"Excuse me, do you speak English?" I asked the desk clerk.

"Yes, may I help you?"

It was Munich's busiest week of the year, and I felt ridiculous asking, "Would you happen to have a room available?"

Instead of snorting at my naiveté, he glanced at his watch. "I am holding my last room until six o'clock for a woman who said she would be back. She has two minutes. If she does not return, you can have it."

At six on the dot, he handed me a pen and said, "Please register." Seconds later, a woman rushed in the door to claim the room. A loud, heated argument in German ensued, during which the clerk occasionally turned to me and said, "Don't worry, the room is yours." A few minutes later, the woman stormed out, muttering what I could only guess was a suggestion for him to perform an anatomical impossibility. The clerk seemed unfazed by her remark and went outside to guide Bill to the parking area behind the hotel.

We wanted to explore Oktoberfest on our own before the following night's event, but only if the fairgrounds were easy to find; we'd had enough of driving around in circles. When we came downstairs an hour later, the same clerk stood at the desk. "Thank you so much for letting us have the room," I said. "I'm sorry it caused a problem."

"It was not a problem. That woman looked for a better deal and lost her chance."

"We want to go to Oktoberfest tonight. What is the easiest way to get there?"

The clerk looked perplexed. "The easiest way is to go out the door, turn right, and walk three blocks." Despite our ignorance and lack of planning, we had ended up in the ideal location.

We wandered the fairgrounds in a chilly drizzle, which did not dampen the enthusiasm of the crowds we shouldered past. Our hearty lunch left us wanting only a light snack, so we shared a bag of roasted almonds as we searched for a place to sit down and order a beer. But on this final weekend of the celebration, when companies reserved all the tables for their employees, there were no empty chairs in any of the tents. Disappointed, but knowing we would have a different experience the next night, we raised the collars of our jackets against the increasing wind to prepare for the short walk back to the hotel. We spotted a much smaller tent near the exit that drew us into its warm glow. Long tables of exuberant partygoers, many clad in dirndls and lederhosen, linked arms and swayed from side to side as they sang at the top of their lungs. A man at a nearby table beckoned us, wedged two more chairs next to him, and waved at the barmaid. Within seconds, giant mugs of golden lager appeared before us, and everyone raised their steins and shouted, "*Prost!*" Our hosts spoke little English, but we clearly understood their hospitality. But, before long, the combination of jet lag and beer made me want to lay my head on the table and drift off. Instead, Bill nudged me, and we rose, looked at the expectant group, and said (probably mispronouncing the word), "*Danke Schön.*" The whole group broke out in boisterous cheers. A couple of men stood to give us bear hugs, and all called out, "*Gute Nacht.*"

The next afternoon, we followed Sam's detailed directions to the small apartment building on the city's outskirts, where he, his wife, and two daughters greeted us. To avoid having to drive after a night of partying, we took the sleek modern subway to the fairgrounds. As promised, we received the royal treatment with a private table and a translator. We tasted all the traditional food—*weisswurst*, giant spiral-cut white radishes, and cold pork roast. But as lovely as it was, it seemed a little formal and sterile compared to our spontaneous reception the night before.

Back at the apartment, after the others had gone to bed, Bill and I talked about how much fun this trip had been. "I know I've spent all my time on the boat and have neglected you. You've been patient with me, and I love you very much." I almost cried. Times like these made up for the rough spots in our marriage and gave me hope that our relationship would keep improving.

But, despite enjoying great times and relatively strife-free periods like the one we had just enjoyed, Bill and I occasionally had arguments severe enough to prompt one or the other to mention divorce again. The flare-ups often arose when he belittled me, especially in front of others. But, after a couple of days of silent coexistence in the house or one of us leaving on a trip, the anger subsided, and we returned to the usual ebb and flow of our relationship.

A few weeks after one of these rough patches ended, Bill enthusiastically laid out a new plan. "*LeakiTiki* is OK for a first boat, but I'm ready for a 'real' boat."

"*LeakiTiki* seems real enough to me. And our dock isn't long enough for anything much larger."

"You're right, but I have a solution." *I didn't know there was a problem.* "I found a great condominium community in Boca Raton with a marina. We could buy a unit, rent a sailboat slip, and have the best of both worlds. *Which worlds are we talking about?*

"And how do you plan to pay for this?"

His quick answer told me his proposal wasn't a spontaneous idea. "We'll sell the house and make more than enough to buy the condo and the boat."

South Florida real estate was booming. In the short time since we had bought our house, its value had more than tripled. Even speculators with deep pockets found it hard to snag a property like ours on a deep-water canal. When these individuals found a bargain, they usually tore down the existing house and constructed a two-story mini palace, which they sold for a sizable profit.

Bill's idea forced me to confront my true feelings about sailing. There was one huge positive factor. It provided a respite from Bill's snide, hurtful comments. While on board, he was always patient and kind, even when I made mistakes in handling the boat. His love of sailing seemed to free his mind from negative feelings and behavior. On the other hand, I didn't share his enjoyment; my physical and psychological difficulties continued, and I felt the move to a larger boat would further ensnare me in a lifestyle I didn't think I wanted. Here I was again at a crossroads: stay or leave? Whether from fear or optimism, I once more acquiesced and chose the road *most* taken: I stayed.

I soon realized I should have considered more carefully. Our move into a condo came with the heartbreak of finding new homes for my beloved dogs, who would not do well in a confined space with no yard. It came close to being a dealbreaker. But despite my sorrow at losing my babies, I helped arrange new homes for them. One of Bill's cousins, Margaret, who lived on a large country property in Tennessee, loved German shepherds and eagerly agreed to take Fred but did not want a second dog. Bill's parents welcomed Zach back with open arms, and the orphans recognized and joyfully bounced around their old playmate. Although I knew I'd have occasional chances to be with Zach when we visited my in-laws, I doubted I would ever see Fred again. On one of the saddest days of my life, I kneeled, looked into his intelligent eyes, kissed the top of his head, and said goodbye. He trotted behind me to the truck, expecting to jump in, but Margaret held his collar as we drove away. I cried all the way home and for weeks after.

With difficulty, I adjusted to life without my dogs. From time to time, I thought I felt warm breath on my face when I was in bed and expected to see a canine face inches away when

I opened my eyes, or I would hear the click-clack of toenails on the condo floor but found no wagging tails to greet me when I turned around.

Living in the condo community was a significant lifestyle change. It was less like a residence and more like a posh resort—tennis courts, pool, tiki bar, private beach. Shortly after selling our house, we had donated *LeakiTiki* to the local Boy Scouts Council, so Bill impatiently eyed the empty slip at the condo marina as we waited for our new boat, a Pearson forty-two-foot ketch we named *Moonraker*. When she finally arrived, Bill and I took a long weekend to sail to the Bahamas, a crossing we would make frequently. While I experienced fewer and less severe cases of seasickness on the larger boat, there were times when it came on with a vengeance, especially when we had to sail in less-than-ideal conditions because of limited time. Sometimes, when the gulf stream had "elephants" (large square waves, occasionally visible on the horizon from shore), the resulting chaos of the northerly current fighting against southerly winds made Tilt-a-Whirls and the Mad Tea Party seem like walks in the park.

Moonraker was, in nautical slang, "yare," which meant ship-shape and easy to handle. Still, Bill's insatiable appetite for a bigger boat continued. We had owned *Moonraker* for less than a year when he announced "our" next purchase. I admitted that the newly designed Pearson 530, a fifty-three-foot ketch, had sleek, beautiful lines but also a heart-stopping price tag. To purchase it would require selling both *Moonraker* and our condo, and Bill would fulfill the last step of his master plan—to live aboard a boat.

The first 530, Hull Number 1, was currently under construction at the Portsmouth, Rhode Island, factory and would remain there for demo purposes. Hull Number 2 already had a buyer. Bill negotiated with a boat dealer in St. Petersburg, Florida. We would trade in *Moonraker* as partial payment for Hull Number 3, which would be ready to launch in mid-September 1980.

Because we were future owners, Pearson invited us to the factory to participate in the christening of Hull Number 1. It wasn't every day a boat manufacturer launched a new model, so Pearson pulled out all the stops. Colorful nautical flags festooned the stays of both masts as the boat sat on the slipway, waiting for her first encounter with seawater. Bill Shaw, the marine architect who designed the 530 welcomed the crowd and placed a leafy beech tree branch on her bow, a tradition to ensure the safe return of the vessel after a voyage. The crowd held its collective breath as a young woman on a lift clutched a champagne bottle. Nautical legend held that it was a bad omen if the bottle didn't shatter on the first whack on the hull (or, in this case, a metal cleat to protect the gel coat.) With Solo cups containing red wine poised in the air, the crowd cheered when shards of green glass fell into the protective netting around the bottle. Bill Shaw revealed the vessel's name, *Pionero*, in honor of the artisans from the Azores Islands whose exquisite craftsmanship made the boat unique. We were honored to be aboard *Pionero's* maiden sail. Conditions were perfect for her to attain her hull speed (the maximum speed a sailboat can achieve) of nine knots, a bit over ten miles per hour.

Back home in Boca, we prepared to sail *Moonraker* to the St. Petersburg dealer, which was a requirement of our contract. After an uneventful sail to the Florida Keys, we motored under the sixty-five-foot fixed bridge at Channel 5, just southwest of Lower Matecumbe Key and into the Gulf of Mexico. Under sail and making good time, we suddenly encountered a series of violent squalls during the night. I was terrified as the boat began to drift into shallow waters where it could run aground, leaving us stranded and the boat badly damaged. To prevent this, Bill furled the sails, dropped anchor, and ran the engine continuously. Once the storms passed (fortunately, not before), the engine died and failed to restart even though the gauge indicated we had ample fuel. "Well, I didn't want to do it this way, but we'll have to sail under the Skyway Bridge." Bill said, his voice edged with fatigue. It had been only three months since a freighter rammed into the piling of one of the spans of the bridge, collapsing it and killing thirty-five people. It would have been tricky enough to pick our way through with our engine running, but it would require local knowledge to manage this under sail, which Bill didn't have.

"Can't we get some help?" I asked, frightened out of my mind. For once, Bill listened to me. He radioed the Coast Guard, which sent a vessel to tow us to the yacht basin. An inspection revealed that an easily replaced split hose had prevented fuel from reaching the engine.

We sold our condo to a couple from New York who couldn't be bothered to shop for furnishings for their *fourth* vacation home and asked us to add our furniture, kitchenware, dishes, and linens to the price. We made more money on the sale than we dreamed, and we were also spared the hassle of liquidating the contents.

At a small vintage beachfront apartment in Pompano Beach, awaiting the completion of our boat, we considered several names, but we couldn't agree on one. With nothing much to occupy our time, we got hooked on reruns of *Star Trek*, one of our favorite shows. In one episode, Scotty, the *Enterprise's* engineer, warned Captain Kirk against pushing the starship beyond warp speed 9. "No starship has ever exceeded that speed, and we may break apart," Scotty warned frantically in his signature brogue. We looked at each other excitedly, with identical thoughts in our heads. The 530's hull speed was nine knots. Nine knots—*Warp Nine*? It was perfect!

Bill decided it would be an epic adventure to take delivery of the boat at the factory and sail her to Florida rather than pay a professional crew. I couldn't stay silent about this. "You can't possibly think it's a good idea to use a one-thousand-mile voyage as the shakedown cruise (the test to find the idiosyncrasies and vulnerabilities of the boat). And what about the weather? It will be autumn, and sailing conditions will deteriorate if we wait beyond September." I begged him to ask at least one of our sailing friends to come along to augment our crew, but he brushed aside my concerns. Sure enough, *Warp Nine* didn't come off the production line until the end of October, a month and a half late.

I had secured vacation time based on the expected timeline of mid-September, so I scrambled to swap vacations with other flight attendants to get the November weeks I needed, sacrificing my Christmas and New Year's weeks in the process. There was little wiggle room in the time frame to return to Florida because I had precisely three weeks off before my first post-vacation trip. "Don't worry about it. It won't take longer than twelve days to make it to Florida." Bill's cavalier attitude irked me. He had managed to get four weeks off and had much more flexibility than I did.

Taking the advice of an engineer at Pearson, we installed an autopilot (which we named Charlie), roller furling on the jib (to prevent having to negotiate a slippery deck in bad weather), self-tailing winches, and a state-of-the-art navigation system, measures that would make it easier for only two people to manage a large boat. We purchased premium foul weather gear and enough food and beverages to last well beyond the ten to twelve days we planned to be underway. My tendency to become seasick weighed heavily on my mind. With our tight schedule, there would be little opportunity to get off the boat for relief. Fortunately, my doctor prescribed what I considered a miracle drug, a newly available scopolamine patch, to prevent seasickness. The procedure was to place a patch behind my left ear for three days, then a new one behind my right ear for the next three, and to continue this for as long as I was on the boat. When I tested a patch a week before our departure to check for side effects, I noticed dry mouth, itchy skin, noticeable spaciness, and fleeting images at the corners of my eyes that disappeared when I turned my head to see them. I readily accepted these minor conditions in exchange for not being nauseous.

Our departure date, November 3, was a cloudless Indian summer day. *Warp Nine* glided on the mirrored surface of Narraganset Bay. I could almost believe she was euphoric to be in her element. After so much consternation about embarking on this trip, I, too, felt exhilarated to be on our way—so much so that I didn't apply a patch behind my ear. Why take the unnecessary chance in these idyllic conditions of being ditzy or seeing things that weren't there? But as we rounded the breakwater to enter the Atlantic Ocean, I realized I had made a terrible mistake. Two-foot head seas—waves that flowed straight at us—slammed into the bow in close succession, sending me to the railing again. With more nausea on the way, I went below (which intensified my discomfort) and applied a patch. But it was too late; scopolamine is a preventative, not a cure. The only things that stayed in my stomach for the next twenty-four hours were fruit-flavored hard candies I had purchased as an afterthought when we shopped for food and supplies. Even water came up the minute I drank it, a condition I feared could lead to dehydration. Bill, who always believed my seasickness was in my head, was exasperated that I couldn't help him manage the boat. *Hey, buddy, I tried to warn you.* At last, the scopolamine took hold, the nausea subsided, and I felt somewhat giddy that I could move around without my insides coming up. At the same time, the wind shifted, and we clipped along with a beam reach (the wind at a right angle to the boat) and a much more comfortable ride.

Once the seasickness subsided, I found a spot to brace against the raised side of the cockpit near the wheel. I had read about half of the eleven-hundred-page *Shogun*, a pastime that distracted me from anxious thoughts of being in the middle of nowhere, while I alternately checked instruments and scanned the horizon for ships. At the same time, trustworthy Charlie steered and kept us on course. The next three days of our journey were picture-perfect. We clipped along under ideal conditions as I cooked bacon and eggs, grilled cheese sandwiches, and casseroles without discomfort. We clinked our beer bottles and toasted a great cruise as the sun set in a blaze of red and gold—red sky at night, sailor's delight.

Offshore of Cape Hatteras, North Carolina, the situation changed. The sky remained cloudless and bright blue, but our anemometer indicated a wind speed of twenty-three knots that blew from the southwest, only a few degrees starboard of the bow. The breaking crests of ten-foot seas sent spindrift into the cockpit, and we had to shout to each other above their roar. Bill trimmed the sails so we could sail close-hauled (as close to the wind as possible), and our speedometer registered an astounding ten knots. I could picture Scotty, somewhere in space, shaking his worried head!

Uncomfortable and frightening as these conditions were, I felt encouraged that we were making speedy headway—except that was only an illusion. Repeated readings from the satellite navigation system revealed that, contrary to the feeling of moving forward at breakneck speed, we hadn't advanced a single meter. The Gulf Stream, broader and deeper off the Outer Banks of North Carolina, ran at about four knots in the same direction as the wind. The cumulative effect was so strong we were fortunate not to have lost ground.

Bill tuned into a NOAA (National Oceanic and Atmospheric Administration) radio frequency to determine how soon the wind would shift to a more favorable heading. "It sounds like we'll have to put up with this for another eight hours or so. Then we'll get a nice beam wind that will scoot us out of here."

Conditions didn't change after the expected reprieve even though NOAA had not altered its forecast. Bill's fatigued and worried face sent my fear meter soaring. We had few options to escape from these nerve-racking conditions. While *Warp Nine's* specs made her ideal for ocean sailing, her sixty-five-foot mast and nearly seven-foot draft challenged navigating the shallow Intercoastal Waterway. And even if we wanted to go that route, Oregon Inlet, the closest entry point, had a fixed bridge that was too low (at the time) to go under.

Night fell. The crests of waves leered at me with frothy faces, every thud convinced me a piece of the boat was breaking off, and ghostly voices moaned in the rigging. *Warp Nine* rode a rollercoaster where every wave sent her on a steep ascent, followed by a sudden heart-stopping dip when we slid off the crest into the trough. Because we were sailing in shipping lanes, one of us had to always remain in the cockpit to look for other vessels, but when we took turns going below, we achieved only a facsimile of sleep. By the following morning, we were exhausted and achy from bracing for hours against the onslaught of waves.

"What do you want to do?" I asked.

"I'm so tired I can't think straight. I've got to get some sleep."

That was not what I wanted to hear. "Why don't you go below and try? I'm OK for now," I lied.

As I watched him descend and stretch out on the settee, I huddled into my corner and escaped to the world of Lord Toranaga and the English pilot Blackthorne. When I glanced below, I saw the rise and fall of Bill's chest as he slept.

Less than ten minutes later, however, he sat up, moved to the ladder below the hatch, and peered upward into the cockpit. *So much for sleep.* He climbed up and squinted in the bright sunshine. "Where are the rest of the crew members?" he shouted.

"What did you say?" I was sure I hadn't heard him correctly over the din of the wind and waves.

He repeated testily, "Where-are-the-rest-of-the-crew-members?"

Goosebumps rose on my arms. "Bill, I don't know what you mean. You and I are the only ones on this boat."

"No, they're supposed to furl the jib," he snapped. "If you'd watched the foredeck instead of having your nose in that book, you would have seen them!" *What is he talking about, and why is he so angry?*

At that moment, I wanted not just my nose, but my entire body transported to feudal Japan or anywhere but on this boat with a man experiencing a mental breakdown. Several scenarios spun through my mind, each grimmer than the last, as I struggled to deal with this dangerous situation. I couldn't handle the boat alone, and if I tried to call the Coast Guard for help, would he block my access to the radio? Was he far enough gone to jump overboard? To harm me? I needed to humor him as I tried to think of a solution, so it was time to put on my Flight Attendant Face as all hell broke loose.

"I haven't seen them, but I promise I'll watch for them," I said calmly. "Why don't you try to get some sleep? I'll wake you up when they get here."

He gave me a skeptical glance but descended the ladder and laid down again on the settee while my mind raced through possible courses of action. About five minutes later, he rose again and stretched. He climbed the ladder, and I prepared for what might come next.

"Wow, I feel better," he said, smiling broadly. "I finally got some good sleep. How long was I out?" *What the hell?* He noticed my incredulous expression and said, "What's the matter?"

"Why were you talking about other crew members and how I was supposed to watch for them?" I was near tears at this point, as much from relief as from fear and frustration.

He eyed me with grave concern. "What are *you* talking about? Other crew members? Are you OK?"

171

At first, he refused to believe my account of our conversation. Finally, he acknowledged that he must have been sleepwalking. To someone who prided himself on always being in control, this was, indeed, an eye-opening revelation. "We're turning around," he announced matter-of-factly. Ten hours later, we tied up safely in a Chesapeake Bay marina.

After we slept as long as we could, we stepped off the boat and struggled to walk on solid ground. (This strange phenomenon is called "land sickness.") We stayed in the marina for two days, enjoyed delicious restaurant meals, and rested as much as possible. Once we replenished our supplies, we resumed our journey slowly southward on the Intercoastal Waterway. Charlie took a break as we carefully navigated the dredged channel, and we sounded three short airhorn blasts to request tenders to raise the bridges and allow us to pass through. Under power, we glided through beautiful marshlands where wading birds stopped fishing to gaze curiously at our vessel. We re-entered the Atlantic Ocean at Morehead City, North Carolina, accompanied by three dolphins, which we took as a sign of good luck.

The remainder of the voyage was free of incident except when Charlie went on strike off the coast of Savannah and refused to resume his duties. We hand-steered the boat from that point, a task made easier by calm sailing conditions. Eighteen days after leaving Rhode Island, we entered Hillsboro Inlet at high tide around seven p.m. and motored to our new home at the Sands Marina in Pompano Beach. We made it back just in time for me to pack my layover bag and then, overwhelmingly fatigued from the long voyage, leave for my three-day trip the following morning. As I grabbed my purse and suitcase, I glared at Bill, sound asleep and sprawled luxuriantly over on my side of the bed, not a care in the world.

Chapter Twenty

M y job required continuously "being on my toes," "nipping things in the bud," "staying in the loop," "keeping an even keel," "foreseeing the unforeseeable," and any other trite expression one can come up with. However, specific incidents happened so frequently that they, themselves, became clichés.

It's Greek to Me

Mettez votre tasse sur mon plateau, s'il vous plaît. Flight attendants may as well have said this French phrase to some of our less experienced passengers because they didn't understand it in English: "Please put your cup on my tray."

As passengers finished their meals and started their desserts, the flight attendants delegated to pour refills of coffee strolled the aisle with a coffee pot in one hand and a small tray in the other, on which sat a dozen cream containers along with a plastic glass filled with sugar and sweetener packets. An empty spot on the tray was just the right size for a coffee cup.

Even if our arms could reach as far as the meal tray at the window seat to refill the passenger's cup, the chance of missing the target was too great. The safer procedure we used was to have the passengers place their cups on our tray so we could bring them close to us, where we had more pouring control. Then, we extended the tray back to the passenger.

"Would you care for coffee?" I asked the passenger who sat at the window.

"Yes, I would."

I extended the tray to him, and he took cream and Sweet'N Low from it. A few seconds passed while we stared at one another, each waiting for the other to do something. To break the standoff, I said, "Please put your cup on my tray."

The passenger looked confused and wondered what the heck I meant. "It is on my tray," he protested, pointing at the cup.

"No, on *my* tray." I tried to gesture, a nearly impossible feat with a coffee pot in one hand and a tray in the other. The passenger beside him picked up his neighbor's coffee cup and set it in the right spot.

"Oh, sorry," the passenger said, his face red at his lack of travel sophistication.

"It's OK." I smiled and extended the full cup back to him.

Attempting to reclaim a measure of worldliness, he smiled and said, "Merci beaucoup."

Pay No Attention to the Woman Behind the Curtain

Except for the L-1011, which had a lower level entirely separate from passengers, our airplanes offered no place to escape for a little break except in the galley with the curtains closed. But (and I always suspected this was intentional), the curtains seldom covered the opening. A single curtain was too narrow to reach all the way across; a double never quite met in the middle.

It didn't matter anyway because even if the curtains fit perfectly, passengers ignored the drawn drapes and pulled them open without a second thought. I might be sitting on top of a meal carrier taking a well-deserved break when a face peeked through the curtain and, ignoring the more accessible flight attendant working in the cabin, said, "I hate to bother you, but..."

If there were leftover meals, the galley furnished a "private" area where flight attendants could eat. Inevitably, after we closed the curtains as far as we could and prepared to dig into our omelet or chicken breast, a passenger whipped them open and said, "Oh, you get to eat, too!" They didn't want anything in particular; they only needed to voice this amazing discovery aloud.

Since so many flight attendants heard this comment, it became a catchphrase. We would sit in a nice restaurant on a layover, happy to be on the receiving end of service after a long day of meeting the needs of others. We talked about incidents on the flight and how much we enjoyed being in Boston, Seattle, or wherever we were. Then, when the food arrived, we proclaimed in unison, "And we get to eat, too!"

Confound It!

Another common occurrence involved passengers' difficulties with the lavatory doors. I felt the problem lay in their perception of an airplane as a high-tech futuristic conveyance on which a simple doorknob turn or a push where it said "push" couldn't possibly open the door. It had to be more complex than that.

I observed passengers pulling out the ashtrays next to the doors and trying unsuccessfully to push them back in until they clattered on the floor. Or they repeatedly pulled on the door only to see it tighten instead of opening. "Is somebody in there?" they asked in frustration. After I gave them a chance to master the task independently but saw that their struggle might last the entire flight, I pushed the door open for them.

Most had the good grace to laugh at themselves, but some were irritated. "Why do they make the doors so hard to open?"

Several remarks came to mind, but I said, "It certainly makes you wonder, doesn't it?"

Selective Hearing

It annoyed me when a passenger wouldn't remove his earphones when he saw I was asking him a question. "What would you like to drink?" I saw the annoyance on his face that I had perhaps interrupted the intricate plotline of *Ace Ventura: Pet Detective* and prepared for his shouted reply.

"WHAT?" The purpose of the metal contraption I stood behind was obvious. It held an ice bucket, plastic glasses, and a coffee pot. If those clues were too subtle, he saw me hand a napkin, a bag of peanuts, and a Sprite to his seatmate.

I wanted to say, "What do you think I asked you? 'What do you call a male ladybug?' No, I asked you what you want to drink."

Instead, I did a pantomime of removing earphones from my head as the woman beside him chuckled and rolled her eyes. In response, he shrugged his shoulders with a look of resignation that said it wouldn't be possible for us to communicate. I had reached the same conclusion and released the brake on the cart to move on to the next row.

"HEY," he shouted in the decibel range of a rocket lifting off at Cape Canaveral, "I WANT A JACK DANIELS ON THE ROCKS!"

What Did You Call Me?

There are several ways to get a flight attendant's attention. "Miss," "Ma'am," "Sir," or (less desirable) "Stewardess" are acceptable forms of address. There are also unacceptable ways—yank on the back of the flight attendants' aprons (or worse, their skirts or pants) or stick your arm out in the aisle as if to stop a train from plowing through. But the worst thing to do? Yell, "Waitress!" We saved up all our icy gazes for such passengers.

I don't mean to disparage waitstaff; I truly respect them. I know it's a skill not everyone can do efficiently and competently. But, while serving food and drinks was the most noticeable flight attendant activity, it was far from the primary reason we were on board the airplane. During initial training and subsequent annual refreshers, we drilled on the skills needed to ensure passenger safety—from evacuating a smoke-filled aircraft to dealing with a hijacking and many more duties that had nothing to do with martinis and chicken cordon bleu. Waitstaff doesn't do those things. It was like calling an engineer a handyman or an elementary school teacher a babysitter. All those professions require skill sets that are not outwardly interchangeable, and I've never once heard a customer in a restaurant attract the staff's attention by yelling, "Stewardess!"

Coffee, Tea, or Peas?

Despite many commonalities, some passengers were unique. Those who became unforgettable didn't sit quietly the entire flight, engage in pleasant chit-chat with the crew, or say "please" and "thank you," actions which would make them part of the vast majority of the courteous but forgettable flying public. Instead, passengers who were cranky, loud, irate, obnoxious, drunk, smelly, or otherwise objectionable could be sure that flight attendants would never forget them, even if they tried. Every flight attendant had a rogues' gallery of candidates for Worst Passenger in Aviation History.

When we shared accounts of these unpleasant characters with our coworkers, we did so with a bit of one-upmanship. "That's pretty bad," the listener would admit, "but let me tell you about the creep I had on *my* flight last week." We conjured up fantasies about things we might say or do to such passengers on the last flights of our careers because, how could there be repercussions? We cracked ourselves up with witty retorts we knew would never come out of our mouths.

But a coworker, "Elizabeth," surpassed anything we could have imagined with her response to a passenger. Only a few eyewitnesses know the details of her last flight (I wasn't present), so what follows is pure speculation. While I've fabricated many details, and her nemesis is a composite of some of the worst passengers I had throughout my career, her final act as a flight attendant is purportedly true.

On a full dinner flight from Atlanta to San Francisco, Elizabeth took her turn to work in first class. The double-aisle L-1011 had thirty-two first-class seats in a two-by-two-by-two configuration. The passenger who sat in 5D, a center seat on the right aisle, was one of the unforgettable passengers. Let's call him Mr. Big. His dress was impeccable—sharply creased khakis, a pink Hugo Boss shirt, and Gucci loafers without socks—and his appearance suave—suntanned face framed by expertly-coifed salt and pepper hair, eyes veiled by aviator sunglasses. Mr. Big's appearance and demeanor screamed, "Look how wealthy and important I am." During boarding, he snapped his fingers at Elizabeth as she assisted another passenger and shouted, "Hey, Honey, how about a drink here?" This remark was just the beginning.

After takeoff, Elizabeth began the service as usual, pushing her beverage cart into the right aisle to serve pre-dinner cocktails. As she rolled closer to row five, she heard Mr. Big loudly bragging to his hapless seatmate about his superior business acumen. He had just closed a multi-million-dollar deal with a less astute businessman, "The sucker never knew what hit him," Mr. Big chuckled.

Elizabeth arrived at Row 5 and asked Mr. Big what he would like to drink. "You don't have what I like to drink. I drink thirty-year-old Glenfiddich, but I guess I'll have to settle for the same rotgut you gave me on the ground. Gimme a double scotch on the rocks."

When she returned to the galley, Elizabeth listened without comment to her two coworkers' remarks on the passenger's rudeness. Next, she pushed her meal cart into the aisle, served fancy salads with hearts of palm, asparagus spears, and edible flowers, asked each passenger for their choice of salad dressing, and spooned on the customary amount. As she served Mr. Big, she braced herself for his next barrage. "Hey, Hon, do you think you can spare more than that dribble of salad dressing, considering what I paid for this ticket?" With a forced smile, Elizabeth took the plate from his extended hand and added a generous portion of honey-mustard dressing.

"That's more like it." Mr. Big grinned and looked around to ensure everyone had witnessed his power play.

After they picked up the salad plates, the flight attendants served dinner. Each meal cart contained several oblong aluminum pans, some with entrées and some with side dishes. There was an equal number of steak Diane, chicken Kyiv, and grilled salmon with no extras to cover the possibility that all passengers might want the same choice. And this, unfortunately, was the problem Elizabeth encountered. After she served her last steak entrée to a passenger in Row 4, she wheeled her cart back one row. "Sir, would you like chicken Kyiv or grilled salmon this evening?"

He scowled. "I just heard you offer steak to the guy sitting in the row in front of me. That's what I want."

"I'm sorry, sir, but I don't have any more steak."

"Isn't this just great?" he snorted. "American never pulls something like this. They value my business, so I always get what I want."

Elizabeth remained calm as he glared at her for a few moments, expecting she would either grovel or miraculously pull out a steak from … somewhere. Still, she knew she could not appease him with further apologies and waited for him to cease his tantrum. Glumly, he said, "I guess I'll have to settle for the salmon."

"Would you like a twice-baked potato and some peas?" Elizabeth interpreted his petulant silence as a "yes," so she placed the fish on the plate, used her tongs to add the potato, scooped up the standard serving of peas, and set the plate on his tablecloth.

He uttered the fateful words as she was about to move her cart to the last row. "Since I didn't get what I wanted, the least you can do is give me more than a measly spoonful of peas!"

For a moment, Elizabeth looked like a combat veteran with a thousand-yard stare, but then she focused on the remaining contents of her meal cart. "PEAS?" she shouted as startled passengers throughout the cabin stopped chewing mid-bite. "You want more peas? Well, here. You can have all the peas."

She removed the aluminum pan of plump, bright-green legumes and turned it upside down above his hundred-dollar haircut. The cabin was deadly quiet as Mr. Big sat stunned and watched little pellets roll off his head onto his petal pink shirt.

The Flight Attendant in Charge emerged from the galley, horrified at the scene. "Go to the lower galley, now!" she hissed as Elizabeth calmly maneuvered herself to the back of her meal cart and left the first class cabin and her career behind.

Once the story got around (minus my made-up details), many of us re-evaluated our last-flight fantasies. While I still thought up stinging retorts and snarky putdowns, I conceded that Elizabeth had outdone everyone by ending her last flight in a spectacular shower of peas.

Pet Sounds

There were, of course, other unforgettable passengers; those who put dirty diapers directly in the seat pocket, those who planted their bare feet high on the bulkhead for all to see (or, even worse, clipped their toenails), those who refused to comply with simple requests, like fastening their seatbelts, and those who smuggled live contraband onto the plane.

Until around 1990, no fur babies were allowed on board except guide dogs, so pets had to ride in a pressurized compartment in the plane's cargo area. That didn't mean they never traveled in the cabin, though. Sometimes, I spotted a passenger clandestinely pushing a moving object into a bag on their lap. I usually looked the other way if no one else was in the row. However, I had to confront the situation if the culprit's actions were blatant and attracted the attention of others.

"What do you have in the bag?"

"Nothing."

"It looks like something's moving in there?"

"It does?"

"Look, I know you've got a pet in the bag. And I'm sure you know animals aren't allowed in the cabin. I sympathize with you, but that's the rule. I'll have an agent meet the flight to discuss this with you." I was not sure what happened during those chats; it was probably just a stern warning not to do it again. Or there may have been a system of demerits that ended up on passengers' "permanent records." I never found out. Eventually, airlines changed their policies to allow small pets to come on board as carry-on luggage (for a fee) with certain restrictions. The pet container had to be small enough to fit under the seat in front of the passenger, provide adequate ventilation, allow the animal to stand up and turn around, and have a secure latch to keep the door closed. This last restriction certainly did not guarantee that the enclosure was not opened. In the "give an inch, take a mile" school of thought, some passengers felt they had carte blanche to release pets from their cages. "You need to keep your dog in its kennel at all times," I admonished many passengers who cuddled a small ball of fur in their laps. The responses were predictable.

"Princess was crying, and I didn't want her to disturb everyone."

"The gentleman next to me doesn't mind, do you, sir?"

"I have to give Charlie his medicine."

"Fluffy is claustrophobic."

"You ought to be ashamed of yourself for making Buster stay inside a cage."

I swallowed my shame (and amusement at the creativity of some of the responses). I requested that the captain have an agent meet the flight to administer those mysterious consequences to the passenger.

The All-Time Best Comment from a Passenger Ever!

Not all unforgettable passengers left a negative impression; some offered delightful surprises. One passenger gave each flight attendant a rose. Another brought a big box of candy to share. Still, others made a point of telling us how much they appreciated our service. And a stressed young mother thanked us effusively for helping her deal with her colicky baby.

Yet, one passenger stands out. I encountered him on a flight after a very short layover, where I reluctantly crawled out of bed in answer to a four thirty a.m. wake-up call. I felt like I had only been asleep for a half hour. My friend Susanne and the other flight attendant on our crew looked sleep-deprived, too, as we slumped in our hotel lobby chairs and waited for the courtesy van driver to load our bags. I didn't even have the energy to get a complimentary cup of coffee from the set-up in the lobby— not that it would have made a dent in my fatigue. We walked through the almost empty Indianapolis airport, knowing that our passengers would arrive soon for the flight to Atlanta, probably well-rested and ready for their day.

As the Flight Attendant in Charge, I stood side by side with Susanne, who was working first class, and we robotically greeted the passengers as they filed on. All we could muster was the slightest trace of a smile as we monotonously repeated, "Good morning, welcome aboard; good morning, welcome aboard." But in response to this lackluster greeting, one gentleman unexpectedly cut through our malaise when he offered us a beautiful, warm smile and, without a trace of insincerity or irony, said, "Well, good morning to you too, Delta sky goddesses!"

I couldn't stop smiling for the rest of the day!

Chapter Twenty-one

Six steps. That's all it took to walk the width of my living space; an average compact car could squeeze sideways into the boat's salon. I had never lived in such a small space, not even in my dorm room in college. But contrary to my expectations, I adjusted well to boat life. That's not to say there weren't any challenges, one of which occurred every time I prepared to leave for a trip. I needed to transfer my suitcase from the boat to the dock, which might seem simple on the surface but, in practice, was quite precarious. I first had to perform a tricky maneuver where I pressed down on a mooring line with my foot to pull the boat close enough to the dock that I could step off. Once I was off the boat, I repeated this action to bring the boat close enough to the dock to grab my suitcase from the deck, which required a perfect combination of balance and strength. I didn't always succeed on the first try (or the second or the third). Most flight attendants had to factor traffic into the time it took them to drive to the airport; I had to add "capture the suitcase" time. Bill completed this procedure in one smooth move, but I feared that if I tried his method and failed, Crew Scheduling would not be happy to hear that I would be late because I was soaking wet.

Occasionally, I lost a bag of groceries if I tried to board carrying two at a time. I was grateful to the helpful harbor master's assistant who rowed around in a dinghy to retrieve things that didn't sink immediately. One such item elicited a snicker from him—an economy-size jar of Vaseline. I could see his imagination running wild at the thought of how we might employ this item, but in reality, I put it to efficient use by coating eggshells to extend their unrefrigerated shelf life.

I became a more competent sailor. Instead of the dread I once felt at the prospect of spending hours on the water with no land in sight, I made a game of figuring out when I'd spot our destination on the horizon, just where I expected it to be. Bill's and my respective flying seniority provided enough flexibility to cruise to the Bahamas or the Keys at least once a month.

Our most remote destination was San Salvador, the easternmost island in the Bahamas, where Columbus first set foot in the New World. When we dropped anchor in Fernandez Bay and climbed down the swim ladder to get into our dinghy, we spotted two shade-seeking barracudas lurking near the keel in the boat's shadow, a sight repeated everywhere we moored. After we secured the dinghy on the beach, we hiked a short distance to the Riding Rock Resort, where we scuba-dived on breathtakingly beautiful coral reefs in crystal-clear waters. Clownfish, queen angels, yellow and blue tangs, and sergeant majors darted among giant yellowfin and black groupers in a riot of color. We spotted four-foot green sea turtles paddling across the staghorn, brain, and undulating soft corals. The next day, Bill returned to the resort alone to dive in the crevices of the underwater walls. I'd made progress with my phobias, but the idea of wedging myself into a tight underwater space was still the stuff of nightmares.

We hitched a ride in the back of a vintage Ford pickup to a house where a woman sold delicious homemade *souse* (pronounced "sowse"), a savory stew with pigeon peas and rice. We learned at the local bar which locals had fresh-baked bread for sale even when empty grocery store shelves awaited the weekly mail boat delivery of supplies from Nassau.

But despite our generally pleasant trips, we still encountered occasional sailing mishaps. Sandy, Paul, and Mom came to Florida for Christmas and New Year's in 1982, and I invited them to stay on the boat and take a Christmas cruise to Key West. While we wouldn't have all the traditional dishes of a fancy home-cooked meal, I planned to roast a turkey breast in the galley oven, accompanied by mashed potatoes, green beans, cranberry sauce, and pumpkin pie, and we would enjoy Christmas dinner in a truly unique way.

We departed our slip at ten o'clock on Christmas morning. Since the forecast called for light winds out of the southeast, limiting our speed to around four or five knots if we sailed, we ran the engine instead to shorten the trip. Navigating Hawk Channel further south would also be easier and safer under power. This four- to five-mile-wide section of the navigable waterway lay between the Keys and the outer barrier reef that protected the channel from the Atlantic Ocean. Hundreds of colorful floats dotted the water during lobster season, making it look like a minefield that couldn't decide if it was picturesque or perilous. The floats were attached to submerged lobster pots, and it took precision to steer around them to avoid snagging their ropes in our rudder.

Around five p.m., we passed Fowey Rocks, where Hawk Channel begins. The sun had been hanging just above the horizon for several minutes and then, typical of the tropics, suddenly dropped out of sight, leaving streaks of orange, pink, and violet in its wake. We'd have twilight for a little longer. Dinner turned out better than I expected, even though we had to eat in shifts in the salon so that someone would always be topside.

When night settled in, clouds obscured moonlight and stars, depriving me of a favorite pastime, identifying constellations. At ten o'clock, as Paul and I sat watch in the cockpit while the others slept below, we heard only the drone of our engine in the deep stillness. I'm not sure what drew his attention, but Paul grabbed my arm and, with a gasp, pointed toward the stern, where we saw a hand or a claw grasping the top of the transom and trying to climb into the boat. I should note that Paul is an attorney and fits precisely how most people would picture someone in that profession—intelligent, well-spoken, logical, fact-oriented, prag-matic—not someone prone to "visions" or flights of fancy. I yelled for Bill, but whatever we saw disappeared when he climbed up to the cockpit. He shined a flashlight into the wake and several yards behind us in a wide arc, where we saw—nothing!

"But it was there!" I insisted.

Bill shot back. "It's impossible for a person to latch on to a sailboat going seven knots, let alone scale the transom. And no creature can do that either. It must have been one of your sco-polamine hallucinations."

"I'm not wearing a patch, and neither is Paul," I insisted angrily. Why couldn't he believe us?

With a heavy sigh and a shake of his head, Bill went back below.

An hour later, I noticed the running lights on the sides of the bow had gone out, and a quick check revealed the same was true of the stern and mast lights. Numerous commercial vessels navigated Hawk Channel, and we were in danger if they could not see us. Again, I summoned a sleepy Bill to the cockpit.

"Maybe the gremlin you saw did this," he said sarcastically. "I'll see if I can fix the lights."

No sooner had Bill gone below to investigate than Paul and I heard a new sound, the low hum of another vessel's engine. In the distance behind us to the east, we could make out the shape of a ship, and to our alarm, we saw that it, too, had no running lights, only a faint glow where the bridge would be. This time, my shouts awakened Sandy and Mom, who came to the cockpit.

"Help me raise the mainsail," Bill shouted to me. "Paul, grab all the flashlights from the wet locker behind the ladder. We've got to shine a light on the sail so they can see us!"

While we all aimed at the upper area of the canvas to illuminate our presence, Bill grabbed the air horn and gave it five short blasts several times in a row. None of these measures prevented the small freighter from continuing its path frighteningly near us. It overtook us within 250 feet to port. The rusty, no-name ship looked derelict and rode low in the water. We never saw anyone on the bridge but escaped a catastrophic broadside!

Once we averted the crisis, Bill replaced a fuse that restored our lights, and we furled the mainsail. We could think of only one reason a vessel might want to sail undetected in the middle of the night—a cargo of illegal goods. As to the mysterious intruder, Paul and I never determined where it came from or where it went (but it was there).

Despite such frightening experiences, sailing also provided numerous positive encounters with interesting people and customs. While off Eleuthera in the Bahamas, Bill and I anchored near a thirty-foot sloop where a couple and their three teenage kids from Georgia were vacationing. Bill shouted an invitation. "Come over around six for dinner."

I was unhappy and muttered, "And just what are we going to feed them?"

"The guidebook says there's a grocery store nearby. Hop in the dinghy."

A friendly butcher behind the meat counter filled our order for two cut-up chickens to grill on the hibachi. When we returned to the boat and removed the brown paper, I saw that the chicken pieces still had feathers. Obviously, we weren't at the Publix back home! It took over two hours to pluck and clean them before our dinner guests arrived. That was also the day I stopped eating chicken for several months.

At the Fort Jefferson anchorage in the Dry Tortugas west of Key West, we used the currency of the realm—packs of cigarettes—to trade for shrimp from fishermen on commercial trawlers. We met a couple who had been cruising all over the world on a twenty-five-foot yawl for over twenty years, and they showed us how to make conch ceviche. Boaters were a friendly, helpful bunch.

Unfortunately, this idyllic period didn't last. With increasing frequency, Bill reverted to his verbally abusive ways even when we were sailing. When I returned from a trip and knew Bill was not flying, I faced three possibilities, and my stomach knotted up as I drove home, wondering which it would be. He might greet me warmly and bring my suitcase on board or be on his second or third drink and immediately lash out at me for real or imagined transgressions. The third possibility was the worst. He might remain absent all night, a scenario that came with the possibility he was with another woman. He and I often went to a pub in Pompano Beach where a flirty bartender all but crawled into his lap whenever we came in, or it could be someone else I didn't know about. His behavior angered and frightened me, but mainly, it made me incredibly sad and depressed.

Bill had recently transferred to Detroit to fly the 727, an opportunity made possible when Southern, Hughes Airwest, and North Central Airlines merged to become Republic Airlines. Many former Southern employees commuted to Detroit, and sometimes five or six of them chipped in to rent a "flop pad," an apartment where they could spend the night before an early sign-in or the night after a trip that got in too late to make it home. Bill shared his place with a couple of pilots and three flight attendants, one of whom was named Patty.

Just as he had done years earlier with Karen, he constantly talked about Patty. Bill was at least twenty years older than she, so I doubted Patty felt attracted to him no matter how much he intimated she was. Nevertheless, I was annoyed to have her constantly thrown in my face. Over the years, I had had opportunities to have affairs (which I declined), but I had never bragged to Bill about the propositions I received. His frequent references to his flirtations (or whatever they were) sickened me.

At the same time this was happening, I flew an L-1011 trip with several close friends. A regular part of our layover routine was enjoying margaritas in the penthouse bar atop the Huntley House Hotel in Santa Monica. Layovers were the one opportunity I had to vent my problems to ears willing to listen.

"Things are getting worse again. It's like he has a split personality. Sometimes, he's sweet and loving, but more and more, he hurts my feelings and makes me feel like I don't do anything right. I can't wait to leave on my trips to escape him."

"You've tried so hard," replied one of my friends, sympathetically touching my hand. "Do you think you should leave him?"

I responded with a sardonic chuckle. "Do you know how many times I've threatened to do that? He ignores me because he knows I have nowhere to go."

"What do you mean? You have your own money, right?"

I divulged the truth. "I turn over my paycheck to Bill, and he pays for everything. I've never had financial independence."

I sipped my drink and averted my eyes from their astonished faces.

One of the women, recently separated from her husband, had rented an apartment of her own. "Believe me, you'll know when the last straw comes," she said. "Don't let 'no place to go' be the reason you stay. You can move in with me whenever you want to. All you need to do is call and say, 'Linda, I'm on my way.'"

Bill and Patty were flying together in August, and he invited her (with no advance notice) to spend the three days between their trips on the boat. When I met her, her naiveté convinced me she was an innocent pawn in his game. To test my perception that he was being cruel for cruelty's sake, I invited my close friends Carole and Dick to go on an afternoon sail with us, so I could get their impression of Bill's behavior. At one point, Bill turned the helm over to me while he took Patty's hand and led her to the bow. Heads close together, they talked and laughed for a long time as Bill occasionally brushed the hair away from her face. Carole and Dick's conclusion: "This was an Oscar-worthy performance strictly for your benefit."

The seesaw of emotions during nine years of marriage had left me sitting on the low side of the board far more often than the high. I no longer had the stamina nor frankly, the willingness to force myself upward again. Appeasement didn't work. Bill used it like a mountain climber uses an ice axe to further his ascent, never asking if I might like to climb a different slope. If he no longer wanted to be with me, why didn't he say so instead of acting out this juvenile and pathetic charade? I couldn't ignore this latest of countless "last straws." As he and Patty prepared to leave the next day, I waited until she was out of earshot to give Bill my news.

"I'm moving off the boat before I fly my next trip. When you come back, I'll be gone."

He flashed a contemptuous smile. "Right."

As she left, Patty hugged me and thanked me for a lovely stay, after which I watched them get into Bill's car and drive away. Then, I picked up the phone and dialed.

"Linda, I'm on my way."

Chapter Twenty-two

The flood of relief I felt driving away from the marina was like an encouraging pat on the back from my guardian angel; at last, I had made the right decision. A month-long stay with Linda gave me the time and space to adjust to a life filled with the kind of freedom I barely remembered ever having. Living in a space where the floor didn't sway was a joy, and I had room to swing my arms around without bumping a wall. Linda and I went out to eat when we felt like it, danced at a popular hotel bar (where neither of us sat down all night), went to movies on a whim, or just sat in the living room watching TV or reading. Sometimes, I imagined I smelled teak oil or stainless-steel cleaner and felt exhilarated upon realizing I no longer had to spend all my "off" time laboring on the boat. But as much as I enjoyed staying with Linda, I knew I needed to find an apartment of my own. I had opened a new checking account in which I deposited my two recent paychecks. However, I still needed money from Bill's and my joint account to pay the deposit and first month's rent for a new place.

Bill had called me only twice since I left, once to tell me I had left a pair of shoes on the boat and the second time to say several pieces of my mail were delivered to the post office box. In neither of these conversations did he say, "Can we talk?" or "I miss you." Instead, I noted a familiar undertone of anger that conveyed he was the aggrieved party and would not take any responsibility for the breakup. He met me at the bank to remove me from the joint account and, after disputing the amount he owed, wrote me a check.

Even though, in retrospect, our turbulent relationship had been doomed from the start, after nine years of marriage, it came as a fresh shock when I realized we were no longer a couple. While we weren't yet divorced, there would be no reconciliation. Bill was already dating someone, and I presumed this had started before we split. Instead of the bartender I had suspected, it was the hostess at the Sands Marina restaurant, right under my nose.

As I began my search for a new place, I was lucky to fly with a coworker who had recently married and moved into her husband's condo. She had been looking for a new tenant and was excited to learn I wanted to check out her place. Her unit's décor was lovely, and her asking rent was reasonable. She left her living room furniture, so I only needed to buy a bed and a small dinette set. With my housing needs taken care of, I began exploring previously unavailable interests. One of these was, of all things, country-western dancing.

Several years earlier, Bill and I had seen *Urban Cowboy*, a movie that introduced audiences to Bud and Sissy. To determine if Bud is a "real" cowboy, Sissy asks him if he knows how to two-step, and when Bud nods his head, she says, "Wanna prove it?" And off they go, gliding around the dance floor at the famous Gilly's nightclub in Pasadena, Texas. The movie started a craze around the country as cities, large and small, opened nightclubs that mimicked the ambiance of Gilly's and Fort Worth's Billy Bob's. Some clubs upped the ante, if they could afford the insurance premium, and installed mechanical bulls that were a magnet for customers—many drunk—to demonstrate their nerve and coordination (or lack thereof). While riding bulls wasn't something that interested me, the dancing looked like such fun that I tried to persuade Bill to take lessons, but since this was entirely out of his bailiwick, he refused.

Now able to make my own choices about friends and recreation, I hung out with a flight attendant, Kathie, who had interests like mine. She lived nearby in Davie, a unique Western-themed town, home to the largest rodeo east of the Mississippi. We invited our mutual friend Lynn to the Orange Blossom Festival at the Davie Rodeo Arena, where we attended afternoon and evening rodeos, browsed craft booths, and enjoyed various types of entertainment. We watched a group of about a dozen people called the Country Kickers perform choreographed two-step, Cotton-Eyed Joe, and line dances for the crowd. Their enthusiasm was contagious, and the audience clapped along as the dancers strutted and twirled in their cute matching outfits. The three of us looked at each other and said, "We should do that!" At the end of the performance, we spoke to the leader, who said she would be happy to take us on as dance students.

What started as a lark became an obsession. We spent every night we weren't flying at a country nightclub called Cowboys. Kathie and Lynn, who were flying together at the time, kept their skirts and boots in their cars to drive directly to the club, change clothes in the restroom, and get on the dance floor as quickly as possible. At first, we learned all the latest line dances because they didn't require partners, a commodity that seemed to be in short supply. Although Kathie and Lynn soon met men who became their steady dance partners, it wasn't until Kathie persuaded her next-door neighbor, Jack, to take lessons that I had one. All four of us caught on quickly. After two months of instruction, we joined the Country Kickers and performed at fairs and other events.

Still, despite my new friends and activities, I found being single uncomfortable. I felt like an oddball eating alone in a restaurant or being in a group of couples. I'd had a man (or men) in my life since college, and relationship failures didn't change my desire for male companionship. Yet the idea of starting from scratch was unsettling. To protect my bruised ego, I maintained casual relationships even though I knew this route would not likely lead me to the loving partner I still dreamed about. I began a juggling act that rivaled the star attraction at a circus. When the captain of a large motor yacht at the Sands Marina, someone I often chatted with when I lived on the boat, asked me out for dinner, I went and continued to see him. While on a layover in Atlanta, I met a man at a nightclub whose work sent him around the country, and we got together once or twice a month in various cities. After I flirted with a passenger from Dallas whose sales area included South Florida, I dated him whenever he came to town. And an introduction to a fellow guest at a friend's wedding reception led to another liaison. But after a few months, I realized that this pattern was unhealthy both physically and emotionally, and I needed to stop. Fortunately, I found the motivation to do so, and it came from the most unexpected place imaginable—my need for a new car.

When I moved off the boat, all my possessions (except a few in a storage locker) fit into my 1976 Cadillac Seville. Years spent in two inhospitable environments, the airport employee parking lot where jet fuel drifted down on the cars and next to the marina with its salt-laden breezes, had robbed the car of its former beauty. Tiny rust spots sprouted beneath the door frames, and its once silver metallic luster had turned a dingy gray. Mechanical problems began to pop up one after the other.

By the spring of 1984, I had to decide whether to purchase tires for an automobile that was picking my pocket like a subway thief or buy a new vehicle. The second option filled me with angst. I had never shopped for a car by myself. Despite my efforts to appear experienced and worldly, I knew I might as well stamp "Sucker" on my forehead in big red letters when I walked into the showroom.

Kathie came to the rescue when she mentioned that her father, Phil, was friends with the owner of an Oldsmobile dealership and had secured a sweet deal for her on a new Cutlass. She was sure he'd do the same for me and arranged for him to accompany me on my search. I picked up Phil on the appointed day and drove to the dealership.

"Do you know what model you want?" asked Roger, the owner. "Not really. I want something reliable and not too expensive," then jokingly, "and it's OK if it's sporty and cool-looking too."

"I think I have just what you're looking for. It's a brand-new model called the Calais. I have one on the lot right now that doesn't have a lot of extra bells and whistles, so I can give you a good price on it. It's light metallic blue."

Light metallic blue? Beautiful!

My excitement grew, but I maintained a disinterested expression. I had learned that much about negotiations from watching TV and movies. We climbed into the car and spun around the streets behind the dealership. I loved how the vehicle handled; it seemed just the right size. I knew I wanted it, but I braced myself for the sticker shock that was to come. Phil persuaded Roger to offer a generous trade-in allowance on the Seville, much higher than I expected. And since Roger was the man in charge, he didn't have to "check with my manager" and return with a jacked-up figure for the bottom line.

I sounded more excited than I wanted to. "I'll take it!"

"Do you need to arrange financing?" Roger asked.

"Yes, I do."

"Then I'll turn you over to our finance and insurance manager, who will take good care of you."

The manager was at lunch, so I drove Phil back to his condo and thanked him for securing such a great deal for me. I felt proud I had made my first major independent purchase, even though I had relied on some masculine help. All that remained was to work out the details of the loan. When I returned to the showroom, I asked to see the finance manager, confident we would complete this final step quickly. A nice-looking man emerged from his office, extended his hand, and said, "Hello. I'm George Davis. Come right in. I'll have you ready to go in no time."

As we walked into his office, my newfound self-assurance faded, and a wave of nervousness overcame me. It was good I had chosen the perfect car, but I needed to work payments into my budget (ugh—a word I wasn't used to thinking about!). Mr. Davis sensed my apprehension and interjected casual conversation as he asked the personal questions required for the paperwork.

"Will your husband be on the loan, too?" he inquired.

"No, we're getting a divorce," I replied. I still smarted when I had to say this.

At one point, I noticed him taking furtive glances at the necklace I wore which had a small gold charm, a pair of cowboy boots. "What's the significance of the boots?" he asked. "Do you ride horses?"

"No," I said, amused at the mental picture of me, literally shaking in my boots, as I sat in a saddle high off the ground. "I do country-western dancing."

When I said this to people, most responded, "Oh, so you square dance?" Mr. Davis surprised me when he said, "Like two-step and line dance?"

"Yes! Do you dance too?"

"I like to dance and enjoy country music, but I don't how to do country-western dancing. It looks like a lot of fun. Do you ever go to Cowboys?"

Again, I was surprised. "Yes, I do, very often. Do you?"

"Oh, occasionally—I can't believe I've never seen you there." He paused. "I would remember if I had."

Is he trying to come on to me? Sounds like he hasn't pulled out the old pick-up line manual recently!

I looked at him more closely as he swiveled his chair to return to his computer. I had already noticed gorgeous light blue eyes that twinkled when he smiled, a sandy, well-trimmed mustache, and now, as I looked at the back of his head, I saw he had really nice hair.

"Well," he said, all business again, "I just need your signature on these papers, and you can drive your new car home."

Once I signed the last form, he handed me the keys, we shook hands, and I thanked him for making this part of the process comfortable for a novice like me. I hopped into the car in front of the dealership and pulled onto Federal Highway to head north. The car purred, and I couldn't help smiling with satisfaction about my new purchase. That is until I looked at the dashboard and saw the speedometer needle flopping back and forth between zero and five miles per hour, even though I was going about thirty. *What the hell?*

I took a right off Federal onto the next side street, turned around in the driveway of a convenience store, and headed back to the dealership to confront the last person I had encountered. I marched into Mr. Davis's office, seething with frustration and outrage. "Nice car you just sold me. I hadn't gone two miles when the speedometer stopped working," I exclaimed.

"What?" he replied, his eyes wide in disbelief.

My voice escalated in pitch and volume, "So, you can either tear up those papers I just signed or get me a car that works!" Even though I realized this wasn't his fault, I couldn't help myself—the more I talked, the more I fumed.

Quietly, without defensiveness, Mr. Davis rose from his chair and said with genuine concern. "I promise I'll take care of this. Let's drive the car over to service."

The technician delivered the bad news, "It's a faulty computer module, and we don't have a replacement. We'll have to order one this afternoon, and since it's Friday, we won't be able to install it until next week."

Mr. Davis, who, by this time, insisted I call him George, said, "I'm so sorry this happened. I'll set you up with a loaner until we fix your car."

But I wanted *my* car, not a loaner, and pouted like a petulant child. I explained how inconvenient this was because starting Monday, I had two two-day trips back to back that would only allow me to return to the dealership the following Friday. Had I been thinking logically, I might have realized I would have little time to drive the car because of my work schedule.

"You won't have to come back here," he assured me. "I'll arrange for someone to deliver your car when it's fixed and swap it for the loaner. It will probably be ready on Tuesday. What time do you get back from your trip?"

"I'll be home about seven o'clock," I said, "but I have to get up early Wednesday morning to fly my second trip. It's probably better if I wait until Friday to get it," I admitted reluctantly.

George looked thoughtful. "You're in Plantation, right? I live next door in Davie, so I could bring it to your place Thursday night. That way, I can be sure the hand-off goes smoothly."

There was that twinkle in his eyes again. "I'll call before I head over to be sure you're home."

"OK," I sighed, resigned that I wouldn't have my sweet little Calais for another week.

"I have your number," he laughed.

You also have my social security number, driver's license info, and annual salary. At least I knew if he was interested in me, it wasn't for my money.

As I drove the loaner home, I considered my encounter with George. Something drew me in. He was easygoing even when under fire from me, and we shared at least one common interest. Plus, I decided he should win "Employee of the Month" for his extra steps to ensure I had a good experience with his dealership after a rocky start.

Considering his kindness, it would be rude to simply exchange keys with him on Thursday and usher him out the door; maybe I should invite him to stay for a drink. However, I realized my stash of spirits consisted of a lone bottle of Absolut vodka (my drink of choice) in the freezer. If I stocked up, I could confidently offer him anything he might want. After a run to Albertson's, I returned home with a liquor bonanza—bottles of chardonnay and merlot, scotch, bourbon, Canadian whiskey, rum, tequila, gin, and various mixers—enough to stock a small cantina. I was ready.

As promised, George phoned at seven thirty Thursday night and said he would be at my place in a half hour. When he arrived, he had another document for me to sign, and we traded sets of keys.

"I appreciate your personal delivery service," I said, "Do you have time for a drink?"

"Sure, that would be great. What do you have?"

"Oh, just about anything," I responded casually,

"Vodka on the rocks would be perfect."

I smiled as I thought about my recent desperate run to the liquor department. *Of course, he's a vodka drinker!*

We sat in my living room, sipped our drinks, and made small talk. George wanted to know if it was tiring to fly all the time and which were my favorite cities; I asked him where he was from (few people were native Floridians) and if he liked working at the dealership. About thirty minutes later, he said he needed to be on his way, so I thanked him again and walked him to the door.

I liked George and sensed he might like me too, so I wondered if he would call, but days passed without a word. *Maybe there's a rule at the dealership against dating customers.* Kathie, Lynn, and I (along with Jack) went to Cowboys with our usual regularity. Each time, I scanned the crowd to see if I spotted George and felt mildly disappointed when I didn't.

My attempt to maintain multiple relationships had become more a chore than a pleasure. I doubted I could sustain this pattern over the long term. Even though I barely knew George, my gut (which I had ignored in the past to my peril) told me he was different from the other men I went out with, more aligned with my personality and tastes. I decided that if he ever did call, and if we were as compatible as it seemed we might be, I would let the relationship evolve slowly. *What if he has some secret passion like skydiving that I don't know about yet?*

Two weeks after he delivered my car, he phoned. "Hi, this is George Davis—from the Olds dealership. (*Oh*, that *George Davis*.) I wanted to check that everything is good with the Calais." When I told him how much I loved the car, he said, "Well, that's good. I'm glad." There was a pause. "Listen, I'd like to see you again. Would that be possible?"

"I have a question to ask you before I answer yours."

"Sure, what is it?"

"Do you now, or have you ever, wanted to sail around the world? Or, for that matter, do you own or want to own a boat?" I could picture his bewildered expression.

After a moment, he responded, "No, and no. I have a friend who has a boat, and I enjoy going out on the Intercoastal with him occasionally, but do I want to own a boat? Never. Why, are you a sailor?"

"Just a recovering one," I laughed. "And yes, I'll go out with you."

"Great! What's your favorite restaurant?"

I thought for a moment. My immersion in the country music scene had centered on clubs catering to a pseudo-sophisticated crowd. I'd never seen the gritty side depicted in the lyrics of classic country songs like the ones I'd listened to in Alabama, and I was curious. "Can you take me to a genuine honky-tonk?"

"Really? OK, if that's what you want, I know just the place."

Rose Al's, in Davie, was an establishment with all the expected characteristics of a dive bar—Formica tabletops, missing linoleum tiles, mismatched barstools, and a jukebox that played Willie Nelson and Merle Haggard in heavy rotation. It wasn't hard to imagine a motorcycle gang storming through the door at any moment and breaking up the place. When we entered the dimly lit room, a couple on the tiny dance floor were drunkenly belly-rubbing to T.G. Sheppard's *Slow Burn*. No fancy two-stepping here.

Almost everyone was smoking, and as we sat at the bar, I was horrified to see George pull out a pack of Benson and Hedges from his jacket pocket and light up. I tried not to sound judgmental as I commented, "I didn't know you smoked."

"I'll put it out if it bothers you," he said, quickly stubbing his cigarette into a boot-shaped ashtray.

I can't have a relationship with a smoker! I detested cigarette smoke and could barely put up with it on the airplane and in public places like this bar. My nose had built-in tobacco radar, able to detect a burning cigarette from incredible distances. Once, as I stood at the front door of a Stretch DC-8 while passengers boarded, I smelled cigarette smoke. Smoking wasn't allowed on the ground, so I rang the back cabin and asked the other flight attendants to track it down. The culprit was in the plane's last row, one hundred and eighty feet away from me!

Because my sense of smell was so acute, I was surprised I hadn't noticed the odor of smoke during my previous interactions with George; he must have used industrial-strength breath freshener and daily laundry and dry cleaning for me not to have picked up on it. We'd have to talk but now wasn't the time.

As more people came in, only a few seats remained vacant, and several customers hovered around us, trying to get the bartender's attention. George stood and offered his stool to a young woman in a ruffled miniskirt and ankle-high cowboy boots. "Thanks," she said. "You're a real gentleman."

The crush of more customers around the bar caused me to feel a little dizzy, and I put my arm across George's shoulders for balance. Inadvertently, I grazed the back of his head, where I felt something hard and metallic.

As casually as possible, I moved my hand away and asked, "What do you have on your head?"

Sheepishly, he replied, "Those are the clips of my toupee."

Oh, my! I remembered my first impression of him and his "really nice" hair. *What other secrets does this man have?*

Chapter Twenty-three

I had never dated a smoker, let alone one who could remove his hair at will, but I still wanted to get to know George better. We sized each other up over the following weeks, sharing the details of our lives, from minutiae to milestones. He had been married twice before, which caused some concern. But as he revealed details, his objectivity in admitting his share of the blame in the breakups and the lessons he had learned made me feel less uneasy.

A happy result of his first marriage was the birth of his two children, Chris and Michelle. The kids, now seventeen and twelve, spent six weeks of the summer with him, and he flew to their home in Texas to spend Christmas with them.

He referred to his second marriage as "the lost eighteen months" to a woman who distrusted him so much that she constantly spied on him to confirm his whereabouts. She had children from a previous marriage who could do no wrong, but she resented his kids and took every opportunity to criticize and mistreat them, especially Chris. That marriage had ended two years before, after which he moved from Ohio to Florida for a fresh start. George lived in an equestrian townhouse community in Davie and owned an Appaloosa mare named Dakota. Because his long hours at the car dealership afforded him little time to ride, he thought from time to time of selling her, but Michelle loved riding her on her summer visits. George worked out a deal that allowed the stable owners to use Dakota for riding lessons in exchange for a break on her boarding costs. As he explained this, an idea popped into his head. "Maybe you'd enjoy learning to ride."

"I'll stay on the ground, thank you very much," I laughed, "unless Dakota's saddle has a seatbelt."

Because of Chris's miserable experience during his dad's toxic second marriage, he extracted a promise: George would not remarry until Chris was on his own and free of the specter of another wicked stepmother. George admitted he didn't seem suited for marriage based on his track record. I was surprised when I heard myself say, "I want to get married again if I find the right person." Until then, I hadn't been sure this was how I felt. When I saw George's alarmed expression, I quickly added, "If you think we should stop this before it goes further, I understand." The cards were on the table, but neither of us walked away, and one by one, I broke off my relationships with the other men in my life.

A pivotal moment came when he said, "I think it might be time for you to see me without my toupee, but I'm afraid of what you'll think."

"Oh, I bet it's not that bad," I responded, fervently hoping I was right.

When I stopped by to see him the following day, I walked into his living room to find a balding man standing in the spot usually occupied by George. He looked different, a bit older and a tad heavier, but by no means like the frog prince I had feared. I told a little white lie. "You're just as handsome without it."

A few days before George left to spend Christmas with his kids, Mom, Sandy, and Paul arrived from Illinois to be with me. I was pleased that George's friendliness immediately won Mom over. As much as she had attempted to establish a rapport with Bill, he had never been warm toward her, so this was a welcome change that further solidified my good feelings about George.

In pursuit of our common interest, George and I began going to Cowboys together regularly, and he proved to be a quick study when it came to learning the two-step. My dance instructor also worked with us on waltz, polka, and ten-step. Even though Jack and I continued as partners during Country Kickers exhibitions, I was happy Jack had convinced his new girlfriend to take dance lessons. He and I hoped our respective love interests would gain enough proficiency to join the team soon.

George and I discovered our common interests went well beyond dancing, from nearly every genre of music to theater, movies, books, and art. I used to love to go to Waterloo Hawks baseball games with Dad to see our Chicago White Sox farm team in action. Growing up, George was a fan of the Toledo Mud Hens. Together, we found a new team to support—the Atlanta Braves when they were in spring training in West Palm Beach. It felt liberating to expand beyond my two-note existence with Bill—flying and sailing.

But a question always simmered on the back burner—where is this going? I avoided the subject because we enjoyed our time together, and he seemed to take my silence as permission to maintain the status quo. But at the same time, I felt I needed to move on if he didn't want to be married. One night in early May, he took me to a highly rated French restaurant in Boca Raton. When I asked what prompted him to choose this particular restaurant, he said several coworkers had recommended it. He ordered champagne, and after the waiter filled our glasses, George took my hand and confessed he had changed his mind about marriage. "It was the luckiest day of my life when you walked into my office, and I don't ever want to be without you. Will you marry me?"

I'd thought about it so much that my hesitation surprised me as I realized the immensity of a commitment like this. But my gut screamed, "Are you out of your mind? Say yes!" So, I did.

The lease on my apartment was due for renewal, but George said, "Aren't you tired of lugging your clothes and toiletries to my place when you stay over? I'd love to see your uniforms hanging beside my suits and sports coats." Unlike my apprehension when I moved in with Bill, I felt secure about these living arrangements.

I felt determined to have my wish this time since I hadn't had a "real" wedding with Bill. George enthusiastically agreed, and we worked on details for a country-themed ceremony on August 10, 1985. We reserved a church, created a guest list of about seventy-five people, paid a deposit to rent the clubhouse at his townhouse community for the reception, and hired the house band from Cowboys to provide dance music.

But we soon realized we might have gotten ahead of ourselves, as one detail still terrified George—telling his children he was getting married. When he visited them at Christmas, he mentioned me, but the kids knew he had dated several other women and were not alarmed because they had "the promise." He proposed the perfect solution—he wouldn't tell them. "Once they get to Florida and see how terrific you are, they won't be the least bit upset we're getting married."

"Are you nuts? I don't want to start my relationship with your kids by tricking them into a scenario they're unprepared for." I felt the familiar prickles that popped up when I was at a crossroads and in danger of making a bad decision. "I won't proceed with the wedding unless you talk to them first." His sheepish expression told me I was right. But, he obviously didn't know how to move forward, because he continued to put off the inevitable.

While I didn't badger him, I asked from time to time when he planned to call them. By early June, only a few weeks before their arrival, I convinced him he would feel better if he ripped off the Band-Aid and put the matter behind him for better or worse. He sat beside the phone, eyed it like a coiled rattlesnake, and finally picked up the receiver. I didn't listen to the conversation, but predictably, his son was angry at the broken agreement and threatened to stay home. Michelle's reaction was more forgiving. "It's OK, Dad. Chris and I have Mom and each other, but I know you must get lonely." By the end of the phone call, Chris grudgingly agreed to fly to Florida with Michelle. While George was relieved, I pictured a sullen teenager sulking in his room for the entire stay.

George had another unsatisfactory plan for the kids' arrival at the Miami airport. He suggested that I pick him up at the dealership, we'd meet their flight together, drop him off at work, and then I'd head home with them—alone. I vetoed that, too. I insisted that, at the very least, we have lunch together before he left me on my own with them. On the day they arrived, I dropped him off at the Continental concourse so he would have a little time alone with them while I parked the car.

It took a while to find a spot some distance away. When I finally got inside the terminal, I found them in a little cluster, each with a different expression: apprehension on George, resentment on Chris, and anticipation on Michelle. I put on my old, reliable Flight Attendant Face, but instead of calming down, I began to babble. "Your flight must have gotten in early. Sorry, it took so long for me to park the car; it's a mile away, I'm afraid. Did you have a good flight? I hope you're hungry." Yada, yada, yada. I couldn't stop myself even though I sounded like a manic wind-up doll. When I came up for air, George revealed his own nervousness with what was, by this time, a needless introduction. "Kids, this is Kathi."

We stopped for lunch at a nice restaurant near the dealership. Between bites of my salad, I tried opening gambits that I hoped would start a conversation but which elicited only head nods and terse replies. *Six weeks of this?* George had to go back to work, and instead of the thaw I had hoped for, a sea of icebergs lay ahead with no clear navigational path.

After we dropped George off, Chris moved to the front seat and peppered me with questions about my personal history, which I answered honestly (dodging only a few), as well as my likes and dislikes. Eventually, the topic turned to music. "Do you only like the country bullshit Dad listens to?" I'm sure he hoped for a reaction to his crude word choice. Instead, at that moment, I was thankful that my eclectic musical tastes had drawn me to MTV for the past two years. "Sure, I like country, but I also like Cyndi Lauper, David Bowie, and Duran Duran, among others. Who do you like?" Chris looked surprised.

From the back seat, Michelle piped up. "My favorite singer is Madonna."

"I like her too!" I responded, surprised that a provocative, scantily clad fashion icon managed to do what had seemed impossible at lunch. *Maybe the ice is broken.* When the kids enthusiastically hauled their luggage upstairs to their rooms, perhaps open to enjoying the summer, I blessed the gods of rock and roll for once again creating connections in my life.

Over the next week, the kids and I fell into a comfortable groove that included playfully ganging up on George occasionally. Not only did they endorse our wedding plans, but Chris decided he wanted to be his dad's best man, and Michelle agreed to be one of my bridesmaids.

As the date for the wedding drew near and we attended to hectic last-minute details, a tragic event suddenly took center stage. Throughout July, I worked Rotation 191, a two-day trip on an L-1011 that left around four p.m. from Ft. Lauderdale to Dallas/ Ft. Worth and then continued to Los Angeles, where we had a layover. On the second day, the itinerary reversed, and we arrived back in Ft. Lauderdale at eight thirty p.m. It was, by far, the best trip in the base, and I looked forward to flying it again in August.

The Flight Attendant in Charge was a woman named Franny, whom I didn't know well but whom others spoke highly of. She and her best friend Frieda often flew together, but Frieda had opted for a different rotation in July. Fun-loving and easygoing but an efficient leader, Franny inspired us to make extra efforts to ensure our passengers received outstanding service. By the month's end, I felt as though I had known her for a long time and wished I had invited her to the wedding. But since this friendship hadn't developed until after I sent invitations, I felt awkward about extending a late one, even though the wedding had been a frequent topic of conversation.

Our last trip in July carried over to August 1. As we rode together on the bus to the Ft. Lauderdale employee parking lot, I said, "I've enjoyed the month so much. I apologize for the short notice, but I'd love for you to come to my wedding on the tenth. Bring Frieda, too."

With genuine regret, she replied, "Oh, I wish we could. Frieda and I are going on vacation and will be gone then. We picked up 191 tomorrow so we could drop a later trip and have more time off." Exiting at the first bus stop, she turned and said with a bright smile, "I'll be thinking of you on your wedding day."

The following evening, George, the kids, and I saw the hottest movie in theaters, *Back to the Future*. We all enjoyed it and were still laughing and talking about the crazy plot when we stopped at Albertson's for groceries. Michelle and Chris helped me put things away in the cupboards while George went upstairs to check our answering machine. A few minutes later, when he entered the kitchen, his stricken face sucked the air out of my lungs.

"A Delta plane crashed in Dallas, and the machine is full of messages from people who want to make sure you're all right," he said and hugged my suddenly rigid body. I walked like a zombie to the TV and flipped channels until I came upon an unbelievable sight—the smoldering tail section of a Delta airplane lay tilted on its left side amid a field of debris. A crowd of people, many in firefighter gear, stood near it. The massive size of the tail-mounted engine left no doubt it was an L-1011; the crawl at the bottom of the TV screen confirmed the worst—Flight 191 had crashed short of the runway in Dallas.

So many of my friends flew this rotation on various days, and I struggled to remember who worked it on Fridays. Then I had a flashback of Franny as she headed to her car the previous evening. Franny and Frieda were on that plane. I sent a silent prayer to the universe that there were survivors, but the images on TV seemed to make that unlikely.

If Delta was a family, the Miami/Ft. Lauderdale base was a clan, and I quickly realized I would likely know everyone on the crew. The next day, we learned grim details. Among the dead were the three pilots and five of the eight flight attendants, including Franny and Frieda. Another Miami/Ft. Lauderdale flight attendant and her husband were non-revs and had also perished.

The plane was on its final approach when a sudden storm produced violent turbulence in the landing path of Flight 191 immediately after a Learjet in front of it had landed safely. Later investigation revealed that the Delta plane encountered wind shear, an atmospheric phenomenon associated with thunderstorm microbursts. The overwhelming force of the wind shear made it impossible for the pilots to maintain control of the aircraft. The airplane struck a car on an arterial highway and a water storage tank about a mile from the runway. The rear one-quarter of the plane broke off and skidded some distance from the rest of the aircraft. As more information became available, we learned that only twenty-four people had survived out of one hundred fifty-two on board.

Three days later, on August 5, I reported to the airport to work on Flight 191 and found the somber atmosphere in the crew lounge was like a thick, impervious cloud. When our two dozen or so passengers boarded, a number markedly lower than our usual load of around one hundred fifty, we knew they were nervous about being on the same flight that had crashed. We walked on eggshells to dispel any apprehension on our part and did our best to put the passengers at ease, even as our hearts were breaking. I had no other trips on my schedule until late August because I had cleared time before and after the wedding. Still, when I returned home Tuesday evening, I had no desire to attend to some last-minute details. What should have been happy anticipation had vanished, replaced by a sad and hopeless uncertainty about what to do. All the arrangements were in place, but it seemed grossly insensitive to celebrate in the immediate aftermath of such a catastrophe. However, my friends encouraged me to go ahead as planned. "We need something happy," they said. George told me he would support whatever I wanted to do, but I felt incapable of deciding.

In bed that night, I tossed and turned until I finally fell asleep, only to have one of the most unusual experiences of my life. I awakened in the dark and saw Franny sitting at the foot of my bed. She looked radiant, her red hair accented by a peach-colored dress.

"Franny," I said, "I'm so happy to see you, but I thought you died in the crash."

"I did, but I'm OK."

I asked her a question that had tortured me since the day of the accident. "Did you suffer?"

"I was scared, but I didn't feel any pain."

Tears ran down my face. "I'm so relieved to hear that. You know I'm supposed to get married in four days, but I don't think it's right to celebrate when you and so many others lost your lives. I don't know what to do."

"I do. Enjoy your special day, and have a happy marriage."

Then she was gone. George remained sound asleep by my side.

When I saw Franny, I knew I was dreaming, yet she seemed so real that I could have touched her. My tears were no illusion;

they were still fresh on my cheeks. I later learned I had probably experienced a lucid dream, no doubt caused by stress and emotional trauma. In this state, the dreamer has some degree of control over what the subject says and does. I felt that if Franny had *really* been there, she would have said those exact words. But since she wasn't, my subconscious stepped in to relieve my misgivings and permitted me to get married with less guilt.

Chapter Twenty-four

Our wedding day was one of the hottest of the year—ninety-three degrees—sweltering even by South Florida standards. The post-wedding photographs took longer than we expected, so many of the guests had already arrived at the reception by the time we got there. The first things I noticed when I walked in the door were the anxious looks on the caterers' faces and icing oozing down the sides of the cake. The band members wiped sweat from their faces as they hooked up their amps and mics. Men's sports coats hung limply on a coat rack at the back of the room next to similarly droopy women's jackets. I quickly understood why. There was no air conditioning! Someone told us the manager was trying to find a repairman on a busy Saturday when many customers needed service. Ceiling and rotating floor fans were having little success in combatting the stifling air, and some guests had escaped to the patio where it was slightly less oppressive.

About a half hour later, a harried repairman located the problem, which took another half hour to resolve, but gradually, cool air began to blow from the AC vents. By this time, some guests had departed with apologies that they had "prior commitments." Still, many stalwarts enjoyed champagne, hors d'oeuvres, and half-melted wedding cake until early evening.

Because we had invited several out-of-town relatives to stay overnight at the townhouse, we opted to spend our wedding night at the Marriott Hotel. When we settled into our beautiful room, I couldn't wait to change into more comfortable (and drier) clothes, but I had difficulty pulling off my right boot. George tugged on it, and when it finally came off, we gasped at my grotesquely swollen shin. An angry-looking welt told me this was likely the work of a spider. The culprit had probably crawled into my boot, and with the excitement of the occasion, I hadn't felt the bite.

"Come on. I'm taking you to the emergency room."

"No way! I've had these bites before. They look awful, but I've never needed medical attention." Instead, I kept my leg iced and elevated, resulting in a most unromantic wedding night.

Despite this inauspicious start, George and I settled into marriage, which included a perk unavailable when we cohabitated. As my spouse, he was now entitled to pass privileges, and he embraced the slogan, "Marry me, fly free," with gusto. I trained him on the ins and outs of non-rev travel. Adhere to the dress code—suit and tie or sport coat and dress slacks; never ask for something the crew doesn't automatically offer you; don't request to change seats with a full-fare passenger; and don't fuss if there is a meal shortage and you don't get to eat. Flight attendants could (and sometimes did) report inappropriate non-rev behavior, and I wanted to ensure our privileges remained intact.

If I had a long layover in a city he wanted to visit, George came with me, and this required me to drill additional non-rev etiquette into his head since I could not sit with him. He must not divulge to other passengers that he was flying for free, should limit his alcohol consumption, and never, ever ring his call button unless he was dying. When he was on one of my flights, I seldom acknowledged I knew him and treated him like any other passenger. He complied with all the instructions—except once.

On a trip that included a twenty-two-hour layover in Los Angeles, George came along, planning to go to a California

Angels baseball game with his brother, who lived in Fullerton. On the flight from Atlanta, his seatmate in first class was very talkative, and there was nothing George enjoyed more than good conversation. They talked and drank, drank and talked, even though I gave George "the eye" a few times as a signal to behave himself. His seatmate noticed this extra attention and told George that one of the flight attendants seemed interested in him. He couldn't help himself, "The cute one with the curly hair? I'll bet I can get her to spend the night with me."

The man's jaw dropped. "How do you plan to do that?"

"The direct approach."

George rang his call button, and I responded, highly annoyed.

"I just told Bob I thought you and I should sleep together tonight. What do you say?"

I was angry and mortified, mainly because his remark carried to passengers seated near him who turned to look at us. "Well, that might have been possible given that we're married, but there's no way it will happen now."

About six weeks after our wedding, a devastating accident near our townhouse led to an unexpected change in George's work situation. At about seven thirty a.m., we awoke to a thunderous explosion that sounded like it was in our front yard. Our bedroom windows were open, and we could see that the screens had popped out, so we jumped out of bed, ran to the now-uncovered openings, and saw a strange sight. Snow, or something that looked like it, floated down, quickly covering cars, grass, and blacktop parking areas. We threw on clothes and hurried downstairs to find our two front windows shattered and the sliding glass door to the back patio sideways on its track. Neighbors who looked as shell-shocked as we felt stood in clusters on the sidewalk and chattered excitedly.

Soon, information filtered through the crowd that a muffler shop on our street about a quarter of a mile away had blown up.

Traffic was at a standstill, and the driveway into our community was blocked. Although I didn't have to work that day, George was supposed to be at the dealership by nine a.m. Still stunned, he called Roger, the owner/manager, and described what had happened. "I can't make it in this morning. Even if traffic clears out, I need to get an insurance adjuster here to look at the damage and have the windows replaced," he explained.

Roger was not happy. "Can't Kathi take care of it?"

"It's not that she can't handle it, but we're both rattled. I want to stay here until we can recover a little bit."

In his defense, Roger had no idea how frightening the experience had been, how dizzy we felt, and how our ears still rang a half hour later. We were at the epicenter of an explosion that people within a ten-mile radius felt. On the other hand, we found Roger's indifference to our trauma unforgivable. It came in the wake of George's increasing dissatisfaction with the twelve-hour days required of him (often six in a row) and Roger's constant pressure on him to exceed his already impressive extended warranty sales. Once the initial shock of the blast wore off, we mutually agreed that because of Roger's insensitivity, George would give two weeks' notice that very day. With his extensive connections in the car business, he would have no trouble finding a job with greater flexibility.

George went to the dealership after a quicker-than-expected visit from our insurance agent and a promise that we'd have new windows by late afternoon. He returned home that night, having made his second major decision of the day—to quit smoking. No tapering off, no "just one more." His last cigarette turned to ash, and he threw the crumpled package in the trash.

Ever since I had moved in with George, I had wrinkled my nose when I stepped through the door and caught a whiff of cigarette smoke. He confined his habit to the patio, but the smoke hitchhiked on his clothing and took up residence in the carpet and upholstery. Why didn't I insist he stop as a condition of getting married? Because I didn't want to be *that* person—the one who said, "I love you; you're perfect, now change." *He'll quit when he's ready. He just needs the right motivation.* And today was the day.

His morning routine had been to stop on his way to work to pick up two packs of cigarettes at a 7-Eleven store across the street from the muffler shop. Although miraculously, no one in the convenience store was seriously injured, the explosion caused extensive damage. Eyewitnesses described shattered windows and coffee machines that flew around like missiles. Toppled shelves coated the floor with bags of Fritos and Twizzlers, lotto tickets, cans of cat food, and other strewn merchandise that sloshed around in a sea of orange juice, chocolate milk, and Thunderbird wine. George knew he had dodged a bullet. He might have left the store in an ambulance if he had dropped by a bit earlier than usual. Not ordinarily superstitious, he saw this as a sign not to tempt fate.

The prospect of a smoke-free home thrilled me because I had hated cigarettes since childhood when both Mom and Dad puffed away at home and (almost unbearably) in the car. When Dad returned from business meetings in the Southeast, he had gifts for each of us packed on top of the wrinkled shirts in his suitcase—a doll, a game, a book—always something that delighted Sandy and me. Mom often got a nice surprise too, but there was one thing she could rely on. From the inside pocket of his suit jacket, Dad pulled out two bright red miniature cartons that contained four Winston cigarettes each, one pack for him and one for Mom, souvenirs of the meal services on his flight.

When I began my flying career, I was relieved that Delta didn't offer complimentary cigarettes. However, they did provide matches so passengers could fire up their own smokes. And they could do so anywhere they liked—at their seat, in the aisles and lavatories. Pilots were allowed to smoke in the cockpit. Though it was against Delta's regulations, stewardesses lit up on the jumpseat. The only restriction was no pipes and cigars.

The worst aspect of smoke on an airplane was that it hung in clouds about halfway between the floor and ceiling, right in my face, as I went about my duties. There were times when I was in mid-cabin on the beverage cart and couldn't see the galley in the back. And the more alcohol people drank, the more careless they became; they hung their arms out in the aisle and punctuated their conversations with expansive gestures, flinging ashes everywhere. Flight attendants knew these hazards when we navigated the aisles to do our service. Still, avoiding them was challenging when we carried a stack of dirty meal trays blocking our sight line. Occasionally, I was upset to find a small hole in my skirt or vest where an errant ash had singed the fabric. Given the carelessness of some passengers, it was a miracle there weren't frequent cabin fires or severe injuries to the crew.

One of the most loathsome experiences was a late-night flight from Boston to Ft. Lauderdale that was always full and had a high percentage of smokers. The assault on my nose, throat, and eyes required me to pop into the lavatory frequently to clean my contacts, a temporary fix only because even that little measure didn't prevent bloodshot eyes. I reeked when I got off the plane and had a throbbing ache between my eyebrows. Nothing ever felt so good as when I inhaled a deep breath of fresh air outside the terminal building and, when I arrived home, I stepped into a hot shower and shampooed my hair multiple times to extract the stink that went down to the roots.

Unionized flight attendants at other airlines fought for a smoking ban on airplanes for years. Evidence accumulated about the dangers of occasional exposure to secondhand smoke, but it *constantly* assaulted us. The powerful tobacco lobbies managed to avert proposed regulations that would cut into their profit margins, and they had the backing of airline executives who feared a ban would alienate a large chunk of their clientele.

To compromise with flight attendant unions and other pressure groups, most airlines created non-smoking sections on their aircraft. Hallelujah! Then the happiness balloon went "pffft!" when we saw how this worked in practice. Imagine you are John Q. Passenger who can't tolerate cigarette smoke, so the reservations agent books a seat for you in the non-smoking section. You arrive at your aisle seat in Row 25. But wait, what's this? A plastic sign on your seatback indicates that Row 26 is the first row of the smoking section. How happy do you think you are now? And to whom will you complain? One guess! Passengers fortunate enough to sit in rows some distance from the smoking section still had to walk through the fog to get to the lavatory. Smokers themselves weren't always happy to sit in an area that looked like the aftermath of a volcanic eruption.

After several incremental smoking bans based on flight lengths and destinations, the final nail in the coffin (so to speak) came in 2000 when President Clinton signed a bill that banned smoking on all flights to, from, or within the United States. We were thrilled to see our concerns about exposure to dangerous chemicals go up in smoke.

Chapter Twenty-five

I t's a terrifying scenario. You're hurtling through the air at thirty-five thousand feet when you have a heart attack or a seizure or go into labor. While flight attendants could deal with many health emergencies using readily available emergency equipment such as oxygen bottles and first aid kits, we had little to offer to medical professionals who might volunteer to help with more serious issues. That is, until 1986, when the FAA mandated airlines to carry EMKs (Emergency Medical Kits) that were to be used only by qualified medical practitioners. Soon after, the agency added AEDs (automatic external defibrillators) to the required equipment. These additional resources significantly increased successful outcomes for inflight medical emergencies.

On a full flight from Chicago to Orlando, I learned how vital the EMK was. Among the passengers was a group of about sixty high school seniors on a class trip to the Magic Kingdom. I couldn't help thinking back to my high school days when a bus trip to an out-of-town football game fifty miles from home was a momentous occasion. Things had certainly changed! I was a little concerned about this group's small number of chaperones. However, the kids were polite and orderly as they boarded the airplane, not bouncing off the walls as might be expected of a group headed to the mecca of fun and excitement. Since the agents could not seat the whole group in one block, the kids sat in small clusters scattered throughout the coach cabin.

As I greeted passengers, a rosy-cheeked girl nervously twined a curl around her finger. She said, "My mom wanted me to tell someone I'm allergic to peanuts." She smiled at the boy behind her, who affectionately squeezed her shoulder. Passengers' intolerance of peanuts was an increasingly frequent problem. In extreme cases where a passenger could not be anywhere near peanuts, we might be forced to delay our departure while we removed all the offending little blue and red bags from the aircraft.

"So, how bad is your allergy?" I asked. "Is it a problem only if you eat them, or are you more sensitive than that?"

"Just if I eat them, and even then, it's not too bad. I feel a little short of breath for a few seconds."

I felt a fleeting moment of concern, but I playfully wagged my index finger at her. "No peanuts for you on this flight, young lady. OK?"

"OK," she giggled, and she and the boy continued to coach to find their seats.

That was easy.

Shortly after takeoff, I heard a call button chime. I craned my neck to look down the aisle and saw it came from an area near the girl's seat. With the airplane still on a steep climb, I waited a few seconds until it was safer to get up, and when I reached the row, I saw that the girl no longer looked so fresh-faced. Her lips had a blue tinge; she was unable to speak and was having difficulty breathing. I asked her boyfriend what happened.

"I don't know," he said, shaking. "Everything was OK, and then she like spazzed out."

I spotted the empty wrapper of a Snickers bar in his lap. "Did she eat any of that?" I asked incredulously.

"No, but I kissed her not long after *I* ate it. She'll be OK, won't she?" the boyfriend asked, clinging to his girlfriend's arm and close to tears.

My jumpseat partner arrived. "Page for medical help and call the captain," I instructed. Seconds later, the announcement came over the PA. "Ladies and gentlemen, we have a passenger who needs medical attention. If a doctor, registered nurse, or EMT is on board, please ring your flight attendant call button."

Whenever we paged for medical help, the next few seconds seemed like hours as we waited for a response. This situation required supplies from the EMK, which we weren't qualified to use. If no one offered to help (and maybe even if someone did), we would have to land, but it might be too late to help the passenger. A flight attendant from the back of the plane rushed up with the EMK and the AED just as a frantic chaperone reached the girl's seat. "What happened, Lisa?" But Lisa couldn't respond. I held her hand and said soothingly, "We're going to help you, Lisa," hoping I was telling the truth.

At first, no one rang their call button in response to our request, so I scanned the cabin to see if anyone was rising from their seat. At last, I heard a call bell chime. *Thank God!*. Then I heard another "ding" and another and another. The overhead panels looked like a Christmas tree, and several people quickly approached Lisa's row. The first ones to reach her were a doctor and an EMT.

After I informed them of her peanut allergy and the proximity of the Snickers bar, the EMT ripped the seal off the EMK, grabbed an epinephrine syringe, and handed it to the doctor, who stuck the needle through Lisa's pant leg into her thigh. The EMT strapped the blood pressure cuff on her arm, took out the stethoscope, and monitored her. Lisa breathed more easily in less than a minute, and her color gradually returned to normal. Her boyfriend, now shedding tears of relief, and another teenager in their row reluctantly moved from their seats so that the chaperone and the doctor (with a second epinephrine syringe ready) could sit with Lisa.

Once the crisis had passed, I walked through the cabin and thanked every passenger who rang their call button. Out of curiosity, I asked each about their medical specialty. I was perplexed that almost all of them had the same one. "It's strange there are so many cardiologists on board," I remarked to one of the doctors. "What are the odds of that?"

"Pretty high when there's an important conference in Orlando this week," she laughed. What a stroke of luck!

But on another flight, the outcome was different. A wheelchair nearly swallowed up the tiny frame of an older woman when the skycap brought her on board. She wore practical travel clothes—navy blue knit pants, a white pullover sweater, and sneakers—to be as comfortable as possible from Ft. Lauderdale to Salt Lake City. The journey included a stopover in Dallas/Fort Worth, which added another hour to the already lengthy trip. The skycap helped her out of the wheelchair and handed me her vintage red Samsonite tote bag. It was heavy, and I hoped someone had helped her with it before she arrived at the airport. The skycap told us that because of the light load (about one-third full), the agent had blocked the other two seats in her row so she could more easily get in and out. Janie, the Flight Attendant in Charge, glanced at the name on the wheelchair request slip and asked me to help Mrs. Hanson to her seat.

With her white permed hair, rimless glasses, and lined face, she was the very definition of "grandma." She looked remarkably like the woman on the wrapper of Grandma's Cookies. I smiled, thinking perhaps we had a celebrity on board. She held on to the seat backs for balance and slowly followed me to her seat about five rows from the back. *Why did the agent seat her so far from the door? She must feel like she's on an army recruit training hike*. But I understood when she asked, "Is the restroom nearby?" Apparently, there were no unoccupied rows near the lavatory at the front of coach. "Yes," I said. "There are two of them four rows behind you. Be sure to let one of us know if you need help. The call button is right above you." She slid over to the window seat and settled in, and I placed her tote bag under the seat in front of her. When I assisted her with her seatbelt, there was slack around her waist, even when I fully tightened it. I reached up for two pillows to place behind her back, and she thanked me.

"Do you think we'll get to Salt Lake City on schedule? My daughter and granddaughter are picking me up, and I don't want them to wait too long." I told her the weather looked good the entire way, and we shouldn't have any delays.

It was my turn to work in first class. After completing the meal service, I peeked into the coach cabin to see how the service was coming along and to help out if needed. With so few passengers, the crew had finished serving breakfast. Janie and Karen picked up meal trays while Nancy offered second coffees. The passengers were involved in typical pastimes—they watched the movie, read, typed on their laptops, napped, or gazed at the landscape below. There had been no call bells, so there was little to do except cruise through the cabins every ten minutes to check on the passengers.

One of the advantages of a low passenger count was that no one needed to wait very long if at all, to use the lavatory. On heavy flights, inevitably, a passenger took their morning constitutional as a long line of inconvenienced passengers formed near the door and waited for the red "occupied" sign to go out. "Are you sure someone is in there?" one or two always asked. Oh, yes, I was sure. And I might have added, "You won't want to go in there when they come out." We sometimes attached a pillow pack of coffee to the coat hook inside the lavatory as a makeshift deodorizer in cases of lethal stench. The company strongly objected to this practice as an inappropriate tool, but we did it anyway. Upper management wasn't on hand to suffer the noxious fumes. However, long lines weren't an issue on this flight; things might have turned out differently if they had been. On my way to the back galley to chat with Karen and Nancy, I noticed Mrs. Hanson was watching the movie screen, and I asked her if she'd like a headset so she could hear the sound. She smiled. "No, thank you. It looks kind of silly. I don't need to hear it to follow the plot."

I laughed. "You're probably right!"

About fifteen minutes from landing in Dallas, the captain turned on the seatbelt sign. Janie's announcement asked passengers to stay seated for the remainder of the flight. While stationed at the back galley, Karen noted that someone was in the rear left lavatory but figured whoever was inside would have emerged when she returned to her jumpseat. She walked up the aisle to check seatbelts and then lingered at the mid-galley to await the final check of seatbacks and tray tables.

Five minutes later, the seatbelt light chimed twice, followed by Janie's announcement that we would land shortly. She and I had already returned coats to the passengers in first class, checked the cabin, and secured the galley. We had just buckled our seatbelts and harnesses when the interphone rang. I wiggled out of my shoulder straps to pick up the handset. Karen's frantic voice: "A passenger has passed out in the aft lav. I unlocked the door when I didn't get a response to my knock, but she's on the floor, unresponsive, and I can't get the door open all the way." I relayed this information to Janie, who called the cockpit while I raced down the aisle to the back of the plane. Having picked up her handset at the middle jumpseat, Nancy was a few steps ahead of me.

The lavatory door had two hinged panels that opened inward like a telephone booth. When we carefully nudged the door open as far as it would go, I saw the tiny figure crumpled on the floor.

"Mrs. Hanson," I yelled, "are you OK?"

There was no response and no movement. Karen and I pushed the quick-release levers on the side of the door, which was hinged to the frame. As the unwieldy door tumbled toward us, Mrs. Hanson slumped into the aisle.

I shouted, "Somebody get the first aid kit." Nancy quickly brought one, ripped off the seal, and handed me the CPR pocket mask while I heard Janie page for medical help. Kneeling beside her, I confirmed that Mrs. Hanson was not breathing. I checked for a pulse and, not finding one, tilted her head back, placed the mask on her face, and prepared to begin CPR. Her face was gray, her skin was cool to the touch, and I knew her unblinking eyes could not see me, but I had to try. As I was about to begin, a doctor arrived and checked her vital signs. He asked for a flashlight and shone it into her eyes. Her pupils remained large.

"There's no point in CPR. She's gone," he said quietly.

The captain had decided to proceed with the landing so that additional help would be available quickly. Janie notified him of the passenger's death and told him we would put Mrs. Hanson in a seat in the last row. However, the captain relayed a message from the ground not to move her due to the circumstances of an unattended death. Instead, we put a pillow under Mrs. Hanson's head, covered her with a blanket, and closed her eyes. Janie asked me to sit in a jumpseat in the rear galley instead of the one in first class so I could help Karen keep the area clear once we landed.

When we arrived at the gate, many passengers, out of respect and a few out of curiosity, were uncharacteristically slow in gathering their belongings. One or two looked back and mirrored Karen's and my stricken faces. A county official and the EMTs boarded the plane and asked to see Mrs. Hanson's carry-on luggage. Her worn tote bag contained numerous prescription bottles, mainly heart medications, a blood pressure monitor, and, heartbreakingly, several small gift items loosely covered with tissue paper. The EMTs gently lifted her onto their gurney and wheeled her to the jetway and down the exterior stairs to their waiting vehicle. As the four of us stood together at the front of the plane, numb and silent, we saw a familiar face approaching from the gate area. Ken, a well-liked flight attendant we had all worked with in Miami, was now a supervisor in Dallas. He hugged us and said he would arrange replacements if we wanted to go home rather than continue the trip. I considered Ken's offer. If I went home, I knew what George would do: hold me in his arms, tell me he understood my sadness. He'd say, "It wasn't your fault; you did your best." But George hadn't been there.

Heads lowered, each lost in thought, we refocused on one another's faces, and it was clear we had all reached the same decision. Only the four of us could truly understand the impact of this event. We would stick together, offer one another support, and try to process this tragedy. The flight attendants who were taking the flight to Salt Lake City came on board and, like close sisters and brothers, expressed their sorrow at Mrs. Hanson's death and the trauma we had experienced. We headed to our outbound flight to San Diego, where a new group of passengers would receive the best service we could provide, never knowing our hearts were broken.

That night in our favorite beach restaurant, as the sun set in the harbor, we sadly raised our glasses to our little grandma and grieved for the loved ones who awaited her arrival..

Chapter Twenty-six

Looking back on George's decision to leave the Olds dealership, I wish someone had whispered, "Be careful what you wish for." While both of us were on board with his plan to seek new employment to have more time off, the tradeoff was an unsteady income. As a new car salesman at a Chrysler store, his monthly checks fluctuated from barely adequate to a mere dribble, a problem exacerbated by an auto workers' strike in the fall that dried up inventory.

The house payments had been manageable with his previous income, but they quickly became burdensome and finally impossible. However, I knew nothing about it because George kept this problem to himself. We maintained separate checking accounts and split the household bills. Since the townhouse was in his name only, he assumed responsibility for the mortgage. After several months of sending partial payments or missing them altogether, he confessed the problem.

I was furious. "Why did you wait so long to tell me?" I yelled.

"I kept thinking things would get better at work and I'd be able to bail myself out."

"That might have been possible three months ago, but now…" Angry tears ran down my cheeks. "Why would you keep something so important from me?"

He sobbed, "I'm so sorry. I didn't want to admit what a loser I am."

If he had hoped for a sympathetic hug and a "There, there, everything's going to be all right," he was disappointed. I turned my back on him, ran upstairs to what would soon *not* be our bedroom, and slammed the door.

The following day, I called the mortgage company to see if we could work out a solution, but it was too late. They told me they would send George an eviction notice and auction the property. In a last-ditch effort, Paul flew down from Illinois to attend the sale in hopes he could purchase the townhouse and sell it back to us, but a higher bidder won. George lost our home in foreclosure.

I felt devasted and mortified. I couldn't believe he had let this happen and that I hadn't known. While my credit remained intact, George's was in shambles, and the situation created a crisis in our marriage that I wasn't sure we could overcome. Secrets and poor communication had bedeviled all my relationships. I admitted *I* was the loser for thinking this one would somehow be different. After a heated, tearful discussion, George agreed to hand over his paychecks to me, and I took charge of paying all the bills while uncertain if I wanted to remain married to this man.

With my home life in such turmoil, responding to passengers' needs and complaints with a smile was difficult. It made me think of the day my dad died, and I had to walk to a nearby drugstore to buy a pair of pantyhose. The cashier snapped at me when I struggled to find the correct change. "Hurry up! There's a line of people behind you." I wanted to yell, "Shut up! Don't you know my father just died?" Like the cashier, the passengers had no idea what I was going through. In addition, I missed out on the usual outlets of jumpseat discussion or commiseration over a glass of wine because I was too ashamed to tell anyone but my closest friends what had happened. When people questioned why we moved from our lovely townhouse into an apartment, I explained that since George no longer owned Dakota (he had sold her before we got married), living in an equestrian community seemed silly. It wasn't a lie, but it wasn't the truth either.

George suffered, too. He was miserable in his sales job. He lost his customary enthusiasm with customers. His sales numbers plummeted, and his increasing unhappiness dragged him into a demoralizing downward spiral. George regretted his departure from his old job and, I knew, harbored some bitterness at my encouragement for him to leave. When our relationship seemed about to drown, one of George's old friends stopped by to see him at work and threw a lifeline.

"Hey, I don't know if you'd be interested, but I know a guy who needs a business and insurance manager, and I told him about you."

"What dealership?' George asked, disinterested.

"It's not cars; it's RVs."

"I don't know anything about RVs. Why would he want to hire me?"

"Because you're the proverbial salesman who can sell sawdust to lumber mills. You can learn what you need to know about RVs, but no one can teach the skill you have, and I told him that."

Later that day, George learned that his proposed role entailed the kind of work he had done at the Olds dealership (which he enjoyed), plus filling in on sales occasionally. His schedule would require him to work some nights and Saturdays but included three weeks of vacation. He could accumulate days off and take them in a block if he wanted extra time to go somewhere.

When he told me the details of the job—its salary and flexibility—I was skeptical because it sounded too good to be true after so much bad news. But George dived into his new job with gusto, his upbeat attitude returned, and I began to relax. With the return of a reliable source of income, I gradually regained my trust in him. We found a small house in Davie we could afford on my income only.

Unfortunately, after only two years with the RV dealership, I noticed telltale signs of dissatisfaction and restlessness. Having stayed at the same company for eighteen years, I found this hard to understand but accepted it as a personality difference. However, a possible alternate explanation presented itself one evening while I was watching a favorite TV show. He picked up the remote and, without a word, changed the channel. "Hey, I was watching that," I said testily.

"Oh, sorry," he said, returning the TV to my show. Then, half-jokingly, "Maybe I have ADD (attention deficit disorder)."

I had never heard of this condition in adults, so I did a little research. A book I borrowed from the library included a self-evaluation that George agreed to take. Sure enough, he had many characteristics of the condition—problems with focus, restlessness, and occasional impulsivity (like changing channels). Although none of these tendencies rose to the level of an incapacitating condition, I started looking at his behavior through a new lens.

George's good fortune continued when a friend proposed they start an LLC to sell extended warranties and aftermarket products to car dealerships in a three-county area. *Not this again! Unreliable commissions.* However, after meeting his prospective business partner (who already had experience in the field) and reading the business plan they put together, I gave George my blessing. Happily, the new business yielded even more flexibility while providing a steady income that was higher than his previous one.

With much less stress in our lives, George and I discovered more interests we shared. His great-grandmother was Shawnee, and he felt an affinity for Native American art and culture. George's fascination sparked pleasant memories of learning about Indigenous Americans in fourth-grade social studies class and drawing pictures of the distinctive shelters each tribe used. We decided to delve into studying Native American populations together. We began our exploration close to home at the Miccosukee reservation southwest of Miami near the Everglades. This excursion whetted our appetites to learn about native culture, art, and food in other areas of the country, so we took a vacation to New Mexico, where we quickly discovered the appropriateness of the state's motto, "Land of Enchantment."

Throughout the trip, as we visited gift shops, museums, and markets, we learned about the characteristics that distinguished the traditional art of the Navajo, the Zuni, and other Pueblo groups from one another. We indulged in affordable Christmas ornaments, pottery, and jewelry and splurged on a painting from an upscale Santa Fe art gallery. Everywhere we went, we found delightful painted wood knick-knacks—howling coyotes, cacti, and lizards—and on the flight home, we discussed the possibility of creating our own line of artwork as a side business. Our creative juices flowed as we explored producing similar items and selling them at South Florida's numerous weekend art and craft shows. When we added up the materials and equipment required, we found the cost reasonable, so shortly after we arrived home, we took the plunge and embarked on our new cottage industry.

George cut shapes out of half-inch pine with a bandsaw, and I sanded them and rounded the edges smooth before I painted them with colorful designs. We built our inventory and developed new ideas—bears, snakes, rows of pots, napkin holders, and picture frames. When we felt we had enough pieces, we debuted at a Town of Davie-sponsored art and craft show on the rodeo grounds. "What name do you want on your placard?" asked the show coordinator. George looked at me and shrugged. "I don't know. How about 'Santa Fe Dreamin'?" And so, our little gig began. We enjoyed brisk sales in Davie, which nearly depleted our inventory. Soon, other area shows accepted us, including several of the prestigious juried Las Olas Art Fairs in

Ft. Lauderdale. We went as far afield as Orlando, where we won a prize for the best 3-D art.

While we rarely did more than break even, we enjoyed this hobby, and it gave us an excuse to make more excursions to the Southwest to look for new ideas and enjoy the laid-back atmosphere. We looked forward to these trips and experienced near-flawless travels to and from New Mexico—until the one time we didn't.

After carefully checking the passenger loads, I saw we had an excellent chance to make it from Ft. Lauderdale to Albuquerque via a Dallas connection by dinnertime. However, the cancellation of an earlier flight from Ft. Lauderdale to Dallas resulted in a swarm of passengers to the flight George and I had hoped to board. While waiting in the gate area of the next Dallas flight, I engaged in a habit I had developed over the years when non-revving—mentally counting passengers in the gate area to gauge our chances of getting on the flight. It didn't look promising, but when two passengers failed to respond to a page over the PA system at the last minute, we gratefully took their seats. When we finally got to Dallas, we raced to our Albuquerque flight—the last one that night—and were, again, the final passengers to board. The flight had only a dozen or so empty seats. Even so, we were dismayed to find ourselves in the most uncomfortable ones on the plane—the row in front of the coach galley jammed up against the bulkhead. George slid over to the window. I sat rigid and bolt upright between him and a largish man on the aisle in a seat that didn't recline—not one centimeter.

Oh, well. It's only an hour and a half flight. I'll survive.

The plane pushed back from the gate, taxied toward the runway, and stopped. I looked out of George's window just when a streak of lightning flashed in the distance. I shuddered as I thought how this type of weather had been responsible for the crash of Flight 191 at this very airport, and I felt relieved when we heard a PA. "Folks, this is your captain. We have reports of severe weather in the area, and the airport has suspended operations. We don't know how long this will last, but we'll keep you posted." *Not good to be delayed, but it's safer.* I noticed the passenger sitting next to me conversing with a man across the aisle who had all three seats to himself. I wondered why my seatmate didn't move over there so we could all spread out a little. As the minutes slowly ticked by, the man continued his across-the-aisle conversation, and my discomfort and irritation with him mounted, but non-rev protocol forbade me from suggesting that the man change seats. I whispered to George, "It doesn't take a rocket scientist to figure out he'd have more room across the aisle." George patted my arm and smiled sympathetically.

Forty-five minutes later, we took off, and I struggled to retrieve a book from my carry-on bag under the seat in front of me. Reading made me sleepy, and the drone of the two men's voices in the background caused me to nod off. My nap ended with an abrupt jolt when my seatmate stood up and stepped into the aisle to stretch his arms and legs, a contented look on his face.

I glared at the oblivious man. *Yes! That's what it feels like to have elbow room, and you can have it for the rest of the flight if you change seats!*

My derriere had spread a bit into his vacated space until he plopped down again and forced me to retreat. Fortunately, the captain announced we'd land in ten minutes. *Thank goodness this misery will end soon.*

The guy next to me said to his friend, "Are you headed back to Los Alamos tonight?"

"Yeah, if the car rental is still open."

"Can I catch a ride with you? I'm supposed to brief some NASA engineers first thing in the morning."

I could hardly believe my ears; I had been wrong. Indeed, the man *was* a rocket scientist and still hadn't figured it out!

Chapter Twenty-seven

Our trips to New Mexico dwindled as we saw the popularity of Southwest décor die down. After some discussion, we decided to dissolve Santa Fe Dreamin'. My disappointment was short-lived, however, as a new, exciting work opportunity arose. Delta acquired Pan American's transatlantic and shuttle routes in 1991 and began operating them toward the end of the year.

As with past mergers, there would be some downsides. Combining two airlines' fleets of planes might be a nuts-and-bolts issue. In contrast, the merger of their people is complicated and emotionally fraught. While the outlook for long-term employment usually improves for everyone, it comes with an upheaval in the lifeblood of each group of employees: seniority. This issue affects every aspect of the job—monthly schedules, salary, vacation, and the ability to change locations—to name a few. Strict date-of-hire isn't fair if one group has considerably more long-term employees than the other; neither is the placement of the employees of the defunct airline on the bottom of the surviving carrier's rosters. So, the method used to meld seniority lists in all departments is a contentious issue often settled by arbitration or a court decision. Each of Delta's mergers entailed unique circumstances. Although my system-wide ranking sometimes lowered, I usually remained close to my position on the base seniority list, the one that affected my day-to-day life most.

We learned that Miami would gain two international routes—one to London Gatwick and one to Frankfurt. After completing special training in Atlanta, several friends and I worked on our first international flight.

Rather than putting us up in London, Delta chose Brighton, about an hour's drive from Gatwick Airport, for our layovers. Our hotel sat across the road from the rocky beach, and right outside the building, we found charming, narrow brick streets and lanes with unique gift shops and ethnic restaurants. The layover wasn't complete without trips to Boots Pharmacy and Marks & Spencer to purchase items unavailable at home. Our Frankfurt trips sometimes included a stay in Wiesbaden at the Schwarzer Bock Hotel, famous for its spa with a mineral water swimming pool, and numerous nearby restaurants with gastronomic delights. On one of these trips, I invited George to come along, and we spent the forty-eight-hour layover with my friend Carole and her husband, Dick. Along with Debbie, another flight attendant on our crew, we rented a car and visited as many places as possible. We drove a couple of hours to Würzburg on the Main River and then to charming and fascinating Rothenburg. This medieval town boasts intact walls, even after centuries of nearby warfare. Strolling the cobbled streets, I mused, "Do you think we'll run into Pinocchio?" In response to my companions' perplexed expressions, I explained, "This is the spot that inspired Walt Disney artists to create the movie's backdrops."

I loved international flying and continued to bid for London and Frankfurt for over two years until I noticed the three-day trips were leaving me tired and achy. "I wish it didn't take me so long to recover after each trip," I remarked to several coworkers.

"What do you mean?" one asked, puzzled. "I have a little jet lag the day after the trip. That's all."

"Me too," said another. "How long does it take you to get over the trip?"

"Three days. So, I only have one good day between trips," I replied, realizing from their surprised looks that my experience was not like theirs. I became concerned that the trips were not the only reason for my symptoms.

An incident on one of my days off convinced me I was right. It was chilly for Florida, around sixty-five degrees, when George and I went to an air show at the Opa-Locka Airport. As we walked across the open space between the parking area and the flight line, I stuffed my hands in my pants pockets to warm them up. When I pulled them out, both were a splotchy purple. "Oh, great! Something must have melted in my pockets, but I can't figure out what it is." George examined my hands and rubbed his thumb across the discoloration. "Honey, there's nothing *on* your skin; that *is* your skin."

Mystified and frightened, I made an appointment to see a doctor, and after a series of blood tests, I learned I had lupus. This diagnosis explained the source of my fatigue and the sensitivity of my fingers and toes to cold. It also made me realize I might need to give up international flying to protect my health and, instead, fly less taxing domestic trips again.

My choice became easier when Delta discontinued the London and Frankfurt routes from Miami. Many of my friends who had grown to love international flying opted to commute to Atlanta, Cincinnati, or New York, where they had a wide selection of destinations. However, my previous three years of commuting to Chicago, plus my new diagnosis, made me decide to avoid added stress in my life.

Around this time, we received big news in the family arena— Chris and his girlfriend Rachel were expecting a baby. Two weeks after Emily was born, George and I flew to Texas to meet her.

Michelle, Chris, and Rachel (with Emily swathed in a blanket) met us at the airport, where George made a beeline to the little bundle in Rachel's arms. He lifted the cover from Emily's face and instantly fell in love. As difficult as it was to accept, we knew our busy schedules might make visits to see our granddaughter few and far between even with our pass privileges, so George came up with an idea. "I'll wear Paco Rabanne (his favorite fragrance) whenever I'm around her," he said. "That way, even if it's a while between visits, she'll remember me by my scent."

I had read somewhere that because the olfactory nerve is close to the most primitive part of the brain, smell is the sense that evokes the most powerful emotions. I wonder if George read this, too, or if he just had an instinct about it, but we learned a few years later how well it worked. Three-year-old Emily and her mother passed the Dillard's department store perfume counter, where a man had just sprayed a cologne sample on his wrist.

"Mommy, he smells like Grandpa," Emily declared as Rachel glanced over to see the man return a Paco Rabanne sampler to the counter.

With the hubbub of the family visit behind us, our lives seemed quiet and boring after we returned home, so we brainstormed about a new side business we could do together to replace Santa Fe Dreamin'. It didn't take long to figure it out. We both loved music, especially oldies. George had a talent for imitating the signature choreography of famous Motown groups and demonstrating how they differed.

"Now, the Temptations had the most intricate moves," he explained while executing a velvet smooth jazz box, tight twirl, and fluid arm movements. "The Four Tops were a little more basic, stepping from side to side with their arms swinging from the elbow. And the Pips…who can forget them pulling an imaginary train whistle on *Midnight Train to Georgia*?" He even included the Supremes in his repertoire, mimicking their dramatic outstretched arms with upturned palms on *Stop! In the Name of Love*.

So, we embarked on another adventure and started a mobile DJ business we named "Rewind Entertainment Services," which specialized in oldies and contemporary country music. Our first customers were friends who sought entertainment for birthday or anniversary parties. If the hosts desired, I contributed some of my skills with line dance lessons at country music parties. Our base expanded as word spread about Rewind, and we even played at a few nightclubs. One December night, we DJed a toga party at a private home where the hosts wanted us to play only disco music (I never figured out the connection). We set up our equipment on the screened patio near the sliding glass door opening into the living room, and guests moved freely from one area to another. It got chilly as the evening wore on, especially for the toga-clad guests, most of whom eventually migrated inside the house. We thought the hosts might invite us to move inside with the crowd, but we realized this wouldn't happen when a couple of guys moved our speakers inside and closed the sliding door behind them. Through the glass, we watched the guests do the Hustle and shake their booties in the warmth of the house. We had started Rewind so we could spend time with one another. We looked at each other and laughed as we realized that on this night, that meant shivering together as we turned into icicles on a deserted patio in December.

Chapter Twenty-eight

Get up at zero-dark-thirty or fly later in the day? I weighed the pros and cons when it came to trip selection. With early sign-ins, I had to get up at four a.m., but most likely, my aircraft would be at the gate, clean, stocked, catered, and ready to go. With late afternoon or evening trips, I could run errands or accomplish a few chores before I had to go to work. Still, the chance was much higher for the inbound aircraft to encounter a delay that resulted in a shorter layover or triggered a reroute.

I usually opted for early trips to arrive at the layover in time to see a bit of the city or relax before dinner. But one month, I bid for a trip that left Ft. Lauderdale at seven p.m. for Atlanta and then, after switching planes, wound up in Chicago for a twelve-hour layover. The flight attendants on the inbound flight served dinner; that flight was usually full with over two hundred passengers. One evening, when I arrived at the airport, I saw that Operations had posted a message to check with them— never a good sign. "We received communication from the flight crew that the inbound aircraft encountered severe turbulence en route and will need a mechanical inspection when it arrives," the Dispatcher informed us. "The outbound flight will be delayed a minimum of forty-five minutes."

In cases like this, everyone pulled together. Two flight attendants on my crew immediately went upstairs to help the gate agents assist passengers who would miss their connections due to the delay. When the rest of us saw on the monitor that the plane had landed, we went to the gate so we could board as soon as the passengers got off and assist the cabin service crew to clean and restock supplies.

The agent walked down the jetway to meet the airplane as it pulled into the gate. A few seconds later, I smelled a pungent odor from the open jetway door as the first few passengers emerged, faces grim, and walked swiftly away from the gate area. The odor became pervasive as more passengers deplaned, all visibly shaken. Most had red and yellow goo on their clothes, which we quickly identified from its appearance and smell as lasagna, the main course of the coach dinner service.

I peered through the jetway door and saw that passengers had tracked globs of pasta, cheese, and tomato sauce onto the carpet. Our outbound passengers, who had been patiently or impatiently waiting to board, took wide-eyed note of the scene. Some quickly gathered their carry-on items and headed to the ticket counter, certain the flight would be canceled or to escape the nauseating smell.

The final ambulatory stragglers exited the jetway, and I saw through the window that a fire and rescue vehicle had pulled up to the exterior jetway stairs—a precaution or a necessity? A long line of wheelchairs awaited the plane's arrival, and several headed down the jetway, leaving half a dozen more as backups. The first wheelchair to return held a frail, white-haired man clutching a sickness bag; in another sat a mother holding a screaming toddler on her lap while a young boy sobbed and clung to her arm as he trotted next to her.

We headed down the jetway, anxious to learn from the flight attendants what had happened and to check out the state of the cabins. As bad as the jetway looked, the spectacle that greeted us inside the aircraft was far worse. Lasagna was everywhere—on the floor, the seats, the tray tables, the windows. Unbelievably, even a few deposits shimmered on the ceiling. The smell was made worse by sporadic areas where passengers had gotten sick, and we struggled to stifle gag reflexes or not become ill ourselves.

We learned that the flight attendants had just finished serving the coach meals when the airplane encountered what's sometimes called (erroneously) an air pocket. After spending so many years terrified of the slightest movement on a plane, I learned that turbulence, while frightening and uncomfortable, was seldom dangerous. But this had been the rarer kind caused by atmospheric conditions that combined in one exact moment and in one precise location to create the unforeseeable perfect storm of severe turbulence. The passengers experienced what felt like freefall. All the meal trays lofted from the tray tables and levitated momentarily, then landed with a thud as they jettisoned their contents all over the aircraft and the passengers. Those who did not have their seatbelts fastened also took a momentary ride in space. Fortunately, the meal and beverage carts, which weighed hundreds of pounds, remained stable, and the flight attendants squatted on the floor, clinging to them to avoid smashing against the seats or the carts themselves. Two flight attendants in the rear galley, who did not have any means to steady themselves, had been thrown to the floor, and EMTs were examining them for injuries. As I gazed at the chaos in the cabin, I pictured a demented artist filling a tank with pureed pasta and airbrushing the entire cabin.

After thoroughly checking the airplane, the mechanics determined there was no structural damage. The flight had to be canceled anyway because of the state of the cabin. For the plane to be ready for service again, it took a double crew of cabin service cleaners all night to painstakingly clean every surface, change every seat cover, and deep clean the carpet.

The debacle also triggered distressing memories of a horrific flight I had been on in 1986, nine months after the crash of Flight 191. Even with the stigma of that ill-fated flight (renamed Flight 139), I flew the rotation because it remained one of the best trips in the base. That afternoon, the plane was only half full, and the flight was routine until we neared Dallas. The captain announced we were in a holding pattern because weather conditions had halted arrivals, and he asked the flight attendants to remain seated because of the possibility of rough air.

The passenger who sat directly across from my jumpseat at the front right door said nervously, "This happens in Dallas quite a bit, doesn't it?" I wondered if she asked because she knew this used to be Flight 191.

"It sure seems to," I agreed in a light conversational manner. "The weather in Dallas can change very quickly. I hope we won't have to hold very long."

Despite my casual remarks, I felt a jolt of fear. Even though I had learned to rein in my flying anxiety over the years, it had obstinately remained under the surface, ready to pounce. And this situation felt eerily like a potential rerun of a tragic event. I often thought of Franny, Frieda, and the other flight attendants who lost their lives on Flight 191, how they had experienced similar weather conditions and had probably had the same conversations with passengers, unaware that these exchanges would be the last they would ever have.

I had confidence in the cockpit crew—all three pilots had years of experience and I'd flown with this same crew a few weeks earlier. Like all pilots nationwide who flew the L-1011, they had undergone enhanced training after Flight 191's crash to learn to identify potential microbursts and evade them. This training and the installation of Doppler radar systems at airports and in cockpits over the next few years were positive outcomes of the accident.

"Folks, we have a break in the weather, so we've received clearance to land, and we're lining up for our final approach. Make sure you have those seatbelts securely fastened."

Seconds later, heavy rain began to pelt the fuselage as the skies blackened, and suddenly, it felt like a giant hand tugged at the airplane to pull it from the sky. The woman across from me gripped her armrest, and I instinctively reached for one that wasn't there. Instead, I sat in the brace position (knees together, feet planted firmly on the floor, back and neck pressed against the headrest, and hands under my thighs). Still, I felt disconnected from any solid object, and panic forced its way in even as I maintained a neutral expression. Then, blaring through the cockpit door only a few feet from my jumpseat, I heard an electronic warning sound like a police car signaling a driver to pull over—whoop, whoop—followed by a recorded voice saying, "Pull up! Pull up!" This was the GPWS (ground proximity warning system), an alert for approaching terrain. The terrorized face of the woman across from me flashed the same question I asked myself—are we going to die? My friend Carole's voice, barely audible, drifted from the jumpseat at the front left door. "Kath?" I braved a sideways glance out the window and immediately wished I hadn't. Treetops appeared not far below us, and I knew that, in seconds, we would dive into them.

Everything around me seemed to be in slow motion, including the plane's descent, the sound of the engines, and the changing expressions on the passenger's face. I felt peacefully calm. I remember thinking, without fear, "So this is how it ends." But even though I had accepted my imminent demise, fortunately, the pilots hadn't. Suddenly, the plane rose steeply like a rocket from a launch pad, and returned to a normal angle in smooth air. The sun appeared as we banked away from the airport. Some passengers wept, a few threw up, and many still had their eyes shut tight like the woman across from me. I emerged from a dreamlike state, disoriented, unable to fully comprehend I was still alive.

Seconds later, the captain made an announcement. "Ladies and gentlemen, I'm sorry for that rough ride a few minutes ago (*what a master of understatement!*). Just as we were about to land, a storm cell developed in our path, and we had to make a 'go-around' to escape it. Everything is under control, but the airport is closed again. We're diverting to Houston to sit it out until we can head to Dallas again."

Once we arrived at the gate in Houston, all the passengers got off the plane, and I speculated that the rental car counters would probably encounter a stampede. Some passengers would never board another airplane. I wasn't sure I wanted to. The flight attendants gathered in first class while cabin service resupplied the plane and disinfected areas where passengers had become ill. I seemed to be the only one experiencing uncontrollable shaking as I dealt with the realization that my worst childhood nightmare had nearly become a reality. I put on my uniform sweater and rubbed my hands together briskly. Carole hugged me. "It's OK, we're safe now." And slowly, the trembling subsided.

The pilots explained that they had found themselves in an almost identical situation to the one 191 had encountered. However, our flight had a much different outcome due to their recent training. "I never want to be in that pickle again!" said the captain. The other two pilots nodded solemnly in agreement.

To my surprise, all but a handful of passengers returned at departure time. As they hesitantly filed back onto the plane, the pilots stood at the door to answer questions and alleviate their anxieties. After a short flight to Dallas, we learned the unwelcome news that, because of the irregular operations created by the storm, we weren't off duty yet. The captain passed along the message he received from Reroute. "Unbelievable! They're making you work the continuation of Flight 139 to Los Angeles."

We would have to act like nothing had happened for another three hours.

Fortunately, the flight to Los Angeles was uneventful, and after a just-legal break at a motel near LAX, we flew back to Dallas the following morning with the assurance we would get a longer rest there before returning home the following day. When we reached the gate, we tidied the airplane in preparation for a new flight attendant crew to relieve us and work the continuation to Tampa.

A cabin service worker who came onboard to restock supplies chatted with one of my coworkers. "I hope you weren't flying through here yesterday," he said. "We almost lost another L-1011."

"What do you mean?" she asked, afraid to hear his reply.

"Flight 139 almost bit the dust when it tried to land, just like 191. We could see it from the ground, but somehow it gained altitude and headed away."

"I was on that airplane."

The man's jaw dropped. "God bless you," he said before turning to tell others on his crew what she had said. They completed their duties in silence, occasionally stealing furtive glances at the "miracle" flight attendant.

She shared this conversation with the rest of us at dinner that night at our Dallas hotel. Physically and emotionally exhausted, we sat silently for a long time as we processed our brush with calamity. I thought again of my friends on Flight 191 and how the lessons learned from their deaths had saved our lives.

Chapter Twenty-nine

Unique situations, humorous and not, were everyday occurrences for my coworkers and me. I was constantly surprised (and sometimes amused) at our ingenuity in problem-solving, a skill that occasionally spilled over into our off-duty lives.

Bad Ice

Any flight attendant would agree that Bad Ice was one of the biggest annoyances we encountered. This ice had nothing to do with inclement weather, winter, or flight safety; it was the substance in our ice buckets. We took most situations in stride— adaptability to constant change was a prerequisite to success as a flight attendant—but few things were more exasperating than Bad Ice. Good Ice, on the other hand, put us in a buoyant mood even if our feet ached, we had to keep moving our cart to enable passengers to go to the lavatory, or a little kid repeatedly rang his call button and his mother made no attempt to make him stop.

Bad Ice made the beverage service interminably longer than necessary, especially when it took the form of big opaque chunks that looked like they had dropped off the eaves of somebody's house. In winter, there were bags of fused ice; in summer, there were bags of half-melted ice. With the former, a good whack on the galley counter would sometimes break it into a usable form—not technically Good Ice—unless doing so ripped the bag and caused a wet, slippery mess on the floor. The bags of bad summer ice were mainly water. After draining the bags, we could offer passengers only one or two cubes because what remained was nanoscopic. Sometimes, during a beverage service, we would encounter a massive glob of Bad Ice that required an on-the-spot operation, a deft touch, and a high degree of finesse. We banged a juice can (never a carbonated beverage that could later turn into a geyser when opened) against the iceberg to break it apart. The trick was to not use too much force, which would split the can open, leaving us with an unusable mess of sticky orange or red ice—the baddest of Bad Ice!

On the other hand, Good Ice was a thing of beauty that could lift our spirits on even the most tedious flight. Those perfectly sized crystal-clear little cubes lay ready to be scooped up effortlessly and anointed with Coca-Cola or Johnny Walker Red as we whizzed through the service. Passengers likely never think about the ice in their drinks—it's just ice. But to a flight attendant, Bad Ice can freeze out all hope of having a good flight!

Smorgasbord

When I began flying, there were only a few varieties of special meals—kosher, diabetic, low sodium, and bland (which many passengers thought was descriptive of all airline food).

As the years passed, choices expanded to satisfy nearly every dietary need—vegetarian/vegan, gluten- and lactose-free, low carb/fat/calorie, fruit plate, and even child and baby meals. Where special meals were once a rarity, their popularity steadily increased. For example, over half of the two hundred passengers ordered special meals on one of my flights from Atlanta to New York. I certainly didn't begrudge passengers' desires for food that met their needs. However, some admitted to ordering a special meal expecting something more appealing than the standard fare. Often, they were disappointed.

Sometimes, we flight attendants experienced frustration when the pre-flight list of special meals differed markedly from the list of passenger orders the agent brought us before closing the door (I never understood why this mismatch happened so frequently.) We were left to solve an exasperating jigsaw puzzle with missing pieces. Someone who ordered a diabetic meal might be forced to stare at a big slice of chocolate cake on the regular meal they had to accept because their special meal was missing in action. Or a vegetarian might skip a meal altogether rather than eat only the salad on a roast chicken tray. In those cases, we mustered every ounce of diplomacy, and the occasional "treat" from the liquor kit or a meal voucher to use in the terminal to ensure passengers didn't leave the airplane with a bad taste in their mouths.

Celebrities

Famous people fell into three loose categories. Some acted as if the crew should bow down in adulation to them; some happily engaged in conversation; others wanted to keep a low profile and not be fussed over. It was usually evident which category they fell into when they boarded. On one of my flights from Tampa to Los Angeles, Frankie Avalon, Connie Stevens, Suzanne Sommers, Diahann Carroll, Erik Estrada, and Fabian were all returning home after touting their product lines on QVC, a televised shopping network based in Tampa. They were so affable that they invited the entire first class cabin to join their little party, and everyone had a great time!

Many other notables boarded my flights including Robert Redford, Glen Campbell, Gladys Knight (with two of the Pips), Danny Thomas, Robert Goulet and Carol Lawrence, Carol Channing,

B.B. King (with Lucille, his black Gibson guitar, in the seat next to him), Robert Plant and Jimmy Page of Led Zeppelin, Jerry Stiller and Ann Meara (with a very young Ben and his sister in tow), Paul Newman and Joanne Woodward, Ted Kennedy, Pete Rose, Joe Namath, and O.J. Simpson (before). Some were more pleasant than others, but, as their hostess, I felt it was my responsibility to protect their privacy, so I never asked them for autographs, did my best to prevent unwanted contact with other passengers, and seldom commented on their individual behaviors to the outside world.

But when asked to reveal my most memorable celebrity, I immediately think of one I encountered in the early 1980s. To preface this story, I confess that before I moved to the South, I would hear people use the phrase "Bless his/her heart" in ways that I found endearingly warm and comforting. But once I had spent time living in Atlanta and Memphis, I realized that some people used the phrase in an uncomplimentary or even derogatory context, as in, "Jim Bob is dumber than a sack of rocks, bless his heart." The comment was usually followed by "God love him," possibly as insurance against damnation for saying such a mean thing. However, I never thought Tennessee Ernie Ford, who tossed off the phrase in his conversational patter, meant it negatively.

You may never have heard of Ernie if you were born after 1970. He was a gospel and country singer who blazed the trail for crossover artists with his hit song *Sixteen Tons*, which topped both the country and pop charts for many weeks in 1955. He also had a popular TV variety show in the late 1950s and early 1960s that I watched with my family every Thursday night when I was growing up. My favorite part of the show was his sign-off. "Goodnight, and bless your little pea-pickin' hearts," he said with a big smile and great sincerity to his vast TV audience—minus any hint of disparagement.

I met Ernie while working first class on a flight from Las Vegas to Atlanta. As my crew arrived at the gate to pick up our paperwork, the agent told us that Mr. Ford would be one of our passengers. While we didn't greet this news with the kind of enthusiasm we would have if Rod Stewart or the Bee Gees were flying with us, we were pleased to welcome Ernie, whom we all remembered fondly.

When he boarded, Ernie took the aisle seat while the man traveling with him (who we learned was his long-time manager) sat in the window seat next to him. Right away, this told me that Ernie was approachable to his fans, and he reinforced this impression by greeting and shaking hands with some of the coach passengers as they filed past his seat. We offered Royal Service on the flight, which featured prestige catering in first class. Ernie was one of the most gracious and appreciative passengers I have ever served, full of compliments for the flight attendants, the service, and Delta Air Lines, in general. Once we cleared his tray table, he rose and walked into the coach cabin to chat with other passengers, after which he returned to first class and came to the galley with an unusual request. Some people he'd been talking to wondered if he could sing his signature song over the PA system. My friend Linda, the Flight Attendant in Charge, thought a minute, then said, "I don't see why not." Since she was busy catching up on her flight report, she asked me to escort Ernie to the front jumpseat. Once we sat down and I handed him the microphone, he seemed to go into another state of consciousness as he tapped his toe to an inner beat. Then, right on key, his beautiful, rich bass-baritone voice began the familiar lyrics of *Sixteen Tons*. I looked at him in awe, remembering those nights I watched him on the tiny screen of our living room TV, hardly able to comprehend that here he was, singing that iconic song while I sat right next to him. His voice transported me to the comfort of my childhood as I listened in a mild trance until enthusiastic applause throughout the airplane brought me back to the present.

Because we were nearing Atlanta, Linda said, "Mr. Ford, you should probably return to your seat now for landing."

"Is there any way I can sit here instead? I'd like to land backward once in my life."

Linda was hesitant, realizing this would be a blatant violation of FAA rules. Meanwhile, he looked at her with the childlike excitement of someone asking if he could ride a pony at the county fair. He must have melted her heart because she decided to grant his request and said with a sigh, "OK, I guess it will be all right." At a length of one hundred and eighty-seven feet, the Stretch DC-8 was sometimes challenging for pilots to put down gently. A gust of wind when the wheels were a few feet off the ground could ruin a perfect touchdown, and, unfortunately, this landing was less than stellar, with an uncomfortable hop followed by a hard thump onto the runway. After I made the taxi-in announcement, Ernie asked if he could say something, so I handed him the mic, expecting he might want to thank the passengers and crew for their hospitality. Instead, he took the opportunity to offer a somewhat backhanded compliment when he said, "I don't know about you folks, but I enjoyed both landings those pilots made. Bless their little pea-pickin' hearts."

Hmmm – maybe all those years, he had meant it the other way!

Buckle Up

The jumpseats used by flight attendants were designed by engineers for safety and functionality, definitely not for comfort! The folding contraptions sometimes mischievously whacked us in the butt when we stood up and required us women to glue our knees together if we wore a skirt and sat in one that faced passengers. These seats were more or less affectionately dubbed

"Sharon Stones," a reference to an infamous scene in the movie *Basic Instinct*. While I had always considered jumpseats awkward, I had never encountered a malicious one.

On the 727 aircraft, a set of retractable stairs allowed access through a rear door for ground personnel to service the inside of the plane. Attached to the inside of the door was a double flight attendant jumpseat. One day, I sat in this rear seat beside Ruby, a jovial super-senior flight attendant I enjoyed flying with because of her consistent upbeat attitude and excellent rapport with passengers. Just before we landed in Atlanta, we discussed the need to hit the ground running to make it to our next gate. With only fifty minutes between our arrival and the departure time of the next flight, it was a challenge to be ready to board passengers on time. "We'll probably come into A Concourse and go out of C like usual," Ruby commented. "It's always a hike."

When we pulled into the gate, I unfastened my seatbelt and shoulder harness to disengage the "girt bars" that attached the top of the slide to the floor. These metal pieces allowed the slide to inflate if the door opened—something you definitely didn't want to happen when the plane was parked at the gate. After I had done so, I noticed Ruby was struggling with the large round harness buckle at her waist.

"What's the matter?" I asked.

"I can't unfasten it," she replied as she jiggled the release lever back and forth.

"Let me see if I can get it from my angle." After trying for a minute, I couldn't budge it either.

By this time, cabin service personnel, who stood on the exterior stairs, pounded on the door for us to open it so they could begin their work. I cracked the door an inch and told them they would have to use the forward service door, then called the flight attendant in front and asked her to phone for help.

With the plane empty, I picked up trash and straightened the cabin. No rescuers had arrived, and as I looked back at Ruby, I suppressed a laugh at the absurdity of the sight. She sat with her arms folded, an uncustomary scowl on her face, securely attached to the door. Then, unexpectedly, the door pushed inward and almost squashed her against the wall as she yelled out. Two mechanics came on board with a wide assortment of tools to extricate her and began to work on the buckle. The other flight attendants and I reluctantly left her in this predicament and rushed to our next flight. As it turned out, the mechanics had to dismantle the buckle mechanism completely to free her. Even so, Ruby arrived at our outbound flight with a few minutes to spare, red-faced from her sprint and indignant that releasing her had necessitated unwanted body contact from the two men. This incident could have been tragic if it had happened during an emergency evacuation, but fortunately, it didn't. And none of the passengers on our new flight had any idea that the flight attendant with the big smile who chatted with them as she served drinks might have been forced to fly endlessly all over the system, strapped forever to that evil jumpseat!

Rock, Paper, Scissors

In pre-flight briefings, we decided who would work in each cabin, but once we determined this, there were only minor choices to make. "Do you want to make or take?" (set up meals or run them out). "Do you want to run or stuff?" (pick up dirty trays and carry them to the galley or put them in the meal carriers). We looked at the big picture, saw what needed to be done, and pitched in until we completed the job.

One afternoon, I discovered that this spirit of cooperation and intuitive communication was broader than I realized. Two of my flight attendant friends hosted a Christmas luncheon at one of their homes, and they invited about twenty-five coworkers to attend and bring an unwrapped toy to donate to a local nonprofit organization for its clients. Lunch consisted of various delectable salads served with an ample supply of wine. Afterward, as we all enjoyed our homemade tiramisu and idly chatted about our holiday plans in small groups, our hostesses announced it was time to wrap the gifts.

On the living room floor, next to the mound of toys, were rolls of gift wrap, spools of ribbon, stick-on bows, tape, scissors, and tags. We stood, stretched a little, and found a place on the floor, and, like magic, formed several assembly lines. No discussion, no "who's on which team?" or "Who'll do what?" Everyone found a spot, selected a job, and got to work. We wrapped the toys in no time, and when someone pointed out the ease and speed with which we accomplished the project, one of the guests laughed, "If a group of pilots were in charge, they'd still be arguing over whose seniority entitled them to use the scissors!"

Chapter Thirty

Even though Mom's first non-rev experience hadn't gone smoothly, it didn't deter her from using her pass privileges. She traveled frequently, sometimes meeting me on a layover if it was long enough to do some sightseeing. When she retired from her job at the orthopedic practice in Waterloo, she moved to Normal, Illinois. She felt it was wise to be near one of her daughters as she got older and correctly reasoned that Sandy was less likely to move. Mom's outgoing personality helped her quickly make friends who were always ready for fun activities, from eating at a favorite restaurant to taking day-long outings to explore new places. She volunteered at a hospital's reception desk and worked part-time at a credit agency for several years. Participating in these activities undoubtedly helped to keep her mind sharp.

Nevertheless, when Mom turned seventy, Sandy and I noticed early hints of memory impairment. At first, the lapses seemed simple absentmindedness—bills piled up on her desk, she didn't remember where she parked the car at the mall—but they gradually worsened. Not only did she lose track of her car, but she got lost driving home or drew a blank when asked about a recent event.

She repeated stories of things that happened in her childhood in vivid detail. "Did I ever tell you about our hired man on the farm? He returned from World War I with shell shock and couldn't bear to be around people. But my father hired him because he was excellent with horses." Yes, we'd heard that story over a hundred times and several others as well.

In stark contrast to her detailed stories of growing up, she had few memories of Dad. She didn't recall her move to North Carolina with Sandy to be near him at Fort Bragg during World War II, nor the return train trip to Iowa once he had deployed to Europe. She had no memories of family vacations or long-time friends from Waterloo. It was as if that part of her life had never happened. When asked where she lived before her move to Illinois, she looked puzzled. "I've always lived right here." Because we knew that people with dementia experience this pattern of memory loss, Sandy and I feared Mom might be suffering from this condition.

On one of my visits, I saw an alarming decline, probably more noticeable to me than to Sandy and Paul, because I didn't see her daily. It became clear that she could no longer live alone. As far back as Sandy and I could remember, Mom's instructions regarding her future had remained the same. When the time came that she could no longer be independent, she wanted to be "put out to pasture," a term Sandy and I inferred meant she did not want to go to a nursing home. I think she remembered the bleak sights and unpleasant smells that greeted her when, as a deacon of her church, she visited shut-in congregation members. She never wanted to be relegated to that kind of environment.

Sandy and Paul decided to have her move into their home so we could honor her wishes as long as possible. Though they anticipated this change would not be easy, they were unprepared for the significant disruptions in their lives—compromised privacy, increased planning in order to attend a meeting or social event. They were inveterate travelers and had left me in the dust years before with the number of places they had visited, but this kind of travel became impossible. That is until George came up with a plan to give them respite now and then. He suggested we use my pass privileges to fly Mom to Florida periodically for multi-week stays. When I pointed out that with my work schedule, he'd often need to oversee her care, he assured me he could handle it. Mom had liked George from their first meeting, though she sometimes called him "Bill." That didn't bother George at all. He was used to my making the same mistake now and then! George sometimes gently teased her, and she seemed to enjoy it, often coming up with a zinger response that made all of us laugh. I rolled my eyes in exasperation when Mom told her childhood stories. George listened patiently and attentively no matter how many times she repeated them.

We soon had our Florida-Illinois hand-off system down pat. Sandy and Paul drove Mom to O'Hare, checked her in for the flight, and waited for George and me to arrive from Ft. Lauderdale. Then George, Mom, and I non-revved on the next flight back. We reversed the process when we returned her to Illinois, sometimes renting a car and driving to Normal to spend a few days before we headed home.

Over the years that we shuttled Mom back and forth, there were surprisingly few glitches because I meticulously checked flights to be sure we would get on them. One time, though, things did not go smoothly when the three of us flew to Florida. The nonstop flight to Ft. Lauderdale from O'Hare was full, so we had to catch a connecting flight through Cincinnati, where one of those dreaded non-rev scenarios occurred. We arrived in Cincinnati to find that the Ft. Lauderdale flight had filled up, forcing us to run the entire length of the terminal to get on a flight to Miami, departing only ten minutes later. Mom was in a wheelchair, so while I raced ahead to get our boarding passes, George pushed Mom's chair as fast as he could for roughly a quarter mile. After that impressive feat of athleticism, George bragged that he held the record in his age bracket for 'The Fastest Time in the 400 Meters While Pushing 130 Pounds'.

As Mom's cognitive problems progressed, I found it increasingly challenging to maintain my patience and sometimes became so frustrated that I had mini meltdowns when George and I were alone in our bedroom. It was hard to accept that after being my caregiver, travel companion, confidante, and supporter (even when she thought my choices were wrong). She was the person who needed care now, and I was failing in that role.

"Why am I always so upset with her? I know she can't help it, but sometimes I want to scream."

"It's because you compare her to how she used to be," he responded. "You're not a horrible person for feeling the way you do. I have more patience because I have a little distance, not the lifetime of memories you have with her."

When I returned from a trip, he told me about their activities in my absence. Mom listened with great interest as if hearing about them for the first time. Sometimes, they ate out or went to a movie, although Mom never remembered what they saw. "That's OK," George said. "She enjoyed it while she watched it." Once or twice, he took her to the Davie rodeo, where he struggled to keep up as she trekked spryly across the parking lot toward the arena. However, it was unclear if she knew where she was.

There were times when she said the most unexpected things, as she did one evening when our friends Debbie and Dean were at our house for dinner. Out of the blue, Mom proudly announced, "I can stand on my head." We all looked at her in stunned silence until Dean said, "Well, I'd pay good money to see that." Mom chuckled along with us but, by this time, probably had no idea what we were laughing about.

One night, when I returned from a two-day trip, Mom was already in bed. "Something unusual happened tonight," George said.

I sat on the couch next to him. "Oh, no. What?" Visions of catastrophes filled my head.

"Nothing bad, just surprising. We were watching the news tonight, and there was footage of that blizzard in the Midwest.

I nodded. That storm had been responsible for a reroute on my trip.

"Your mom said, 'I'm sure glad I don't have to deal with that anymore.' I wasn't sure what she meant, so I said, 'No, you definitely don't have to worry about snow in Florida. Then she said, 'No, I mean when I used to fly all the time.'"

"What?" I asked, puzzled.

"When I said, 'Oh, you used to travel a lot?' she looked at me as if I were the stupidest person on earth and replied, 'Well, of course, I did when I flew for Delta.'"

"No way! What did you say?"

"I started to laugh but stopped when I saw she was dead serious, and I said, 'Marge, Kathi's the one who flies for Delta—you never worked for them.' She was indignant, and for a second, I thought she would take a swing at me. 'I most certainly did, and it was the happiest time of my life.' Somehow, I covered my astonishment, and when I said, 'Oh, sure, I'd forgotten about that,' she calmed down."

How did he become so wise? With his example, George taught me an essential lesson about dementia. There's no reason to correct someone's memory of a person or event. It doesn't matter if they have it wrong, and it only creates stress and more confusion when you tell them their recollection is incorrect. I guessed Mom combined her travel experiences, including when Sheila rescued her in Chicago, and her trips and layovers with me to produce the "memory" of being a flight attendant. We told Sandy and Paul about Mom's newly discovered past career. They found it amusing until one day, after their minister visited with Mom, he said, "I never knew your mother used to be a stewardess. I bet she has lots of stories." Yes, indeed!

Around that time, Delta was gearing up for the 1996 Atlanta Olympics. As the official air carrier, they planned to increase frequency on many routes. They considered calling back retired flight attendants to augment crews on the expected full flights. When I told a few of my friends about Mom's delusion of a flying career, most commented about how bad that must make me feel. Except Nina. "Say, maybe your mom could come back and help pour coffee," she said with mock seriousness. As I pictured that scene, I couldn't help but laugh.

As the years passed, it became more challenging to manage Mom's needs. With Sandy and Paul working, Mom was alone during the day except for Kelly, an energetic wire-haired fox terrier. They got along well, but one day, in her excitement at a ringing doorbell, Kelly accidentally scratched Mom's hand, which bled profusely. The caller at the door was a friend who had arrived to take Mom to lunch but instead called Paul to tell him about the accident. He came home immediately and took Mom to the emergency room. Other minor incidents occurred—an unexplained bruise on her leg and a carton of milk left on the counter all day—that made us realize Mom needed more supervision than we could provide. A friend of Sandy and Paul's who worked in the healthcare field helped us find a cheery-looking care facility that, we hoped, would not resemble the dismal setting she had dreaded all her life.

Other than complaining about "that other woman" (her roommate), Mom seemed to adjust well to her new environment. A photographer took Polaroid pictures of family groups during a Christmas party for the residents. Sandy posed with Mom, and when she saw the photograph, Mom pointed to Sandy's image and said, "There I am, but who is that standing next to me?"

Dementia is called "the long goodbye," and we did, in fact, lose Mom a little more every day. In the spring of 1996, she developed pneumonia and went to the hospital with a poor prognosis. George and I came to see her for what turned out to be the last time. When I entered her room, she greeted me cheerfully. "Would you like to look at a magazine?" she asked, ever the gracious hostess.

"No, Mom, I'm here to see you," I said, holding back tears. She died the next day, four days before her eighty-sixth birthday.

I was grateful I had not dealt with Mom's decline alone. George had been my rock as he helped me navigate the wild up and down emotions I experienced. He taught me so much in Mom's later years—how to savor the good days when things went smoothly and to remain sane and composed on those days when they didn't. His easy manner and loving patience demonstrated far better than any "how-to" book the best way to face the scourge of dementia. Little did I know I would need to use those lessons again only a few years later.

Chapter Thirty-one

After twenty-seven years in the air (was that possible?), I realized I had turned into a lotus eater like those in Homer's *Odyssey*, happily apathetic to changing my lifestyle. Long gone was the idea that I would fly for a couple of years before pursuing my life's "true work." I had a dream job; it was interesting, paid better than many other occupations, provided generous time off, and didn't even seem like work despite challenges from time to time. Why would I want to mess that up? I learned I was not alone in wondering if I'd thrown away the opportunity for a different career path. Many flight attendants had abandoned previous lofty goals—teaching, nursing, research, even medical school—in favor of a comfortable status quo.

I couldn't deny that every September, even after so many years, I felt a twinge of nostalgia for academic life. Sandy was a professor at Illinois State University in Normal. If one of my visits coincided with the start of the fall semester, I browsed the campus bookstore, leafed through the psychology textbooks, and wondered if I had made a mistake in not pursuing a field I had fallen in love with during my first year of college. But in the wake of those musings, I'd have a layover where I attended a Broadway matinee, got in for free at a popular Las Vegas nightclub show, or strolled the beach in San Juan, and my desire for change would vanish. Then, by chance, I flew with someone who would soon complete her master's degree in mental health counseling at Florida Atlantic University in nearby Boca Raton. As she spoke glowingly of the faculty and the program's quality, the feelings I thought had drowned in a sea of contentment suddenly broke the surface and refused to dive back down.

"How do you manage to go to classes and fly, too?" I asked her as we took a short break in the galley. I had always told myself that flying and completing a degree were incompatible. She gave me a "you've got to be kidding me" look and said, "With your seniority, you can easily arrange your trips to make it work. All the classes are during the week, so you'll probably have to fly on weekends, but it's a small sacrifice to accomplish a goal that's important to you. When did you first know you wanted to pursue a counseling career?" *Oh my, she's good!*

After I reflected on her comments, I still wasn't sold on the idea but decided to discuss it with George. "I may not want to fly until I drop," I told him. "It would be great to have another career ready to go when the time comes."

As I expected, he said, "Do whatever will make you happy. You always have my support."

Because my friend spoke so highly of the program at Florida Atlantic, I investigated the course of study there and the requirements for admission, one of which was passing the GRE (Graduate Record Exam). I had achieved a less-than-stellar score on the exam when I took it during my senior year of college. While I had done well on the verbal part of the test, I failed the math section miserably, and my skill in that area had certainly not improved in the intervening years. I had only two months to prepare before the next testing date.

If I was going to pass, I needed to give my full attention to preparation. Instead of socializing on my layovers, I toiled over test preparation manuals and re-taught myself basic arithmetic and then advanced algebra. The hard work felt exhilarating as I used my brain in uncustomary ways. It paid off. I passed the test on the first try. Florida Atlantic University accepted me into its M.Ed. program in Mental Health Counseling. Ahead of me lay a grueling sixty-credit-hour program with two practicums and an internship, but now I was determined to fulfill the promise I had made years earlier to acquire an advanced degree and embark on a new career when the time came.

I felt ready for the course of study that lay ahead. I'd always loved to listen to people's stories, and my obvious interest drew them in, particularly if they faced a problem or difficult choice. It was easier to help others avoid pitfalls than to stay clear of them myself! However, I needn't have felt so unique. On the airplane, I was no different from a bartender, priest, or hair stylist in their milieus. In an era with few options to connect with others—no anonymous chat rooms, no online self-help groups—people turned to resources nearby when they had to let off steam or work through a thorny issue.

I had listened to hundreds of problems when flying with coworkers. So had others. The interaction was so common that it earned the nickname "jumpseat therapy." Forced physical proximity tended to break down communication barriers. Who better to understand what a fellow flight attendant was dealing with than someone who might have struggled with a similar situation? I remembered how instrumental such conversations had been in my decision to leave my first husband.

But these discussions weren't confined to my coworkers. Sometimes, a passenger would approach me in the galley, especially on long flights. "Could I ask you something?" they might say, sensing my willingness to listen, and they always found an empathetic ear. While I sometimes gave in to the impulse to be "Dear Abby" (here's what *I'd* do), for the most part, I asked questions that helped them crystallize their own thinking.

I was glad I didn't know what was in store for me one winter afternoon on a full flight to Dallas. While we waited to depart Ft. Lauderdale, Dispatch informed our pilots that DFW operations were shutting down because heavy snowfall was accumulating faster than ground crews could plow it. Air traffic control delayed our takeoff so they could slot us in for a landing when the airport reopened. However, once we neared our destination with no let-up in the weather, we spent another hour in a holding pattern. Just as the pilots considered asking permission to divert to another airport, they received clearance to land. But that was only the start of what turned into a hellish marathon. Departing planes needed de-icing before heading to the runway. Usually, the de-icing process was routine, with mechanics towing aircraft to an area expressly set up for the procedure. However, due to the heavy snowfall, planes had to remain at their gates far longer than usual, resulting in fifteen or more aircraft on the ground with no place to go. The cumulative result for us was that the journey from Ft. Lauderdale to Dallas, which should have taken three hours, took nine, nearly five of which were spent on the ground after we landed. We could have been in London in that length of time!

The hours dragged on as we waited for our turn to pull into a gate. We wanted to offer passengers beverages, but they milled about the cabin, which made it impossible to pull a cart into the aisle. To help ease the frustration and pass the time, I parked the cart near the rear galley and set it up like a bar where passengers could line up to order drinks. But it turned into more than that, and I wished I had a sign like Lucy Van Pelt's in *Peanuts*: Psychiatric Advice 5¢. Besides asking for beverages, many passengers vented irritation, fear, and indignation at this unprecedented delay. The crew did their best to keep the mood as calm and stress-free as possible while, at the same time, controlling the level of alcohol consumption.

Our efforts almost unraveled when, after four hours of waiting, a passenger noticed a plane moving ahead of us on the left side. "What's up?" he asked angrily. The captain came on the PA. "Folks, you may have seen another Delta airplane going past us. It has a passenger with a medical emergency and is being cleared to a just-vacated gate. We're still waiting." A cacophony of shouts erupted. "Hey, I've got a medical emergency, too." "I'll knock someone's teeth out if that's what it takes to move." A passenger entered the galley and eyed the emergency exit. "I've got to get out of here," he yelled.

The Flight Attendant in Charge was in first class and didn't hear the commotion, so I picked up the mic. "Ladies and gentlemen, everyone is tired and frustrated about this delay. Your flight attendants are, too. We share your desire to get off this plane as soon as we can, but the ability to do that is out of our hands. Please understand that if you create a dangerous situation on the plane, your behavior will result in legal problems for you and further delay for everyone else when we reach a gate. Let us know what we can do to make you as comfortable as possible, and we'll all get through this together." The grumbling died down, and some passengers thanked me for defusing the more belligerent comments and behavior.

At one point, I noticed a man standing a short distance away, observing me as I served beverages from my makeshift bar/ counseling booth and chatted with passengers. When the line finally tapered down, he hesitantly approached me. "This delay has my head spinning," he said. "I like how you're able to calm people down. Do you have a few minutes to talk?"

"Of course."

"I didn't want to be on this flight, but my dad is in the hospital, and the doctors don't expect him to make it much longer. Even though he and I haven't spoken in years, I felt a need to come to Dallas to see him. But now, with this delay, I'm scared I might be too late to talk to him. And the weird thing is, I don't even know what I want to say."

His emotions were all over the map—guilt, anger, disappointment, self-reproach, regret. We talked intermittently, interrupting our "session" several times as I continued my duties with other passengers. I asked gently probing questions and reflected his answers back to him for clarification. By the time we pulled into the gate, he had realized that the cause of the father-son rift was ancient history, and he wished he had not let it fester for so long. He truly loved his father, would miss him, and prayed it would not be too late to tell him. He shook my hand and said, "I can't thank you enough." I felt emotionally drained but grateful I could help him.

Occasionally, on other flights, passengers exhibited telltale signs of fear. Some sat rigidly in their seats with their eyes shut tight; some clung to the armrest for dear life (as I had always done—and still did occasionally); some ordered drink after drink. All shared one wish: to be somewhere else, even in a dentist's chair, having all their teeth pulled. I understood what they felt— the pervasive fear that logic could not penetrate. Sometimes, I said quietly, "You're doing great," or "You should be proud of yourself."

Often, they looked shocked that apparently I could read their minds but grateful that someone understood their misery. "How do you do this for a living?" they sometimes asked. "Aren't you ever afraid?"

I flashed a conspiratorial smile and said, "When I've finished my service, I'll come back and let you in on a little secret."

Chapter Thirty-two

I should have thought through my educational goals more carefully. I understood it would be difficult to introduce school into *my* life, but I didn't realize how much of an impact it would have on my partner. My pursuit deprived George of vacations, short getaways, and even spur-of-the-moment movies or dinners out if I had to make a presentation the following day, but he never complained. He was proud of me and encouraged me to continue toward my goal even when I thought I would never achieve a balance between work, school, and home life. "There's an end to this," he said, "and we'll be able to return to a more normal life after you graduate."

George was right. I did learn to juggle multiple balls until one of them tossed me a nasty curve that I never saw coming and knocked me to the ground. One late afternoon, George was in a rush hour traffic jam on Federal Highway in Ft. Lauderdale, a busy thoroughfare he traveled daily. As he turned off to the west, the angle and intensity of the sun nearly blinded him. While he was stopped at a traffic light, George suddenly lost strength in both arms and felt disoriented and nauseous, and when the light turned green, he couldn't budge. Frustrated drivers honked and yelled at him, which intensified his confusion. Thankfully, a good Samaritan exited his vehicle, helped George move his car safely to the shoulder of the road, and, when George refused the man's offer to call an ambulance, stayed with him until he felt better.

When George got home, he told me about the incident in detail. "I could hear everyone yelling, and I remember thinking, 'Shut up! You try driving when your arms don't move.'" I was concerned he might have suffered a stroke, but he rebuffed my pleas to go to the emergency room and offered an alternative explanation for what had happened.

He had recently made yet another job change. Instead of selling extended warranty programs to car dealerships, he started working for a business that supplied marine after-market products to boat dealers. His vast territory—Lake Okeechobee to Key West—required him to spend long, tiring days in the car. He attributed the incident to fatigue and not taking time to eat lunch. With no further problems, we regarded the occurrence as an anomaly and forgot about it.

But a few months later, he had another worrisome experience when we visited his family in Ohio for Thanksgiving. As we changed into our non-revving clothes for our flight home, he said, "I don't know what's wrong, but I can't tie my tie. I'm all thumbs, and I can't remember how to get it started."

A sense of dread came over me, but I maintained an upbeat tone. "It's been a busy weekend. Maybe you're just tired," I said, knowing my husband wore a tie almost every day and had never had a problem. He could do it in his sleep. He kept trying without success until, in frustration, he flung the tie on the floor. I didn't know what to do until I spotted our new digital camera sitting on a chair beside the bed. "You've been taking a lot of pictures the last few days. Let's look at what you shot."

Looking over my shoulder, he saw his mom stuffing the turkey, everyone smiling at the dinner table, and his nieces and nephews playing Parchesi on the floor. He laughed out loud at his brother snoozing in front of the TV, oblivious that the Lions were trouncing the Bears. "Hey, I'm a damn good photographer," he declared, casually picking up his tie from the floor and tying a perfect half-Windsor knot.

If these incidents weren't strange enough, he had episodes of erratic speech, or he would struggle to find the word he wanted, which was uncharacteristic of someone as articulate as he.

We talked about the adverse effects his work seemed to be having on his health. "The money's too good. I can't give it up for something else," he protested.

"Baby, the job is killing you."

I was relieved when George decided, reluctantly, to give up his marine accounts and return to the car business, even though I remembered that the unreliability of sales commissions made managing finances more difficult. However, it soon became apparent that his outgoing personality and enthusiasm, qualities that had always made him a top salesman, were gradually diminishing.

He would come home upset and disappointed. "I was sure I had a deal in the bag, but when I was about to close, they walked away." His strength had always been establishing rapport with customers quickly and putting them at ease; I had only to remember my first contact with him to know that was true. But now, with his hesitant speech and mispronunciation of words, customers possibly believed he was drunk and disappeared. He agonized over how to get his "mojo" back. In 1998, after four months as a new car salesman at an Acura store, the dealership let him go for failing to achieve his monthly sales goals. No one had ever fired him, and both of us were shocked and distraught. It took much coercion and reasoning, but I convinced him to see a neurologist. "Maybe there's a simple explanation for your difficulties, and there might be a solution. Don't you want to try to find out?"

Numerous tests—a CT scan and MRI of the brain, EEG, carotid ultrasound, and a complete metabolic blood study—failed to illuminate the problem, so the doctor ordered a neuropsycho-logical evaluation. This is a battery of tests that assesses general intellect and several other areas of brain functioning. It takes several hours to complete and can be stressful, even for people not experiencing neurological problems. George gave up before he finished the entire series. "These tests make me feel stupid!" he declared, frustrated beyond his limit. Based on the results of the portions George did complete, the examiner saw "a pattern of diffuse cerebral impairment."

Over the next fourteen months, four other car dealerships hired and fired him—each time for his inability to generate sales and properly complete paperwork. On a subsequent visit to his neu-rologist, we heard the "A" word as a possible diagnosis. I could not accept that a healthy fifty-six-year-old man had Alzheimer's disease. Not my fifty-six-year-old man, at any rate. But the signs were there; he was confused about which drawer his underwear was in and how to operate the Nokia cell phone he had been using for over a year. I noticed he was not progressing in a book and realized he was probably reading the same pages repeatedly.

One day, as we walked through the mall, George spotted a "help-wanted" sign on the door of a small furniture store and, to my astonishment, stepped in and spoke to the manager. "I need a job, and I've had years of sales experience, but I'm dealing with some memory problems that make it hard to concentrate. If you give me a chance, I'll work my tail off for you." The manager was moved by George's determination and hired him to greet customers and help them find what they needed, but didn't require him to complete paperwork, which would have been nearly impossible for him. After two weeks on the job, George handed me an envelope. "My first paycheck," he said proudly. Unfortunately, although this branch store was doing well, the national company was not and was forced to file for bankruptcy, leaving George unemployed again and despondent.

The cruel irony of the situation did not escape me. This man, who had been such a source of strength when I dealt with Mom's dementia and who had always been patient and kind to her, suffered the same terrible condition. I wasn't sure where to direct my anger, at the universe or at George himself. This was not our plan. Why couldn't he snap out of it and return to normal? Then, the shame of these self-centered thoughts, the same ones I had felt about Mom, overwhelmed me. Had I set this in motion by spending less time with him? I couldn't shake this thought.

A requirement of my master's degree program was to undergo counseling to experience what it's like to be on the receiving end. I had learned some cognitive therapy interventions in my class work that should have been effective in managing the anger and guilt I felt but failed to help. It didn't work to wear both hats—client and therapist—at the same time. Yet, when my therapist suggested specific techniques to me, I wanted to scream, "Don't you think I've already tried that?" I turned to support groups but found no help from them either. I didn't fit neatly into either category of participants—adults my age dealing with parents or much older people dealing with much older spouses. A common refrain was, "He's too young to have dementia." My old friend, jumpseat therapy, had the same limitations because no one could fully relate to my situation.

I switched from flying multiple-day trips to turnarounds on Delta Express, a subsidiary of Delta that offered service between South Florida and the two New York airports, which allowed me to be home at least part of each day. It wasn't long before I recognized that even this change wasn't enough. George needed supervision the whole time I was gone. He often forgot to eat the lunches I left for him, but, more concerning, he had become uncharacteristically clumsy, and I feared he might hurt himself.

I faced a quandary that many parents deal with—pay for daycare to continue a career or stop working to be at home. With few cash reserves, I had no choice but to continue working, so I managed to find a hybrid solution. Delta's highly flexible work parameters allowed me to fly minimum hours while bringing in a reduced paycheck. I hired aides from a home healthcare agency (with money I didn't have) to stay with him on the two days a week I flew, and they remained until I got home in the evening. George hated having these workers in the house and told one of them, "You can go home. I don't need a babysitter." I gained his cooperation by telling him a little white lie (or maybe it wasn't). "I could be in serious trouble with the authorities if someone reports me for not looking out for your safety and well-being."

"You always take care of me," he replied, "and I don't want you to get in trouble." His compliance touched me, reluctant though it was, because I knew that he still watched out for me even in his diminished mental state.

The weather was sunny and mild on December 15, 2000, when I walked into an FAU auditorium to receive my diploma thirty years after I last wore a cap and gown. I needed to attend a pre-commencement reception, so my friends Debbie and Janie brought George to the ceremony. I only wished he could fully appreciate what his sacrifices and support had enabled me to accomplish.

One week later, as if to bring us crashing to earth after a temporary respite, we received the devastating news that George's mother, whom he adored, had passed away. Margie had been diagnosed with Stage 4 liver cancer two years before. Her condition seemed to improve after surgery and several rounds of chemotherapy. George's stepfather had kept the news of her latest setback from us, believing she would pull through, so the news came as a shock. George was inconsolable. When we returned from Margie's funeral in Ohio, George's sorrow left him deeply depressed. I was not faring very well, either. I felt anxious about what lay ahead and whether I could prevent our financial situation from plummeting over a cliff again. However, I couldn't share my concerns with George, which was one of the saddest changes in our relationship. Ever since his lack of forthrightness had created the foreclosure debacle early in our marriage, we had always told each other everything—fears, joys, hopes, wild ideas—but now, with his diminished cognitive and emotional status, we could no longer do so. I yearned for the man I had fallen in love with, the one with the wicked sense of humor, who enjoyed music that ranged from Bach to the Beatles, whose taste was impeccable when he chose clothes for me, who loved to cook, who was ready to go on an adventure at a moment's notice. I had vowed to love George for better or worse. Still, I struggled to feel the same about his replacement, even though I had to accept that the original would never return.

On a Tuesday morning the following September, I left George in front of the TV watching *The Today Show* while I drove a few blocks to the Publix grocery store to pick up food for the coming week. When I walked from the garage into the kitchen and set the groceries on the counter. George called to me, "An airplane crashed into a building."

"What?" Had he somehow switched the channel and landed on an old movie? *Con Air*? *King Kong*? But as I walked into the living room, I saw the TV screen. There, to my horror, I saw what he was talking about. Matt Lauer and Katie Couric spoke by phone to an eyewitness who described what we saw on the screen—vast clouds of black smoke billowing from a hideous gash in a skyscraper. An airplane had crashed into one of the twin towers of the World Trade Center in New York City. Speculation ran wild. Was it a private or commuter plane? The enormity of the gaping hole made that doubtful. But how could a commercial or military aircraft stray so far off course? It was a cloudless, lovely late summer day in New York and, for that matter, the entire Eastern United States.

Less than five minutes after I sat down, eyes glued to the TV, another airplane, caught on camera circling the scene, crashed into the second tower. I couldn't breathe. These were not accidents but intentional depraved acts of unimaginable scale.

As the newscast played the horrible scene on a loop, I could not move nor look away. Thirty minutes after the second plane exploded into the tower, news came that another commercial aircraft had crashed into the Pentagon in Washington, D.C. Simultaneously, there were unconfirmed reports that a fourth aircraft, possibly a Delta flight en route from Boston to Los Angeles, had been hijacked and was also headed to Washington, most likely to strike the Capitol or the White House. We soon learned that this flight was not a Delta plane but United Flight 93, which had been taken over by terrorists but, because of the actions of brave passengers and crew, dived nose-first to the ground in rural Pennsylvania instead of the terrorists' intended target. In addition, there were reports that a half dozen aircraft were unaccounted for. In a strategy to pinpoint other rogue planes, the FAA announced it had closed all the nation's air space and had directed every aircraft still in the sky to land immediately at the nearest airport. Planes that did not comply would be subject to military intervention.

George and I had not spoken for over an hour when he voiced his primary concern, "You're not going to fly anymore, are you?" Was I? This situation fed into my deep-rooted fears about the dangers of airline travel, so I wasn't sure how I felt. I squeezed his hand. "We'll have to see what happens."

In consideration of George's worsening condition, I had been trying for two years to secure Social Security disability for him. Unfortunately, I had encountered only roadblocks, delays, and ineptitude on the government side. The effort had become, without question, the most frustrating process I had ever experienced. I spent hundreds of hours writing letters, making phone calls to anyone I thought could help, submitting paperwork, and meeting with the local Social Security office and the VA. After his claim was denied twice despite letters from three of his doctors that, in their opinion, he could not do work of any kind, I nearly gave up.

In a final effort to obtain the benefits to which George was entitled, I hired a disability attorney who succeeded in scheduling a hearing before an administrative law judge in October 2002. Hoping to manage our expectations, the attorney warned us not to expect a decision on the spot and said it could take several weeks or months for the judge to make a ruling. Much to our surprise, the judge reprimanded the Social Security attorney at the end of the hearing with a firm statement. "You should have settled this at the first filing," he said, trying to control his displeasure. "I have seen few cases in my career that are more cut and dried."

He awarded George twenty-five months of retroactive benefits and ordered monthly payments to begin immediately. I was relieved we had finally prevailed, but fresh heartbreak awaited us.

Chapter Thirty-three

A loud thud from the bathroom jolted me awake. It was the middle of the night, but since I rarely slept soundly anymore, I had heard George get out of bed a few minutes earlier. I opened the door and found him lying on the floor, his limbs jerking in a seizure. I was terrified, but remembering my first aid training, I pulled a towel off the rack, pillowed his head to keep it from banging into the tile floor, retrieved my cell phone from the nightstand, and called 911. When I finished the call, his seizure had subsided, but he appeared to be unconscious. I saw red flashing lights and ran to the front door to let in the EMTs. As the two men lifted him onto the gurney, George cried out in pain.

At the hospital, an MRI revealed that George's left shoulder had sustained multiple fractures. However, it was unclear if the seizure was the cause of his fall or the result of it. I was uneasy when the ER doctor recommended calling in an orthopedic surgeon. While I didn't want George to be in pain, I feared that the anesthesia might worsen his mental damage. When I explained this, the doctor conceded that a conservative approach was the best option, at least for the time being, and fitted him with a casing that immobilized his shoulder. "This is not a substitute for surgery," the doctor warned. "But let's give him a little time to recover from the trauma."

It was the Sunday before Thanksgiving, and I had turnarounds on my schedule for the next two days. The combination of flying and caregiving had already proven nearly impossible. But, now I realized I couldn't work at all with this new development. I called my supervisor's home phone number to discuss my options. She was incredibly sympathetic and assured me I could take the time I needed to deal with the crisis. "Your job will be waiting for you when you can come back to work." With this worry removed, I couldn't have felt more fortunate to work for Delta.

The hospital released George the day before Thanksgiving even though, despite the efforts of a physical therapist, he was unable to walk and had to go home in an ambulance. His hospitalist ordered a medical supply company to deliver a hospital bed and a Hoyer lift to the house. Before leaving the hospital, I had arranged for two private duty nurses, both named Stewart, to begin twelve-hour shifts at our home starting the day after Thanksgiving, an arrangement made possible only because of funds from George's disability award.

From the onset of George's problems, friends had rallied to help me in whatever capacity I needed them. Two of my closest friends, Debbie and Cindy, were always willing to drop everything when I called on them. Debbie was hosting a big Thanksgiving dinner at her house the next day, but even so, she came to help. It was almost midnight when the delivery truck finally arrived. Once the driver set up the bed in the living room, Debbie and I used the Hoyer lift to move George into it.

Thankfully, Debbie decided to spend the rest of the night in the guest room, and I pulled the recliner beside George so he knew I was near him. He dozed but repeatedly woke up in a panic, unsure of where he was. I kissed his cheek and told him he was at home, but I wasn't sure he understood, even though he seemed calmer when I spoke comforting words. He was nonverbal except when he called out my name, which he mispronounced as "Katty." The day crept by after Debbie left the next morning to prepare for her guests. Holiday be damned, I kicked myself for not asking the Stewarts to start until the day after Thanksgiving, unaware of how difficult it would be to manage George's needs by myself. I was afraid to leave his side even to go to the bathroom. When Daytime Stewart arrived Friday morning and took charge, I felt immeasurable relief, and later, I got a decent night's sleep because Nighttime Stewart watched over George. While there was no improvement in George's condition, it hadn't worsened either. But the status quo shattered nine days after he came home from the hospital. As I fed George some chocolate pudding, which he seemed to enjoy, he suddenly became irate and spit it out. His previously indiscernible speech became a spate of swear words, loud and clear. Daytime Stewart tried to calm him down, but this only increased George's agitation. I placed another 911 call, and again, we rushed him to the hospital. Once in his room and sedated, George reached for my hand and spoke in a voice so low I could hardly hear, "Sorry."

A speech therapist determined that George's swallow reflex was compromised and that he was in danger of aspirating food. After the hospitalist examined George, he quietly asked me to step into the hallway. "We need to insert a feeding tube," he said authoritatively. I was stunned and felt too overwhelmed to respond.

"I need to think about it," I managed to say.

The exasperated hospitalist replied, "Well, you can't let him starve to death."

With that horrible indictment ringing in my ears, I went to my car and broke down in convulsive sobs. I had overcome a lot of adversity in my life, but this situation affected not just me but the man I loved. There was only one person I trusted to give me the advice I desperately needed. I headed to the office building of Dr. Roth, our primary care doctor. Without an appointment or phone call, I walked into his office and asked the receptionist if

I could speak to him. She said, "I'll check," and returned a few seconds later. "The doctor is almost finished with a patient, and then he'll be with you."

Dr. Roth had received reports and clinical notes on George's current hospitalization and looked them over as I blurted out, "They want to put a feeding tube in, and I don't know what to do." Dr. Roth said gently, "Here is what I suggest. Ask the hospitalist if he can assure you that a feeding tube will prevent George from developing aspiration pneumonia. Ask him if the procedure will make George more comfortable and restore him to better health. If he's honest, he will answer 'no' to all those questions. A feeding tube has its own risks. It can cause pain and bloating, it can become blocked, and it doesn't always prevent pneumonia. If George can't tolerate it, they may need to physically restrain or sedate him to keep him from dislodging it."

"Will he die if I refuse the tube?"

"Possibly. However, the feeding tube is only part of the issue. The progression of the disease is in its end stage, so you need to be prepared. Did the two of you discuss what to do if this situation arose?"

When George and I had been married for about ten years, we had "the talk." Each of us felt that quality of life was more important than quantity (which was easy to say when we were in our 40s, healthy, and felt like we would have many long years together). We did not want doctors to take extraordinary measures to prolong a hopeless condition. Our conversation so many years ago had come to mind only a few days earlier. Daytime Stewart propped George up in a cushioned chair, and we listened to Motown music, which George enjoyed enough to attempt a

Diana Ross hand gesture as *Stop! In the Name of Love* played. His smile suddenly disappeared, and he said, clearly and distinctly, "I don't want to live like this."

Stewart and I exchanged glances. Had we heard that?

Tears stung my eyes as I struggled to keep my voice steady, "I know you don't, Baby. This must be so hard for you." We had made a promise to each other, and now I had to keep it.

Dr. Roth put his hand on my shoulder. "The hospitalist's goal is to save George, but that may not be realistic nor meet George's needs or wishes. I see hospice as the best option, but it's up to you. Few things are more difficult than facing a situation like this. Do you have a friend or relative who can support you when you discuss this with the hospitalist?"

"Yes, I know just who to call," I replied. "Thank you so much for helping George and me through this."

Back in the car, I called my friend Cindy. She didn't know George well, and I wanted someone calm and objective to be with me. She agreed to meet me in the hospital lobby, where I told her that the time had come to put George in hospice. Cindy walked by my side as I approached the hospitalist. He glanced up from a computer at the nurses' station as I nervously told him my decision, "I'm not going to have a feeding tube put in."

Arms folded, he did not take my refusal well, saying, "Well, I don't know what you expect me to do then."

I began to cry.

"She wants to discuss putting her husband in hospice care. Please call someone to talk to her about that," Cindy said firmly.

The doctor waved his hand in dismissal and walked away. A nearby nurse said kindly, "Please sit in the family lounge, and I'll call someone to talk with you."

After reviewing George's chart and discussing his prognosis with me, a social worker made the necessary arrangements, and an ambulance took George to a nearby hospital with a hospice unit. I was immediately relieved to see that, unlike his previous room's sterile, cold atmosphere, the hospice room looked like an actual bedroom with pale yellow walls, a bright quilt, and cheerful window curtains. I, too, took up residence in the room, leaving only occasionally to take care of things at home.

Friends called, checking in to see how we were holding up; a few visited. Things were the same as ever at work. One coworker raved about the made-on-the-spot pasta dish she had enjoyed in the employee cafeteria at the Dallas/Ft. Worth airport. "I asked the chef for the recipe, and I'll give you a copy." Another gave me details of a nasty confrontation between two passengers about who "owned" the overhead bin above their seats. "I thought we were going to have to call airport security." A third had scored an autograph from George Clooney, her idol. These conversations simultaneously encouraged and depressed me. They reminded me of how much I missed being on the airplane, where even the most challenging circumstances paled in comparison to what I was dealing with now. Sometimes, I tried to cheer myself up by remembering funny incidents I'd had on my flights. One always made me laugh no matter how down I felt...

"What would you like to drink?" I asked.

"What do you have?"

Wearily, I listed the long list of choices. "Coke, Diet Coke, Sprite, Diet Sprite, ginger ale, club soda, tonic water, orange juice, apple juice, tomato juice, Bloody Mary mix, coffee, tea, and water."

"Do you have Dr. Pepper?'

"No, only the drinks I just told you."

"OK. I guess I'll have root beer."

But most of the time, I sat beside George, studying his face to see if there was any sign of awareness of his condition. I would talk to him. "We had a bad thunderstorm last night. Did you hear it?" "I don't think Gene (George's nurse) is here today. He must have the day off." Sometimes, I thought I saw a glimmer of understanding in his eyes, and I started to have second thoughts about what I was doing. What if, somewhere deep inside, he understood his situation and, while unable to voice or indicate objection, disagreed with the decisions I made? But misgivings aside, I knew I was doing what he would choose for himself or for me if I were in his place.

As days turned into weeks, there was no change in George's condition, and my residence in his room seemed surreal. I found myself wishing for this to be over and then mentally whipping myself. The only way for this to be over was for him to die. Is that what I wished for? Was I ready to lose him, despite the circumstances?

Three days before Christmas, eighteen days after George transferred to hospice, I felt strongly compelled to go home for a while after dinner. Sandy, Paul, and Paul's mother were due to arrive the next day, and even though they would understand a neglected house, I wanted to clean it at least a little bit. But it was more than that; I couldn't bear the constant sadness as I watched George slowly slip away, and I needed to flee, if only for an hour or two. Most of the regular hospice staff had taken time off for the holidays, Gene included. In Gene's absence, a very young woman I had not seen before, who looked more like a candy striper than a registered nurse, came to check on George. When I asked if she thought it was all right for me to leave for an hour or two, she assured me it was and promised to call me immediately if things changed.

Once at home, I put sheets on the guest room beds, robotically ran the vacuum, and cleaned the bathrooms. I was about to go back to the hospital when the phone rang. I recognized the young nurse's voice. "I think it's time for you to come back."

As I hurried down the hall toward George's room, a different nurse, one I had seen before, met me in the hallway. She put her arm around my waist and told me George had passed away a short time before I arrived. I walked into his room, sat next to his bed, and stroked his arm, a gesture that always seemed to comfort him but now comforted me. The young nurse who had been there earlier was nowhere to be seen, and part of me will always wonder if she was real. Perhaps her sole purpose was to help him make the passage because it seemed he did not want me to witness his final breath.

I waited at George's bedside for an hour until the funeral home personnel took him away from me. Even after they left, I stayed on, took in the details of what George saw in his last moments, and then gathered our items. Back home, I knew I couldn't sleep, so I busied myself with more chores. Had I dusted the fan blades in each bedroom? Did the kitchen sink need a good scour? A few hours later, I gave in, lay down on top of the comforter, turned out the light, and tried to drift off, but my mind refused to rest as thoughts swirled through my head. Our battle was over. I had survived but would never be the same again. What had I done right? What had I done wrong? How much suffering had he endured and been unable to express, this man for whom conversation had been such a pleasure? Or was he even aware of his circumstances? And the most crucial unanswerable question, where was he now?

I spoke in the darkness, "I just wish I knew you were OK."

Subtly at first and then more pronounced, I detected a distinctive aroma. Recently, George had suffered a bout of oral thrush, and I thought back to seeing Gene gently swab George's mouth with a medication that smelled like bananas. George seemed to enjoy the taste of it, and his face looked relaxed and peaceful. As the fragrance of bananas grew stronger, I believed George was communicating by the same method that had proven successful with Emily years before—scent.

"All right, Baby; all right then."

How could I celebrate the George everyone loved? I found the life-size cardboard cutout of a Wurlitzer jukebox we used for Rewind Entertainment gigs and brought it to the funeral home. In front of it, I put a pair of his cowboy boots and a favorite cowboy hat, homage to the Joe Diffie song, *Prop Me Up Against the Jukebox When I Die*. George had always joked that it was the perfect song to play at his funeral. I couldn't bring myself to go that far, but I did play it at home after the service, where a group of close friends raised their glasses in a toast to him.

At the service, I told the story of how we had met and how, years later, George recalled the momentous day while we walked hand in hand along the beach one morning. He stopped, took both my hands, looked into my eyes, and said, "When I saw you walk into my office, I thought you looked like an angel." He paused as he waited for me to reply. After an awkward silence, he asked hesitantly, "Did anything about me catch your eye?"

"Well," I said, "I did notice how attractive your hair was."

He let out one of the loud, uninhibited laughs I loved so much. "If only I'd known you liked it, you could have taken it home."

Before and after the memorial service, Sandy, Paul, and Paul's mother stayed at the house with me, while Chris, Michelle, and George's other family members stayed at a nearby hotel. Paul had an unusual visual experience that stunned him the morning after the service. As he stepped out of the shower in the small guest bathroom, he turned on the hot water in the sink and prepared to shave. For some reason, his mind strayed to a vacation we had all taken together to the Black Hills several years before

George's problems began. On our return trip across South Dakota to Illinois, George requested that we drive through Pine Ridge, an Oglala-Lakota reservation, because he always wanted to see all aspects of Native American history and culture, even the sad ones. Paul remembered how George had stood respectfully at the Wounded Knee monument in the small reservation cemetery as colorful prayer ties on the chain link fence fluttered in the hot breeze.

As Paul stared at his reflection in the mirror, he thought he saw an image formed in the steam—an Indian chief in a full-feathered headdress. Not believing his eyes and remembering the skepticism that met him and me when we saw the "creature" on Hawk Channel years before, he decided not to mention it. But when the image reappeared the following morning, he called his mother, Sandy, and me in and asked if we could see it. We saw it too. On the third morning, the image had vanished. George had said a final goodbye to us.

It wasn't until everyone went home over the next few days that I felt true loneliness set in. My supervisor assured me I didn't need to return to work immediately, but I needed to be busy. I flew some Delta Express turnarounds to LaGuardia, where nothing had changed. Passengers still complained about short delays and receiving only a bag of peanuts. They left the usual mess in the cabin despite the flight attendants' frequent strolls up and down the aisle with trash bags. These irksome behaviors gave me a sense of normalcy that was absent at home. Even so, I found it easy to stay inside my head and mourn the loss of *my* person, the one I found after so many false starts, the one I learned to trust implicitly, who never changed how he felt about or treated me from the day we met. Even though we were allowed eighteen years together, it wasn't enough. I had lost the two most important men in my life way too soon—Dad at age fifty-seven and George at fifty-nine.

In the following weeks between trips, I turned to tasks I needed to take care of—notifying insurance companies, sorting George's clothes for charity, and removing his name from bank accounts. One day, I stopped by the gym where we had exercised together until his fall and approached the front desk where a muscular young attendant stood.

"I need to cancel my husband's membership,"

"Was there a problem?" he asked with concern.

"He died a couple of weeks ago," I responded and wished I didn't have to provide this information, yet again, to a total stranger.

"Oh, I'm sorry," he replied, looking down quickly to avoid my gaze.

I gave him George's gym ID card, and he filled out a cancellation form, which he then handed me to sign. I noticed that under "reason," he wrote "past away," but I decided not to point out the misspelling.

Two weeks later, an envelope addressed to George with the gym's return address arrived. Inside was a flyer with this heading: "George, we're sorry to see you go. Renew now and bring your body back to life." I felt a punch in the gut, but then I heard George's good-natured laugh and an enthusiastic, "It's a deal!" God, I missed him.

Chapter Thirty-four

September 11, 2001, changed airline travel in ways no one could have imagined a month earlier. It became a stress test for passengers to get from the curb to their seat—long lines, removal of articles of clothing, scrutiny of electronic devices, occasional pat-downs, and new restrictions on items that could come aboard. Even though flight crews had it a little easier with dedicated security lines, they bore the brunt of passengers' anger and frustration.

Increased security measures during flights were a constant reminder to passengers that perhaps the person beside them had evil intentions, especially if they dressed or behaved differently than the norm. If a pilot needed to go to the bathroom, flight attendants barricaded the area between the cockpit door and the lavatory with a beverage cart, facing the cabin like sentinels and scanning for unusual movements. Passengers flying into Reagan National Airport near the nation's capital were not allowed to leave their seats for any reason during the final thirty minutes of the flight.

The terrorist attacks caused severe economic damage to airlines in the immediate aftermath, with bankruptcies, mergers, and losses in the billions of dollars. Airlines struggled for financial survival, and Delta was no exception. One way to save money was to cut the number of flight attendants on each flight to the minimum number required by the FAA rather than maintaining the previous policy of adding an extra flight attendant to enhance service. To combat the sour mood caused by the added workload, flight attendants joked about how "Bambi," the missing-in-action flight attendant, was not doing her share of the work.

With fewer flight attendants needed, the company sought to pare down the number of higher-paid personnel. It offered attractive severance and retirement packages to those who qualified. While many of my friends took them, I wasn't ready yet. Still, I sorely missed flying with my friends who opted to leave, as they were among those who had built Delta into one of the most beloved airlines in the history of commercial aviation. But I was glad I stayed when I learned about an exciting new opportunity in June 2003.

Delta and other airlines participate in CRAF (Civil Reserve Air Fleet). This program augments the Department of Defense's military airlift capabilities during peacetime and wartime emergencies. Commercial airlines, subject to agreements with the government, are committed to providing planes and crews for transporting personnel and cargo in and out of disaster and military mobilization zones when needed.

In March 2003, the United States and some of its allies invaded Iraq, and the Department of Defense recruited CRAF flights to transport troops and equipment into the Middle East for the duration of the operation. With most of the fighting over by May, the military again called on CRAF flights to bring some troops home, and I wanted to be part of that effort. I completed the required special training and mistakenly thought my thirty-three years of seniority would allow me to snag one of the trips immediately. After trying for over a month, I finally secured the most junior spot on an eight-day CRAF trip, which included nine other flight attendants from five different bases. I realized the seriousness of this assignment when I received my Geneva Convention Identity

Card for civilians who accompany armed forces, even though the chance of an incident that would require it was slim.

On June 9, we flew from our respective bases to JFK, where we deadheaded on a flight to Rome and checked in at the Hotel Savoy on *Via Ludovis*. The following day, our crew, including four pilots and one mechanic, made its first ferry flight (no passengers) into Kuwait. To provide a warm, friendly, American-style welcome for our special passengers, we spent part of the six-hour trip decorating the cabins with American flags and red, white, and blue streamers. Once we arrived in Kuwait, ground crews comprised of local airport personnel and U.S. military specialists serviced the airplane, refueled it, and loaded cargo as expeditiously as possible to keep the plane's exposure to hostile actions at a minimum. The catering facilities in Rome had already stocked all the food and beverages for the return flight, including gourmet-quality meals, specially decorated cakes, ice cream, and tons of Gatorade.

We welcomed aboard two hundred and thirty-four camo-clad officers and soldiers who brought everything from backpacks to weapons on board. Later, as we began our service and I pushed my meal cart up the aisle, it encountered an obstacle that prevented the wheels from rolling. I spotted the problem and tapped a soldier's arm. "Would you mind sliding your rifle in a little so I can move my cart?" This scenario was *definitely* not something our instructors had ever mentioned in training, nor something I had ever had occasion to say in my many years of flying.

When we arrived back in Rome, another crew boarded the plane to take our passengers on to JFK, and we returned to our hotel to begin a thirty-five-hour layover. This CRAF trip was our captain's last assignment before retiring, so after resting a bit, the entire crew joined him and his wife, who had flown to Rome separately, to celebrate his milestone. We had the glassed-in sidewalk section of the Hard Rock Café on *Via Vittorio Veneto* to ourselves. We enjoyed a raucous party, complete with the "solemn" presentation of gag gifts and placing a paper crown on the captain's head.

The following day, we ferried another airplane to Kuwait. We bestowed an additional honor on the captain—to "tray surf" on takeoff—a highly-coveted experience arranged by coworkers only on ferry flights. The surfer sat on the floor on an empty serving tray at the front of first class with arms stretched forward and slid down the aisle as the plane rotated upward on takeoff. While this was an unsanctioned activity, it was relatively safe and fun for the honoree and the spectators alike, and we all applauded the captain's flawless performance before returning to serious business.

After completing our second trip to Kuwait in four days, we returned to Rome with another ship full of servicemen. I say "men" because, even though the Army and Marine Corps were slowly evolving to allow women to serve in combat units, there were none among our passengers. Upon landing at six a.m., we said goodbye and, once again, turned over the flight to a new crew headed back to the United States.

We became the handoff crew two days later when we reported to the Rome airport at seven thirty a.m. to meet an inbound flight. It was our turn to fly the soldiers to JFK and return home ourselves. This half-full plane gave the men more room to roam around the cabin, and as we neared the end of the flight, I noticed a crowd had gathered to look out the windows on the plane's left side. "What's so interesting out there?" I asked. Without taking his eyes away from the view, an excited young soldier replied, "Ma'am, we're back in America!"

When I returned to regular trips, I couldn't help but compare the outstanding food service and amenities we provided on the CRAF flights to what was now available on domestic ones, underscoring how drastically in-flight service had changed since my early flying days. As much as I once complained about high-speed meal services, I was sorry to see peanuts or pretzels replace the full meals we had previously served on most mid-haul flights. The service changed, yet again, when we began charging domestic coach passengers on long flights for the food we provided—boxed sandwiches and salads, cheese and crackers, chips, and bags of candy. When first introduced, passengers grumbled at the idea of paying for in-flight food once included in their ticket price. In response to the absence of food, passengers frequently brought on board snacks they purchased at the airport. The resulting effluvia from pizza, fries, onions, curry, and plain old grease was often gag-inducing.

I asked myself if it was time to close the door on this chapter of my life. At the end of 2004, Delta offered another retirement package, and this time, I was ready, so I submitted my paperwork and began to count down the days. But where should I spend my final layover? There was little doubt that it had to be San Francisco, a destination I had loved since I first saw its iconic skyline, so I bid for a two-day trip in January that included a night in my favorite city.

I'd had experiences with my coworkers there that I would never forget. One time, we rented a car and drove to Muir Woods, some sixteen miles north of the city in Marin County. I had seen pictures of the giant coastal redwoods, but none did justice to these magnificent beauties. We hiked a short trail in the park. Then, we stopped at a roadside general store outside Mill Valley to buy sandwiches and sodas before returning to the city. The sky turned gray as we resumed our journey on Highway 101, and upon reaching the Golden Gate Bridge, I saw an incredible sight—a white bank of fog rolling in from the ocean. It was ethereal as it covered us with a fluffy blanket that undulated as if being shaken out by an unseen presence. When traffic slowed to a crawl as the cloud enveloped the bridge, my coworker gripped the steering wheel and declared nervously, "I hope I'm staying in my lane."

On another layover, Debbie and I set out on a three-mile hike from our hotel on Van Ness and California to Golden Gate Park. We had covered quite a distance when a woman we met on the sidewalk warned us we were in a sketchy area, so we reluctantly turned around. Back at the hotel, we checked a map and found we had been only a half mile from our destination. On the next layover, we took a cab to the park and wandered into one of the most famous neighborhoods in the world—The Haight, as locals call it. Past its days as the mecca for flower children, it retained its counterculture vibe with head shops, trendy boutiques, and the Haight-Ashbury Free Clinic.

I had become hooked on Armistead Maupin's quirky *Tales of the City* books. I convinced myself that if I looked hard enough on the streets of Russian Hill, I would find the prototype of Anna Madrigal's sprawling Victorian house. I ran George ragged on one of my layovers as I showed him all the places I loved, finally allowing him to catch his breath at an Italian restaurant in North Beach. We enjoyed a fabulous meal and rode a cable car back to the hotel.

On one rare occasion when none of my crew wanted to do anything except shop, I walked to Fisherman's Wharf and took a ferry to Alcatraz. I knew little about its colorful history, so I looked forward to the guided tour and listened attentively to the park ranger's anecdotes about the imposing site. When I entered the dining hall and gazed around the space, I froze as an overpowering sense of déjà vu came over me. I just knew that I had been there before! I stood glued to the floor until I saw my group moving on, then had to rush to catch up. But my mood had changed, and I did not find it amusing when we entered the solitary confinement cellblock and the smiling guide asked, "Who wants to go inside and see what it's like when the door is locked?" Not I! I stayed as close to the outer wall as possible, fighting an eerie feeling that stayed with me for the duration of the tour. Had I seen the dining hall in a movie? I didn't think so. I later read quite a bit about Alcatraz's history, but I never figured out what happened to me on the Rock that day. There doesn't seem to be a timeframe for me to have been in the dining hall in a previous life—if I believed in that sort of thing, of course.

On January 18, 2005, I left Ft. Lauderdale for the last time as a flight attendant. Cindy was on my crew, and Debbie non-revved on the flights to Cincinnati and San Francisco to celebrate with me. My room at the St. Francis Hotel overlooked Union Square, where years before, I had boarded the Gray Line bus on the day the city opened her beautiful vistas to me. This layover was too short to revisit my favorite spots. Still, it was wonderful to reminisce and share the memories with my best friends.

My eyes got heavy as I lay in bed on my last night, and the ironies of my life paraded through my thoughts. Other than my extreme myopia, shyness, skinny frame, and (oh, yes) terror of flying, I turned out to be the perfect candidate to become a flight attendant. When I began my career almost thirty-five years earlier, I could not have imagined that I would someday retire from a job for which I was so ill-suited. I remembered the first time I heard, "The closest exit may be behind you." In retrospect, so many exit points had turned into entrances to new experiences and opportunities. I had survived the heartbreak of broken relationships but was still mourning my most tragic loss of all—the man I had wanted to spend the rest of my life with. What further adventures would we have had? Travel for sure, but maybe new hobbies and interests or another fun little sideline business. What lay in store for me instead? Perhaps I could resume the training required to become a licensed mental health counselor. Maybe a move to be nearer my family. The sky was *not* the limit. I drifted off.

The following morning, shortly after we took off for Dallas/ Ft. Worth, the pilots rang and asked me to come to the cockpit. Below me lay the beautiful skyline, the Golden Gate Bridge, and Alcatraz in stark relief against the deep blue water. With a broad smile, the captain directed my attention to a text message on an instrument panel screen. I read: "Kathi, Wishing a great retirement to a great gal."

There was no uncertainty about one thing. I was going to miss my Delta Family!

THE END

Works Cited

Goldstein, Michael. "The Triumph of the Roller Bag."
Accessed June 15, 2020, https://www.forbes.com/sites/
michaelgoldstein/2019/04/15/the-triumph-of-the-roller-bag/?s
h=5583dabfaa7e.

Johnson, Kate and Albert Garcia. "'Male stewardesses' just didn't
fly." Accessed February 12, 2008. https://www.latimes.com/
archives/la-xpm-2007-sep-27-oe-johnson27-story.html.

Kraus, Terry. "Ellen Church and the Advent of the Sky Girls,"
accessed August 21, 2014, https://www.faa.gov/sites/faa.gov/
files/about/history/pioneers/Ellen_Church_and_the_Advent_
of_the_Sky_Girls.pdf.

Tiemeyer, Phil, Plane Queer: Labor, Sexuality and AIDS in the
History of Male Flight Attendants." University of California
Press, 2013.

Wickman, Forrest. "How the Gay Airline Steward Became a
Stereotype." Accessed April 18, 2017. https://slate.com/
culture/2013/07/gay-male-flight-attendants-in-im-so-ex
cited-the-history-of-the-gay-steward-stereotype.html.

Winnetka Historical Society. "Before Her Time: Anita
Willets-Burnham's Rolling Suitcase." Accessed September 15,
2018. https://www.winnetkahistory.org/gazette/before-he
r-time-anita-willets-burnhams-rolling-suitcase.

Acknowledgments

I didn't fly solo when I wrote this book, I had a first class crew!

Sharon Schmid not only expertly edited the manuscript but provided priceless insights into how to sharpen my writing. She put the book on a weight loss program, reducing its heft by a couple thousand words. I can never adequately thank her for the hundreds of hours over several years that she devoted to seeing my dream of becoming a published writer come true.

Authors Terri Ryburn (*No Crybabies Allowed*) and Melanie Verbout (*Go Pick* Peas) were the first to hear passages from the book, as we shared and critiqued our writing with one another many years ago. They were an unfaltering pep squad who listened to my ever-changing assessment of the book ("I think it's pretty good;" I think it's garbage!") and offered helpful suggestions all along the way.

My sister, Sandra Harmon, and her husband, Paul Harmon, were early readers and added rich details to our shared history.

Three groups, Women of Words, Longfellow Club, and my book club, indulged me by listening to readings from selected chapters. Their laughter and sadness in all the right places encouraged me more than I can say.

Thanks to Steve Dodge, Chuck Broyard, Pam Dyches, and Debbie Maheras and beta readers, Jane Baldus, Kathy Carroll, Marcia Hamilton, Gina McHugh, and Pat Scala

A special "thank you" to Snookie and Ann for allowing me to share their stories.

Lastly, I'm grateful to my stalwart proofreaders: Terri Ryburn, Melanie Verbout, Greg Meyer, Karen Hanson, Diana Hauman, and Phylis VerSteegh, who never saw a comma they didn't love.

About the Author

Photo by Ralph Weisheit

Kathi Davis contributes to *Pieces from Our Past*, a weekly column from the McLean County Museum of History in the Bloomington, Illinois *Pantagraph* newspaper. She has also performed at the "Next to Normal Story Slam," a periodic event where individuals tell true, first-person accounts before a live audience.

She lives in Normal, Illinois, with her dog Sadie. *The Closest Exit May Be Behind You* is her first book.

www.ingramcontent.com/pod-product-compliance
Lightning Source LLC
Chambersburg PA
CBHW021705120626
46545CB00004B/1416